Praise for *Beyond Human?*:

"Science promises to change, perfect and even immortalize us. But how far can it go without damaging our fundamental humanity? John Bryant supplies a masterly, readable and deeply informed critique of the current arguments based upon extensive original research. Beyond Human? *must be reckoned essential reading for everyone concerned about the deepening chasm between scientific and technological possibilities and ethical, humane and just conduct."*

Professor Allan Chapman, History of Science, University of Oxford

"This is an enjoyable and thought-provoking read, in which John Bryant, a respected plant scientist, sets out the current human condition, taking in scientific, technological, environmental, medical and social perspectives. What's compelling is that this is further positioned against a wider history of human development, which notes the rise and fall of empires, and the development of spiritual and ethical awareness. Whilst freely identifying himself as a scientist and an active Christian, this is no religious polemic, but a balanced 'human' view. It's not 'the biology' of being human, nor 'the spirituality' of being human, but a truly holistic view, with a strong and important message for us to take heed that, while celebrating and making use of what is good, to apply ourselves to solving the problems which beset so many."

Dr Peter J. Lum
U

BEYOND HUMAN?

SCIENCE AND THE CHANGING FACE OF HUMANITY

JOHN BRYANT

LION

Published by Lion Books
an imprint of
Lion Hudson plc
Wilkinson House, Jordan Hill Road,
Oxford OX2 8DR, England
www.lionhudson.com/lion

ISBN 978 0 7459 5396 0
e-ISBN 978 0 7459 5898 9

First edition 2013

Acknowledgments

Every effort has been made to trace the original copyright holders where required.
In some cases this has proved impossible. We shall be happy to correct any such
omissions in future editions.

Scripture quotations are taken from pp. 84, 196, 199: The Holy Bible, Today's New
International Version. Copyright © 2004 by International Bible Society. Used by permission
of Hodder & Stoughton Publishers. A member of the Hachette Livre UK Group. All rights
reserved. "TNIV" is a registered trademark of International Bible Society. p. 167: The
Authorized (King James) Version. Rights in the Authorized Version are vested in the Crown.
Reproduced by permission of the Crown's patentee, Cambridge University Press. p. 232: The
Holy Bible, New International Version, copyright © 1973, 1978, 1984 International Bible
Society. Used by permission of Hodder & Stoughton, a member of the Hodder Headline
Group. All rights reserved. "NIV" is a trademark of International Bible Society. UK trademark
number 1448790. p. 245: The Holy Bible, New Living Translation, copyright © 1996, 2004,
2007 by Tyndale House Foundation. Used by permission of Tyndale House Publishers, Inc.,
Carol Stream, Illinois 60188. All rights reserved.

p. 21: Extract from *Ancient Worlds: The Search for the Origins of Western Civilization* by Richard Miles
copyright © Richard Miles, 2010. Reprinted by permission of Penguin Books. p. 45: Extract
from *Spiritual Fitness* by Graham Tomlin copyright © Graham Tomlin, 2006. Reprinted by
permission of Bloomsbury Publishing Plc. p. 54: Extract from *The Culture of Liberty: An Agenda*
by Peter L. Berger copyright © Peter L. Berger, 1998. Reprinted by permission of Springer.
pp. 80, 85, 244: Extracts from *An Intelligent Person's Guide to Ethics* by Mary Warnock copyright ©
Mary Warnock, 1998. Reprinted by permission of Gerald Duckworth and Co. Ltd.
pp. 93, 103–104: Extracts from "How have I cheated death?" by Tim Wotton in *The Guardian*,
15 February 2011. Reprinted by permission of *The Guardian*. pp. 111, 119, 123, 138: Extracts
from "The Human Genome Project: Tool of Atheistic Reductionism or Embodiment of
the Christian Mandate to Heal?" by Francis Collins in *Science and Christian Belief* 11, 99–111
copyright © Francis Collins, 1999. Reprinted by permission of Paternoster Periodicals
c/o AlphaGraphics. pp. 175–76: Sourced from *Declaration on Euthanasia* published by Sacred
Congregation for the Doctrine of the Faith, Vatican, 1980. p. 176: Extract from Stephen
A. Richards, That Religious Studies Website: www.thatreligiousstudieswebsite.com. p. 176:
Sourced from *Christian Agnostic* by Leslie Weatherhead copyright © Leslie Weatherhead, 1965.
Published by Hodder & Stoughton. p. 181: Extract from Alan Turing's epitaph copyright ©
Alan Turing. Reprinted by permission of The Turing Estate. pp. 181, 201–202: Extracts from
BBC Radio One interview with Kate Bush, reprinted by permission of the BBC and Kate
Bush. pp. 205, 228: Extracts from *Better Humans* by Nick Bostrom, edited by Paul Miller and
James Wilsdon copyright © Nick Bostrom, 2006. Reprinted by permission of Demos. p. 212:
Extract from *Clones, Genes and Immortality* by John Harris © John Harris, 1998. Reprinted by
permission of Oxford University Press. pp. 243: Sourced from *Human Trafficking: An Overview*
published by United Nations Office on Drugs and Crime, 2008.

A catalogue record for this book is available from the British Library
Printed and bound in Great Britain, February 2013, LH26

CONTENTS

Foreword   9

1 Starting from the Beginning   13
1.1 Beyond what?   13
1.2 Being human: the origins and early evolution of humankind   16
1.3 Corn and community, cities and civilization   19

2 The Way We Were   25
2.1 Introduction   25
2.2 Shifting power bases in the ancient world   26
2.3 Religion in the ancient world   27
2.4 Into Europe   28
2.5 Post-Roman Britain   29
2.6 Moving away from Rome   31
2.7 Science, culture and religion   31
2.8 The Industrial Revolution and the age of invention   34
2.9 Science, culture and religion revisited   36
2.10 Into the twentieth century   37
2.11 Some thoughts on the story so far   41

3 The Way We Are   45
3.1 Introduction   45
3.2 Communism and capitalism   46
3.3 Israel and Palestine   51
3.4 The European Union   53
3.5 The 1960s   54
3.6 Northern Ireland   59
3.7 Terrorism and war   61

3.8 Power bases shift again   64

3.9 Science, religion and culture   65

3.10 Human society: fraying round the edges or cracking
       down the middle?   70

3.11 After World War II: a final comment   74

4 Morals, Ethics and Complex Issues   77

4.1 Introduction   77

4.2 Ethical systems   78

4.3 A brief excursion into postmodernism   85

4.4 Application of ethics in medicine   87

4.5 Extending the ethical vision   89

5 Genes, Genetics and Human Disease   93

5.1 Introduction   93

5.2 Early understanding   94

5.3 Genes and medicine: the early years   95

5.4 The new genetic revolution   99

5.5 Science, sequences and sickness   102

**6 Genetic Testing and Diagnosis: The Good, the Bad
and the Muddly   113**

6.1 Genetic testing and diagnosis   113

6.2 Prenatal and pre-implantation testing: wider ethical
       issues   123

6.3 A gene for this and a gene for that   133

6.4 Concluding remarks   138

7 Medical Technology: From Gamete to Grave   141

7.1 Introduction   141

7.2 The art of reproduction: from donor insemination to
       test-tube babies   142

7.3 Gene therapy   149

7.4 Repair, replacement and renewal   152

7.5 Three score years and then   167
7.6 … and then: when am I dead and when may I die?   171
7.7 Whatever next?   177

8 Chips with Everything: Computers, Information and Communications Technologies   181

8.1 Introduction   181
8.2 Alan Turing and the dawn of the computer age   182
8.3 The age of computers: the digital age   185
8.4 How things have changed   186
8.5 Networking   188
8.6 The digital divide   189
8.7 The darker side of digital technology   191
8.8 Concluding remarks   201

9 Transhumanism: Stronger, Faster, Better, Older?   205

9.1 Introduction   205
9.2 Transhumanism: biomedical   207
9.3 Transhumanism: pharmacological   221
9.4 Transhumanism: digital   223
9.5 Transhumanism: biomechanical   229
9.6 The "super-soldier" programme   230
9.7 Concluding comments   230

10 Beyond Human?   235

10.1 Introduction   235
10.2 The angel and the beast   236
10.3 Fair shares for all?   237
10.4 Fiddling while home burns   239
10.5 Better humans?   242
10.6 Postscript   244

Index   246

FOREWORD

*What we call Man's power over Nature turns out
to be a power exercised by some men over other men
with Nature as its instrument.*
C.S. Lewis

Progress in biomedical science has, during the past three
decades, been very rapid. As a (formerly) practising molecular
biologist I have been thrilled with the increased knowledge
we now have of genes and the way they work. We now know
things and can do things that were undreamed of at the
start of my career in science. But acquisition of knowledge
and capability in genetics and in several of the other areas
discussed in this book is now moving so fast that we barely have
time for any reflection on the social and ethical implications
before yet another advance is announced. We should be
concerned about this. Will our knowledge be used wisely, to
the general benefit of humankind or will it lead to further
inequalities in our already divided society? That concern is
well expressed in the quotation at the top of the page, written
in *The Abolition of Man*, published as long ago as 1947. If it
was relevant then, it is even more relevant now. And then
there is the question of whether some uses of knowledge or
some types of experiment are in some way "off-limits". In
popular culture it was very well put by Jeff Goldblum in his
role as Dr Ian Malcolm in the film *Jurassic Park*: "Yeah, but
your scientists were so preoccupied with whether or not they
could, they didn't stop to think if they should." In this context,
it is easy (and correct) to condemn much of the work carried
out by the notorious Josef Mengele and his associates in Nazi
Germany, but what about twenty-first-century science? For

example, is it wrong or is it morally acceptable to use human embryos to generate stem cells or to reject embryos on genetic grounds? Indeed, how do we decide what is morally right or wrong in these areas? Further, if we have a religious faith (I myself am an active Christian), can we in any way rely on that in dealing with these issues, on none of which there is any direct guidance in, for example, the Bible, the Torah, or the Qu'ran? We need to be scrupulously honest here and not try to seek "pat" answers to complex questions.

Thus, it is with such questions and topics in mind that this book has been written. The plan started to emerge over a lunch with Stephanie Heald and Kate Kirkpatrick, both then employed by Lion Hudson. Stephanie had edited a previous book of mine[1] while working for a different publisher. During our lunch meeting she was kind enough to suggest that a more up-to-date book with a broader perspective would be a very timely addition to the literature. I must thank both Stephanie and Kate for their roles in the early stages and am sorry that they both moved on before the plan came to fruition.

I also want to thank the many people who have walked with me at different phases of my bioethical journey. I do not have space to mention them all, but do want to name Celia Deane-Drummond, Steve Hughes, Cherryl Hunt, Linda la Velle, Suzi Leather, Donal O'Mahuna, Christopher Southgate, Peter Turnpenny and Chris Willmott. I want especially to thank my close friend and (in other publications) co-author, John Searle, for those many discussions we have had and continue to have about bioethical topics and for the advice he provided on some parts of this book. I am grateful too for the patience and wisdom of Alison Hull, my editor at Lion Hudson, who oversaw all but the earliest stages of the writing and whose wise guidance and advice has been invaluable. Lawrence Osborn of Osborn Editorial also made some very constructive comments at the copy-editing stage. Finally it is, as always, a real pleasure and privilege to thank my wife Marje, who has an immense interest in the human condition and in the way that science can enhance or diminish it. She has been very interested in and supportive of this project from the very start.

John Bryant
Exeter, October 2012

NOTE

1. John Bryant and John Searle, *Life in Our Hands: A Christian Perspective on Genetics and Cloning*, Nottingham: IVP, 2004.

1

STARTING FROM THE BEGINNING

For the first time since life began, a single animal is utterly dominant: the ape species Homo sapiens. Evolution has equipped us with huge brains, stunning adaptability and brilliantly successful prowess.
Mark Lynas, *The God Species*, 2011

The past is but the beginning of a beginning, and all that is or has been is but the twilight of the dawn.
H.G. Wells, *The Discovery of the Future*, 1902

1.1 BEYOND WHAT?

The title of this book suggests that we are in some ways moving to change or transcend the human condition. However, there are fundamental questions to think about first. If we wish to discuss whether we are moving "beyond human", it is surely necessary to think about what we are going beyond. What does it mean to be human? How do humans function? What are the special features of humans? These questions are complex and invite answers at different levels.

In terms of biology, humans are mammals, warm-blooded animals that nurture their embryos within the body of the female and suckle their young. Thus, many of our genetic functions are held in common with all mammals. Of the animals alive today, the nearest relatives of humans are the great apes, especially the chimpanzees. The evolutionary pathways to chimpanzees and humans diverged about 5 million or so years ago. So, what are the biological features that mark us out as humans? We are bipedal (walk on two legs) but the specific mode of bipedal motion is unique. We have very big brains, three and a half times the size of an average chimpanzee brain, contained in a balloon-shaped cranium. We have high foreheads, but no protruding eyebrow ridges; we have chins and small teeth. Both sexes are relatively hairless; the two sexes diverge from each other in size and musculature. Thus we can define humans anatomically but that is not enough. At the very least we need to add that our large brain size has conferred on us an intelligence far superior to that of any other creature on earth. That intelligence has allowed the development of language, abstract thought, technical and technological skills and thus a general ability to dominate and modify the planet. We also have a strong sense of self-awareness or consciousness of self, although some regard this as just a quantitative difference from the small number of other species which also exhibit some consciousness of self.

However, we have still not defined what it is to be human. We have imagination and aesthetic sense, we have created art and music and we have developed a whole range of activities that have nothing to do with our survival as individuals or as a species. Yes, it is true that hints of these things may be seen in some animals but their development in humans goes far, far beyond anything seen in the animal kingdom. We have a rich emotional life as is evidenced by the wide range of words we have to describe and to define an equally wide range of feelings. Further, we have "emotional intelligence" that enables us to discern the feelings of others. Again, some animals, especially the higher apes (as shown, for example, by the work of Jane Goodall on chimpanzees), do exhibit emotions but we should not exaggerate this to claim that all mammals experience the range and depth of human feelings and emotions.

But there is still more to being human. In general we have a strongly developed moral sense, leading to the concepts of right and wrong. Indeed, many commentators, including the author C.S. Lewis, the ethicist David Cook and the former director of the Human Genome Project, Francis Collins, have suggested that all humans have an inbuilt moral code.[1] Whether or not this is so, it is clear that humankind exhibits altruism that extends far beyond the altruistic behaviours seen in many animals. We do not encounter potentially or actually self-sacrificial behaviour, undertaken consciously and deliberately in order to save the life of a total stranger, in other animals. Such behaviour is indicative of empathy, one of the virtues that characterize human behaviour at its best. Charles Darwin put it this way: "We are compelled to relieve the sufferings of another, in order that our own painful feelings may be at the same time relieved."[2] These words were echoed recently by the Dalai Lama: "… 'the seed of compassion' is the discomfort we experience when we see someone suffering. We are thus impelled to relieve the suffering of another so that our own painful suffering may be relieved."

Our behaviour often falls far short of the best; we are also capable of hostility, cruelty and violence towards our fellow-humans. Nevertheless, the very fact that we can acknowledge this is an indication of our moral sense or moral awareness. We know the difference between right and wrong, even if, too often, we choose the wrong. This brings me to the final, and for some, controversial point in this section. For adherents of the Jewish, Christian and Islamic faiths, the features discussed in this paragraph are indicators of being made in the image of God and able to relate in some way to God. This brings in first the concept of a supreme being, God, and secondly the idea that humans have a spiritual dimension. In twenty-first-

century Britain, many may regard these concepts as archaic
(but see Chapter 3, section 3.9.3). However, a majority of
the world's population are in some sense religious and do
acknowledge a spiritual dimension. Thus, the psychologist
Carl Jung suggested that we all have a "God-image" within
us that is central to our well-being.

I have attempted to define what it is to be human but has
it always been this way? Have we changed since the origin of
our species, over the history of humankind? How has "being
human" panned out over the millennia? We start our search
for answers by considering the emergence of our species,
Homo sapiens, in Africa, and the subsequent spread of the
species over the planet. It may seem strange to start a book
concerned with modern technology by going back so far, but
the general message from the first 160,000 years or so of our
history is an important one. It is that the human species has
changed and there is no reason to suppose that our capacity
for change has disappeared. Indeed, there are clear indications
that it has not and this has obvious implications on whether
or not we are moving beyond human.

1.2 BEING HUMAN: THE ORIGINS AND EARLY EVOLUTION OF HUMANKIND[3]

1.2.1 Back to basics

"Anatomically modern" human beings, i.e. members of the
species *Homo sapiens*, are currently thought to have originated in
Africa about 165,000 years ago. In lifestyle, they were hunter-
gatherers. Social groups consisted of networks of families,
although the latter were not the direct equivalent of modern
nuclear families. It is also surmised that the differences in size
and musculature between males and females allowed division
of labour, supporting the development of larger population
groups. The hunter-gatherer lifestyle is often nomadic or

partly nomadic but the travels of these early humans were unusually extensive. There is evidence for journeys of up to 200 km to obtain and/or trade materials that were needed, for example for tool-making. To put this in context, this is at least twice as far as any hunter-gatherer group extant in the twenty-first century is known to travel. The "travelling man" tendencies of early humans would later lead them to colonize most of the rest of the world. In the meantime, an aesthetic sense was developing. Beads, made from shells, discovered in North and South Africa have been dated respectively at 82,000 and 77,000 years ago. The South African site also yielded clear examples of geometric art. Life was already more than a matter of basic survival.

Tools also became more sophisticated and, over 100,000 years, progressed from hand-axes to spears, harpoons, fishing hooks and sewing needles. The harpoons and hooks enabled them to add fish to the wide range of hunted animals. Many tools show evidence that the tool makers carried designs in their heads and were able to execute them from a range of raw materials.

1.2.2 Out of Africa: the invasion of Europe

As the population of *Homo sapiens* grew, so they started to migrate out of Africa. The means by which they reached the furthest regions of the globe make a fascinating study but here we just focus on the move into Europe. About 47,000 years ago, humans had reached the Near East (which today, somewhat confusingly, is often called the Middle East) and from there it was a relatively short step into Europe. Neanderthals were still there,[4] albeit in smaller fragmented populations. They survived, as far as we can tell from archaeological evidence, until about 30,000 years ago. The specific reason for their extinction remains unclear. From there, *Homo sapiens* went from strength to strength. Weapons for hunting became more efficient while the use of ornaments and other forms of art became increasingly sophisticated and beautiful. Cave paintings, the earliest dating back 31,000 years, were so accurate that it has been possible to gain some idea of the population composition of the various game animals. Further, it is clear that the artists could carry accurate images in their heads because these paintings were executed underground, far from the hunting grounds.

There is one more element to consider, namely religion. It is of course impossible to tell from an ancient skeleton whether an individual had a sense of a spiritual dimension. Indeed, until the invention of writing, the only clues come from archaeological remains. It was about 37–40,000 years ago that representations of unknown beings were first constructed. The earliest were female-like figurines with grossly exaggerated sexual characteristics, suggesting some sort of fertility cult but there were also lion-headed men and other semi-mythical creatures. Soon after this, about 28,000 years ago, the first "ceremonial" burials occurred, with valuable "grave goods" accompanying the deceased person in the grave.[5] Ceremonial burials with grave goods indicate a belief in an afterlife and at this point we can regard *Homo sapiens* as a religious species. That is not to say that religion developed in the same way in all the different populations dispersed around the world but, nevertheless, development of religion seems to have been a general feature of human evolution.

1.2.3 So, are humans special?

We can set the origin and early development of humans very much into an evolutionary framework. This does not diminish us as a species. If other species have come into being by evolution why would we suppose that humans have not, especially with the range of scientific evidence supporting that view? I have also suggested that in the short time during which humans have been on the planet, characteristics like art and religion have also evolved. What I am not saying here is that art, or an aesthetic sense of religion can be ascribed to particular genes that are directly subject to natural selection. Although the general media love the simplicity of an "art gene" or a "religion gene", it is simply not like that. What I am saying is that art and religion have arisen, developed and become more sophisticated as part of human evolution. However, that does not in any way invalidate them.

1.3 CORN AND COMMUNITY, CITIES AND CIVILIZATION

1.3.1 Introduction

We have reached a time when we were still dispersing over the globe. From that point, different populations developed in different ways, both physically and culturally. Differences in physique and skin colour, very much a feature of the wonderful variety of the current state of our species, would feature in that divergence. There are clear evolutionary reasons for these differences but space does not permit a discussion of them here. So, keeping this wonderful variety at the back of our minds, I will focus on the main events that led to the development of civilization and culture in Europe. Other cultures developed in different ways, but our main interest lies with Europe. How did "being human" play out as we occupied this part of the world? What factors affected our development?

1.3.2 The coming of agriculture

At about 10000 BC, a major change occurred in the way that humans obtained their food. Agriculture was invented in the region called the Fertile Crescent, probably in the part that is now northern Syria. Exactly what triggered the change is debatable and, indeed, there may have been several triggers. It is clear, however, that the "founder crops" of agriculture included pulses, cereals and flax, the latter used to make fabric. Excavated plant remains show that humans began to impose selection, presumably choosing the plants that exhibited better yields. Over the centuries, the selection imposed by farmer choice induced some dramatic changes in wheat, so the crop had changed significantly many centuries before the advent of modern plant breeding. Nevertheless, einkorn wheat is still grown in parts of the Near East, albeit that the cultivated varieties are higher yielding than the wild varieties. Further, domestication was not confined to crop plants. Animals were also domesticated, starting with sheep, then cows and goats and, in some cultures, pigs. All this shows humans were moving from harvesting nature to modifying nature, a process that led eventually to the biomedical technologies discussed in later chapters.

The adoption of an agrarian lifestyle had another effect. As noted, many hunter-gatherer communities were nomadic or semi-nomadic, although some lived more settled lives in areas with plentiful year-round resources. Indeed, some commentators distinguish between hunter-gatherers (nomadic or semi-nomadic) and foragers (more settled). However, the agrarian lifestyle demands even more commitment to place because planting, tending and harvesting crops takes several months of the year and this is compounded when crops with different growing seasons are in the mix. Thus communities became more settled and indeed grew larger. We might say that the village had been born.

1.3.3 Cities and civilization

The formation of stable, settled communities probably occurred wherever agriculture was established. However, the next major change in living arrangements was by no means universal. For the first time people started to live in cities. There is a good deal of debate about the age and location of the oldest city, with several different claims as to the identity of the "oldest continuously inhabited settlement".[6] However, there is a difference between a settlement and a city, albeit that one can turn into another. Currently, many experts believe that people started living in cities for the first time in the area known as Mesopotamia (now part of Iraq),[7] between the Tigris and Euphrates rivers (the rivers of Babylon) and also in what is now Syria. In doing so, they laid the foundations of the Sumerian civilization. Richard Miles describes this very vividly:[8]

> ... just under 6000 years ago, a remarkable thing happened. People left the security of their family compounds and tribal villages. They came together... to create something far more complex and difficult: a city, a civilisation... It was this decision that resulted in the creation of Uruk [in Mesopotamia], the mother of all cities.

By this time, religion had become embedded in human life and many of these cities that sprung up around 3800 BC showed clear evidence of temple worship (usually of several gods but with each city having its own special god). Over the next 2–3,000 years, city life in this area thrived. By 3000 BC (5,000 years ago) the population of Uruk[9] was about 50,000 and the city walls were 11 km in diameter; by 2500 BC, 80 per cent of the population of the Mesopotamia region lived in cities with populations of at least 15,000, a percentage of urban dwellers not seen in northern Europe until the Industrial Revolution.

City life led to a greater variety of employment and division of labour. Arts, crafts and music flourished, often in connection with religious practices. The first evidence of the wheel dates back to 3500 BC, although many commentators suspect that it was invented before then, probably in several places. In ancient Mesopotamia, the wheel seems to have been used in pottery-making (the potter's wheel) before it was used in transport. Thus, simple technology and manufacturing were invented. Mathematics was also developed and we see the first evidence of writing at about 3200 BC.

Egypt also adopted city life just a few hundred years after the establishment of those first cities in Mesopotamia. Again, polytheistic temple worship became well established with many of the gods being representations of animals and heavenly bodies such as the sun. The king was also referred to as a deity. As in the Sumerian culture, arts, crafts and music were vibrant, again often in connection with religion. Writing also emerged in Egypt at about the same time as in the Sumerian culture.

The pattern was repeated as agriculture spread from the Near East and the Nile Valley, first into the eastern Mediterranean region, then to southern and south-eastern Europe, north and west through the continent, reaching Britain in about 4000 BC. Throughout Europe, the adoption of agriculture led to a more settled mode of existence and eventually to the establishment of cities. The general pattern was that cities appeared in a region about 4,000 years after the adoption of agriculture. Thus in Britain, the first city (now known as Colchester) was established in about AD 45, although other places that do not qualify as cities date back much further.[10]

The establishment of cities obviously had a major effect on the development of human culture. The various tasks involved in sustaining city life and engaging in what we might call "non-essential" activities required both extensive division of labour and also cooperation between the different groups or individuals carrying out the different roles. Efficient city life meant humans needed to get on with each other within the community. However, that attitude of willing cooperation did not necessarily extend to those in other cities, as will become apparent in the next chapter.

NOTES

1. Immanuel Kant, the eighteenth-century philosopher, wrote in *Critique of Practical Reason* (1788): "Two things continue to fill the mind with ever-increasing awe and admiration, the starry heavens and the moral law within."

2. In *Descent of Man*, 1871.

3. I am very grateful to the biological anthropologist, Cara Wall-Scheffler, for providing much of the information on which this section is based.

4. Neanderthals have had a bit of a bad press. They were not the brutish "cave-men" so often depicted, although they were not as sophisticated as early humans.

5. Interestingly, Neanderthals had buried their dead for several tens of thousands of years before then, which is why we have such extensive fossil evidence about them. However, whether these burials were ceremonial or had a religious significance is difficult to tell. Graves were often decorated with animal horns and bones and in some sites, based on the abundance and variety of pollen in the vicinity of graves, it is thought that they may have been decorated with flowers. The bodies were often buried in the foetal position and there are some indications of body decoration. All these are indicative of ritual and some experts believe that, at least in the later stages of their presence on earth, Neanderthals were in some sense religious.

6. For example, this is often claimed for Damascus (which, at the time of writing, is in the news for very different reasons).

7. Mesopotamia is a Greek word meaning "between rivers".

8. In *Ancient Worlds*, London: Penguin Books, 2011, page 3.

9. Not to be confused with Ur, the ancient city from which Abram (Abraham) left to travel westwards, as reported in the book of Genesis in the Bible.

10. Especially Thatcham in modern-day Berkshire and Abingdon in modern-day Oxfordshire.

2

THE WAY WE WERE

... the charioteer of the human soul drives a pair, and... one of the horses is noble and of noble breed, but the other quite the opposite in breed and character. Therefore in our case the driving is necessarily difficult and troublesome.
Plato, *Phaedrus*, 365 BC

Many and sharp the num'rous ills
Inwoven with our frame!
More pointed still we make ourselves
Regret, remorse, and shame!
And man, whose heav'n-erected face
The smiles of love adorn, –
Man's inhumanity to man
Makes countless thousands mourn!
Robert Burns, "Man was made to mourn: A Dirge"

Those who cannot remember the past are condemned to repeat it.
George Santayana, *The Life of Reason*, 1905

2.1 INTRODUCTION

By the end of the previous chapter, our brief history of humankind had reached the stage where, in the ancient world, our ancestors (at least in a cultural sense) had started to live in cities. Many commentators regard those early Mesopotamian cities as the cradle of Western civilization and so the purpose of this chapter is to look at points along the timeline from that ancient world to our own culture in twentieth-century Britain, and to a lesser extent the USA (we reach the twenty-first century in the next chapter). What have these ancient cities contributed to the way we are today? What were the formative influences on our culture? What does "being human" look like in modern times and how did it get to be that way? Understanding our past is vital to understanding our present. Further, even for today's secular Britain, this understanding needs to incorporate a religious timeline. Our law and our ethical thinking have been very strongly influenced by our Judeo-Christian tradition, as is acknowledged even by atheist thinkers such as Mary Warnock.

2.2 SHIFTING POWER BASES IN THE ANCIENT WORLD

As those early cities developed and grew, they accumulated goods, wealth and resources. Trade routes were established which eventually, as cities sprung up in other regions, went out across south-western Asia to India. Cities joined with other cities to form kingdoms and, as the kingdoms continued to increase in wealth, power and influence, these features could be further enhanced by taking over other cities or kingdoms. As civilization spreads, it is accompanied by the increased sophistication and commitment of resources to warfare. This is a very different aspect of humankind from those positive qualities of altruism, empathy and so on listed earlier. It is a sad fact that humans will slaughter many other members of their own species,[1] often simply because they are not members of the same group or tribe or because one group or tribe has something (e.g. resource-rich land) that another covets.

So, empires grew, became dominant and then collapsed as another empire took over. The whole area, from what is now Turkey, right through Persia, even as far as India, south to the

Persian Gulf, across to the Mediterranean and further south still into Egypt, was in a state of flux for around 2,000 years.[2] Hittites, Assyrians, Babylonians, Egyptians, Persians and Greeks all had their periods of dominance, in some cases more than one.

However, life was not all war. In periods of relative stability, art and culture could flourish (even from Assyria, reputed to be the most fiercely militaristic regime of the ancient world, we have examples of beautiful and intricate bas-reliefs and carvings). In Babylon, under King Nebuchadnezzar II,[3] the city of Babylon itself became a city "that surpasses in splendour any other in the known world".[4] Among other things, Nebuchadnezzar II directed the construction of the Esagila (a complex temple dedicated to the god Marduk) and the nearby seven-storey ziggurat (which is recorded in Jewish writings as the Tower of Babel).

2.3 RELIGION IN THE ANCIENT WORLD

Religion played a large part in the life of these ancient world cultures and cities, with many of the finest buildings being dedicated to religious practice. Nearly all the religions were polytheistic and rulers often added to the pantheon of gods by declaring themselves to be deities worthy of worship. However, we also see the beginnings of monotheism. Thus, when, as described in Genesis, Abram (Abraham) left the city of Ur, with its fine ziggurat dedicated to the moon-god, Nanna, he abandoned the polytheistic religion of the Sumerians to worship the "one true God", effectively establishing Judaism. Monotheism also started to arise elsewhere. In Greece, for example, essentially a polytheistic culture, Plato and Aristotle developed the idea of one God, envisaged as the architect of the world who represented ideal perfection. Ethical codes also emerged during these times, including the Jewish Ten Commandments and the virtue ethics of Plato and Aristotle.

2.4 INTO EUROPE

The Hellenistic Empire established by Alexander the Great
extended as far east as the Punjab in India. Nevertheless,
its power base remained in Greece and thus allowed Greek
influence to extend across the region. The philosophers
Socrates, Plato and Aristotle, who have been so influential in
Western thought, were developing their ideas when Greece
was at war with Persia or later, when Alexander the Great was
pushing the Hellenistic civilization eastwards. Art, literature,
poetry and mathematics flourished, the latter typified by the
work of Pythagoras, Euclid and Archimedes.[5] The Greeks also
enjoyed sport, especially the "games". The "Olympic Games"
were established over 2,700 years ago and were part of a
religious festival dedicated to Zeus, king of the gods. Being
human was, and of course still is, a very multifaceted affair.

The main power base was now in Europe and remained
there when the Hellenistic Empire fell to the Romans in the
period between 146 and 31 BC. Even before then, Rome had
conquered much of Europe, and during the takeover of the
Hellenistic Empire the move north also went on.

In 55 and 54 BC, Julius Caesar invaded Kent and on the
second occasion succeeded in installing a king who was
favourably disposed towards Rome. The actual conquest of
Britain started in AD 43 under the emperor Claudius and was
effectively complete by AD 84. Much of Britain was occupied.
Cities were established (Chapter 1, section 1.3.3); many of our
modern cities still show clear evidence of a Roman heritage.
For example, in the layout of Exeter, the city in which this
book is being written, it is still possible to see the shape of
the Roman city and port and the straight roads that emerged
like spokes from the city gates, one of which I travel along
regularly.

In the meantime, an event that was to change the Western
world, including Britain, had occurred in Palestine: namely

the emergence of Christianity. The new religion, which had, in effect, grown out of Judaism, was based on the person of Jesus Christ – his life, death and resurrection. It spread very rapidly, reaching Europe during the missionary journeys of St Paul. In Europe, Christianity came up against the polytheism of the Greco-Roman world (notwithstanding the earlier leanings of Plato and Aristotle towards monotheism) and the imperial rule of Rome. In Rome, the relationship between the Christian believers and the Roman authorities swung between extremes. However, in AD 313, Emperor Constantine's *Edict of Milan* promoted religious freedom and tolerance throughout the empire and thus Christianity and Judaism could be freely practised. Emperor Theodosius went further by issuing, between AD 389 and 391, a series of edicts that culminated in Christianity and Judaism being the only permitted religions in the empire (thus restricting religious freedom).[6]

2.5 POST-ROMAN BRITAIN

2.5.1 Pagans and Christians

This institutionalization of Christianity within the Roman Empire had little effect on Britain because the Romans left in about AD 410. However, there is evidence that Christianity had actually arrived here in the previous century (and possibly earlier) and coexisted as a minority religion with the pagan religion of the native Celtic tribes and with Roman polytheism. The departure of the Romans signalled the invasion of Britain by, among others, Angles and Saxons, with their own pagan religions. Christianity was pushed to the western and northern fringes but was kept alive by the Celtic saints, among them Aidan, Bede, Brendan, Columba, Ninian and Patrick.

So, when Augustine was sent to Britain by the Pope in AD 597, the country was not entirely pagan, although in eastern and south-eastern England the Anglo-Saxon pagan religions were dominant. However, King Æthelbert of Kent became the first of the Anglo-Saxon kings to convert to Christianity and he gave Augustine some land at Canterbury on which to build a church. A strong alliance between Christianity and the monarchy was created. This event was crucial to the subsequent development of Christianity in Britain and hence to its role in forming British culture. In particular, it gave a foothold in Britain to the way that Christianity was practised in Rome, leading eventually to a great debate at the Synod of Whitby in AD 664. Here it was decided that British Christianity would follow the practice of Rome rather than the practices of the Celtic church.

In the meantime, in AD 622, Islam had been founded at Mecca, another of those events that was to have repercussions down the ages.

2.5.2 Anglo-Saxons, Vikings and Normans

The Angles and Saxons (who invaded Britain in the fifth century after the collapse of the Roman Empire) were later challenged by Norsemen or Vikings (from Norway and Denmark). The Viking raids and invasions started in the eighth century and lasted well into the eleventh. There was an almost constant struggle for power between the two cultures, especially in northern and eastern Britain. However, all this was brought to a halt when Britain was conquered by the Normans.[7] The date of 1066 is probably the best known of all the dates in our history. Some historians have suggested that it was *the* major turning point in British history. Others do not go as far, but all agree their influence on English culture was important. Architecturally, the Normans produced strong, "confident" buildings as can be seen in the many Norman castles and churches or in churches with Norman features. Socially, the Normans introduced a feudal system. Linguistically, Anglo-Norman, a version of old French with clearly visible Latin roots, became the language of the aristocracy and ruling classes. England now had two main spoken languages, Anglo-Norman (effectively French) and English,[8] the latter spoken by the peasantry and lower classes. Long, long before more modern waves of immigration, Britain had been influenced socially, linguistically and culturally from several different directions.

2.6 MOVING AWAY FROM ROME

We now jump forward to the Tudor era and particularly the reign of Henry VIII in the sixteenth century. Henry broke with Rome initially on political grounds (the Pope would not allow him to divorce his first wife, Catherine of Aragon). This led eventually to the establishment of the Church of England and the dissolution of the monasteries. The break from Rome gave the theological reformers a chance to break with Roman doctrine as well as Roman governance. England thus became Protestant. This was not a smooth transition, and it was not until the "Glorious Revolution" of 1688, when William III of Orange, King of the Netherlands, was invited (with his wife Mary) to take the throne of England to save the country from Catholicism, that the situation finally began to stabilize.[9] Following the arrival of William and Mary, Parliament established a constitutional monarchy in Britain. Roman Catholics were barred from becoming monarchs but there was general freedom of worship (and no need any more for "dissenters" to flee to America as the Pilgrim Fathers had done).

2.7 SCIENCE, CULTURE AND RELIGION

2.7.1 Fifteenth to seventeenth centuries

The period of religious and governmental change described above was also a period of cultural and scientific change.

Printing was invented in 1457. The great artist Michelangelo, the astronomer Copernicus and the Protestant reformer Martin Luther were more or less mutual contemporaries, while Shakespeare and Galileo were born in the year that Michelangelo died (1564). It was also the era of exploration, especially by the nations of western and northern Europe, leading to extensive colonization of far-off countries, too often accompanied by pillaging of local resources and subjugation of native peoples.

Consideration of the work of Copernicus and Galileo leads us to Francis Bacon (1561–1626), who set out the requirements for proper scientific enquiry. Intellectual theorizing was not enough. Investigation of the natural world required careful observation, measurement and experiment, and, based on the data obtained by these "empirical methods", hypotheses could be constructed and tested by further observation, measurement and experiment. It is true that other factors, including imagination, intuition and even guesswork, can, and often do, play a role in the development of hypotheses, but all hypotheses, however developed, need to be subject to testing by empirical methods. Francis Bacon is therefore often regarded as the father of modern science in that he formalized scientific method and thus helped to usher in the scientific age.

2.7.2 The Enlightenment

Many commentators also refer to this time as the start of the modern age, linking science with an intellectual movement, *the Enlightenment*, that started in Continental Europe and then spread to Britain and eventually to America. Historians argue about the roots of the Enlightenment. Some trace its origins back to fifteenth-century Italian humanists associated with the Renaissance. We need to note that these were not humanists of the non-religious (or even anti-religious) type that we encounter today. They regarded humankind as the pinnacle of God's creation and gloried in human achievement as an outworking of a God-given status. Others suggest that the Thirty Year War (1618–48), which resulted in religious, social and political fragmentation in mainland Europe, coupled with a marked decline in the power of the Roman Catholic Church, was the catalyst. A third idea is that scientific advances in the late seventeenth century (especially the work of Isaac Newton) provided the initial impetus. From our twenty-first-century perspective it seems likely that all these factors were involved, such that Enlightenment thinking flourished through much of the eighteenth century. The church was no longer regarded as the ultimate source or guardian of learning. Individual humans and humankind in general had great potential. Thus Immanuel Kant (1724–1804) gloried in the fact that ethical codes could be discerned by human intellect ("the moral laws within") rather than being imposed by the church (although Kant certainly regarded himself as a Christian). The power of the church started to decline and although many Enlightenment thinkers were Christian believers, the Enlightenment opened the way for subsequent non-religious philosophies, including atheistic humanism.

During this period, social and political theorists developed the ideals of human autonomy, equality and freedom of the individual that were at the heart of the American Revolution and War of Independence. Some commentators also ascribe the French Revolution (1789–1804) to the Enlightenment, but this is too simplistic. Although Enlightenment values may have influenced the early stages, it is clear that many social, economic and political factors also contributed. The the Revolution went through several stages, including "The Terror" (which certainly did not embody "Enlightenment values"), and even after Revolution ended in 1804, France continued for many years to experience social and political instability.

2.7.3 Gin and Christianity

Prior to the Enlightenment, Britain had experienced two revolutions: the temporary overthrow of the monarchy during Oliver Cromwell's Commonwealth and the "Glorious Revolution" of 1688, which brought William and Mary to the throne. However, during the eighteenth century, social inequalities were very marked and poverty was rife, with about half the population[10] living at bare survival level. Gin drinking was widespread, especially in the towns, providing a cheap way for the poor to forget their problems. Into this situation came Christian preachers and reformers such as George Whitefield and John Wesley. In addition to encouraging a recommitment to the Christian faith, these reformers also worked tirelessly for social justice, not from a secular standpoint (as seen, for example, in the work of the Anglo-American social reformer, Thomas Paine) but from a Christian standpoint. The Christian revival that resulted from the preaching of Whitefield and Wesley was followed by a programme of building schools and hospitals, establishment of charities to help the poor and eventually the abolition of slavery, the latter after the tireless work of Wilberforce and the Clapham sect. It is worth pausing to remember all this as a contrast to attitudes in our current secular age, when "faith schools" are regarded with suspicion by many, Christian charities seen as "biased" and religion in general is thought of as irrelevant at best and dangerous at worst.

2.8 THE INDUSTRIAL REVOLUTION AND THE AGE OF INVENTION

Science continued to flourish following the formalization of the scientific method by Bacon, leading to extensive new information about the workings of the universe. But it was not only in "pure science" that progress was made. Newcomen invented the steam engine in 1712 and manufactured several over the next few years. In 1769, James Watt patented a much more efficient version which could be adapted to drive machinery, such as in a cotton mill. Coal was plentiful and provided fuel for the engine. Arkwright built machines for carding and spinning cotton and adapted them to be driven by water power. His first water-powered mill may still be seen at Cromford in Derbyshire.

Industry was becoming mechanized; transport links were improving through the building of new canals, roads and bridges, which facilitated the movement of materials and products. The Industrial Revolution, widely regarded as starting in Britain in 1750, was under way. It led to extensive migration from the countryside to towns and cities. Many towns and cities, especially in the Midlands and North of England, in South Wales and to a lesser extent in lowland Scotland, grew dramatically in size. In 1750, Merthyr Tydfil was a small village set in green countryside; agriculture provided most of the employment. However, coal, iron ore and limestone were locally and readily available; Merthyr thus became an iron town. Workers poured in, some from other countries including Ireland and Italy, and the population grew, reaching about 8,000 in 1801 and 46,000 by 1851. This made it the largest town in Wales. However, rapid growth of urban populations led to the growth of slums, and many working people lived in appalling conditions, graphically described by Thomas Carlyle[11] and depicted by Hogarth. In general, the Industrial Revolution led eventually to increased standards of living but working-class people did not benefit from this for some time.

By 1850, the industrial age was well and truly here, aided by the rapidly growing railway network. It had spread to America and to mainland Europe and led to the strengthening of capitalism as the predominant socio-politico-economic system (strongly criticized by Karl Marx in *Das Kapital*, first published in 1867). The building in 1885 of the first car (automobile), Karl Benz's *Motorwagen*, paved the way for improved road transport. The invention of the telephone (1876) and the radio (1895) led to much better communications. Added to all this, increased knowledge in many areas of science would lead to further technological advances in the twentieth century. Overall prosperity increased and populations continued to grow rapidly; the population of Europe doubled between the beginning and end of the nineteenth century. For much of that time, following the defeat of Napoleonic France in 1815, Britain was the dominant economic (and military) power, heading the largest empire that the world has ever known.

2.9 SCIENCE, CULTURE AND RELIGION REVISITED

Although, as we have seen, the Enlightenment was not in itself an anti-religious movement, it did open the way for atheistic humanism and for what was called rationalism. In the world of science, many earlier practitioners were Christians, believing that the order and beauty they observed in the universe reflected the work of the creator. However, belief in a creator God is not a pre-requisite for investigating the world. There was a "gap in the wall" such that by the middle years of the nineteenth century, the Christian consensus was weakening.

No single event illustrates this better than the publication in 1859 of Charles Darwin's book, *On the Origin of Species by Means of Natural Selection*. Darwin himself was very clear that he did not regard an evolutionary viewpoint as being incompatible with religious belief.[12] Nevertheless, publication of the book set in train a fierce debate between, on one side, those Christians who read the first three chapters of Genesis in a literal way and, on the other, people with strong anti-religious views. Both these groups viewed evolution as a challenge to a theistic understanding of creation, that the very gates of Eden had been stormed, but while the former group continued to challenge evolutionary theory, the second group, typified by the biologist Thomas Huxley, were happy to remove God from the creation processes. Many commentators regard this debate, and especially Huxley's role in it, as being the origin of the widely held view that science and religion are in conflict.[13]

On a more general level, non-belief became more socially acceptable. As the historian Schaubach put it in 1863, "It is almost as though people want to show how intelligent they think they are by the degree of their emancipation from Bible and Catechism."[14] More informally, Gwen Raverat, writing in *Period Piece*, her account of growing up in Cambridge in the second half of the nineteenth century, recalls the young people's realization that rejection of Christianity and even espousal of atheism was now socially acceptable.

In parallel with this, the German philosopher Friedrich Nietzsche pronounced that God was dead. This may lead to nihilism, but for Nietzsche it meant that humankind became the ultimate source of wisdom. He thus suggested that man can reinvent himself as superman. In ethics, he argued that with no external authority, the individual becomes the arbiter of ethical behaviour. Thus, the only rational approach was to look after oneself, an ethical system known as rational egoism (see Chapter 4, section 4.2) from which can be traced the objectivism of Ayn Rand and the existentialism of Sartre and others (see below and Chapter 4, section 4.2).

2.10 INTO THE TWENTIETH CENTURY

In Britain, the passage from the nineteenth to the twentieth century was marked by the Suffragette movement, one of the most significant social movements of modern times. It seems incredible that it is still less than 100 years since women were given the vote. Government and other authorities, including the Church of England, were implacably opposed to allowing women to vote, and many suffragettes were imprisoned for roles in the more violent or disruptive of their protests. However, at the end of World War I (see below), women were given the vote in The Representation of the People Act of 1918.[15] The successful passage of this Act through Parliament is often attributed to the recognition of the vital role that women played in the war. More generally, this was a key moment in the emancipation of women in this country, a trend that would continue through the whole century. In terms of our value and human personhood, men and women are equal in the sight of God; it has just taken humans themselves (or perhaps men themselves) a long time to realize this (see also Chapter 3, section 3.5).

In the economic and industrial spheres, Britain had started to lose its pre-eminence by the end of the nineteenth century. America began to emerge as a dominant world power and some of the nations in mainland Europe, especially Germany, had also started to develop strongly. Nevertheless, Britain remained a major player and would continue to be so for many years to come. Industrialization continued apace, fuelled by increasing trade and by continuing inventiveness and innovation. One very significant invention was the aeroplane. Following the momentous first powered flights of the Wright Brothers' *Flyer 1* at Kitty Hawk, North Carolina, flying quickly took off! Pioneers of flight undertook daring journeys across the sea, and then across large oceans, and even around the world. It was clear that air travel was entirely practical. By the later years of the century it would become the preferred mode of long-distance transport.

Aeroplanes were also quickly adopted for military purposes and played a role in World War I (think of "The Red Baron") which started only eleven years after the Wright Brothers' first flight. Indeed, the first half of the century was punctuated by warfare, from the Boer War onwards. World War I (1914–18) was marked by the death of 8.5 million military personnel (total for both sides), many of them dying in appalling conditions in the trenches in France, Belgium and the Gallipoli peninsula. A further 21 million were wounded. Looking back on that war from here it is very hard to understand the folly of it all and yet when war was declared in 1914, there were street celebrations in cities across Europe!

Towards the end of that war, Russia, one of Britain's allies, experienced the 1917 Revolution. The Tsar was deposed in February 1917 and the Bolsheviks assumed power in October of that year. As with most revolutions, a power struggle then ensued, but by 1922 the Bolsheviks were able to establish the Soviet Union. In accord with Marxist principles, the Union was institutionally atheist and religion was suppressed. However, other Marxist ideals such as democracy and emancipation of the workers soon fell by the wayside. The Soviet Union thus developed as a one-party state with the workers and other "ordinary" people having very little power. It was interesting that, despite this, many West European academics and intellectuals, including for example Jean-Paul Sartre, espoused Marxism/communism in the inter-war years.

Sartre was also a proponent of a philosophy known as *existentialism*. This was developed from the philosophy of Nietzsche and proposed that any understanding of the world must start with the individual. It has been summed up as existence (of the individual) before essence (i.e. the fundamental nature of things). Individuals find themselves through experience, exercise of free will and choice without needing any external objective truth. This means it is difficult to define experiences and choices in traditional terms of right and wrong. Both Nietzschean philosophy and existentialism have affected more general philosophical and moral thinking in the late twentieth and early twenty-first centuries, as is discussed in Chapter 4.

One other significant event of this era was the partitioning of Ireland, with the south, now known as the Republic of Ireland, finally gaining independence from Britain in 1922, while the north remained as part of what was now the United Kingdom of Great Britain and Northern Ireland. This was one of those events that had echoes down the years, as is seen in the next chapter.

On the wider international scene, it was just 21 years after the end of World War I that Britain and its allies (including the Soviet Union) were once again at war with Germany. Under Adolf Hitler, Germany had adopted policies of racial supremacy, including ruthlessly enforced anti-Semitism. In the years leading up to the war, many Jews fled from Germany, making their homes in several different countries including Britain and America. Our cultural and intellectual life was much enriched by this influx. I have several friends in the science community whose grandparents (or even parents) came to Britain as refugees in the 1930s. One of those refugees was a wonderful German Jewish doctor, Ludwig Guttman, who worked at Stoke Mandeville on the rehabilitation of spinally injured servicemen.[16]

The horrors and atrocities of the war itself have been dealt with extensively elsewhere; I simply want to say two things. First, the war had lasting effects on the psyche of the German people, which have taken two generations to shake off completely. There have also been effects on German science, where, because of the horrors of Nazi eugenic and ethnic cleansing programmes, there has until relatively recently been a great antipathy towards anything to do with genetics. Secondly, the Allies' dropping of nuclear bombs on Nagasaki and Hiroshima revealed the horrific effects of such weapons. Even so, the major powers continued to develop nuclear weapons after the war had ended, such that the possibility of mutual destruction was a major factor in the "cold war" (see Chapter 3, section 3.2). The Allies had won the war against Germany and the axis powers but the collaboration between the Soviet bloc and the "Western" Allies quickly dissipated after victory had been won (see Chapter 3, sections 3.1 and 3.2).

2.11 SOME THOUGHTS ON THE STORY SO FAR

This chapter has been a whistle-stop tour of civilization over a few thousand years. In that time, one of the world's main power bases has moved from the Near/Middle East into Europe and then to Britain and finally to America.[17] Britain's history was shaped initially by successive invasions and conquests and thus she has drawn her culture and ethnic origins from several different sources. Britain developed from a pagan, largely rural, country to a major industrial power in less than 1,800 years. It also became a Christian country and eventually established its own Christian culture and identity separate from that based on Rome. However, by the end of the nineteenth century, the Christian consensus was weakening.

And what of Plato's two horses (see start of chapter)? At institutional and state level, it seems that the horse of ignoble character often has its way. War, acquisition of territory, ethnic cleansing, pillaging of resources and war crimes have all been part of the story and these are doubtless large-scale reflections of individual egoism and cruelty. But the noble horse has also been at work, in countless untold acts of heroism, love and self-sacrifice and in the work of the social reformers, many of them driven by their Christian faith. Plato's analysis, echoed by St Paul, Pascal and many other writers down the centuries, is constantly proved to be true. In Pascal's words, "Man is neither angel nor beast; and the misfortune is that he who would act the angel acts the beast."[18] The next chapter looks at how this has played out in more modern times as we consider "post-war" civilization and culture.

NOTES

1. Indeed, it is often claimed that the human is the only animal that does this, but this is simply not true. Thus, Jane Goodall reports that among chimpanzees there was systematic violence towards members of other groups which included inter-group "warfare" that could last several years. One of the groups she was studying totally wiped out a rival group.

2. Readers who are interested to read a full account of this are likely to enjoy Richard Miles's *Ancient Worlds*, London: Penguin Books, 2011.

3. The Nebuchadnezzar mentioned in the Bible.

4. According to the Greek historian Herodotus, writing in 450 BC (*The Histories*, Book 1, para. 178).

5. Note that Euclid and Archimedes lived in "Greater Greece", i.e. regions of the Hellenistic Empire outside of Greece itself. Euclid was based in Alexandria (Egypt) and Archimedes in Syracuse (Sicily).

6. In AD 395, Theodosius forbade the staging of the Olympic Games in Greece because they were dedicated to a pagan god, Zeus; he also shut the temple dedicated to Zeus.

7. It is likely that my ancestors, and the ancestors of others with Breton surnames, arrived in Britain "on the coat-tails" of the Norman invasion.

8. Kernowek was spoken in parts of Cornwall until the nineteenth century.

9. The initial landing of King William and his troops was in Torbay; to this day, there are many people with Dutch surnames in South Devon, while Dutch-style houses still exist in several villages and small towns around Exeter.

10. The total population was about 6.5 million at the beginning of the eighteenth century but rose to about 9 million by the end of the century.

11. After visiting Merthyr Tydfil in 1850, Carlyle wrote that the town was inhabited by "such unguided, hard-worked, fierce and miserable-looking sons of Adam I never saw before. Ah me! It is like a vision of Hell, and will never leave me, that of these poor creatures broiling, all in sweat and dirt, amid their furnaces, pits, and rolling mills." (Letter to Jane Welsh Carlyle, 16 August 1850.)

12. See, for example, Nick Spencer and Denis Alexander, *Rescuing Darwin – God and Evolution in Britain Today*, London: Theos, 2009.

13. At this point, I need to add a personal note. As a professional biologist I have spent 40 years working directly or indirectly with genes. My work has brought me into specific contact with the process of evolution. I have never seen this as a challenge to my Christian faith. I reject the view that science and religious faith are in conflict and indeed hold that they complement each other.

14. Cited by Eric Hobsbawm, *The Age of Capital*, London: Abacus, 1977, page 294.

15. In the USA, women were given the vote in 1920.

16. See Chapter 9, note 4.

17. I am not forgetting everything that was happening in Asia. For example, China was the world's largest economy for most of the period between the emergence of the Han Dynasty around 200 BC and the start of the European Industrial Revolution. However, I am focusing here on the West because it is directly relevant to my theme.

18. *Pensées*, 329.

3

THE WAY WE ARE

Every gun that is made, every warship launched, every rocket fired signifies in the final sense, a theft from those who hunger and are not fed, those who are cold and are not clothed. This world in arms is not spending money alone. It is spending the sweat of its laborers, the genius of its scientists, the hopes of its children.
Dwight D. Eisenhower, from his "Chance for Peace" speech, 16 April 1953

Everyone… agrees that the church is failing. Even though it may be growing phenomenally in other parts of the world, in Europe at least, its days seem to be numbered. It is not hard to find the reason… It is largely because people have better things to do with their time. Church for many people simply feels boring, irrelevant and unnecessary. And today's culture offers a whole raft of more effective and attractive ways to fill Sunday mornings or find spiritual enlightenment.
Graham Tomlin, in *Spiritual Fitness*, 2006

3.1 INTRODUCTION
While the events described in the previous two chapters provided the foundation for our current culture, it is in the seven decades since the end of World War II that the foundation has been built upon to form our current cultural

norms, on the way that "being human" works itself out today. The vast majority of my readers will not have any memory of World War II and yet, in approaching an understanding of where we are now, we actually need to go back to Europe in 1945. By the end of World War II, Europe was divided by an "Iron Curtain". On the western side of the curtain were the "free" capitalist countries and on the eastern side, the Soviet bloc, countries allied to and under the thrall of communist Russia, led by its ruthless dictator, Joseph Stalin. Germany was divided into the capitalist West Germany and the communist East Germany. The city of Berlin was situated within East Germany but was itself divided into capitalist West Berlin, in which were stationed troops from the main Western Allies, and communist East Berlin, occupied by troops from the Soviet Union (as indeed was the whole of East Germany). Parts of Asia were also partitioned: after Japan surrendered, Korea was divided into two. The south was occupied by US troops and the north by Soviet troops. The division between the two lay along the "38th parallel". This led almost inevitably to the establishment, immediately after World War II, of a capitalist state in South Korea and a communist state in North Korea. International tensions were thus more or less built into the world's political geography and those tensions would remain for several decades. It was not just a clash of ideologies (and it certainly was that) but also a reaction by Stalin and other Soviet leaders to World War II itself: a buffer of "client states" would be a defence against any further attempts to invade the country, following the defeat of Hitler.

3.2 COMMUNISM AND CAPITALISM

It did not take long for those tensions to spill over into actual conflict. The great capitalist powers on one side and the great communist powers on the other side fought two "proxy" wars in south-east Asia. The first was the Korean War (1950–

53), ignited by North Korea's invasion of South Korea. Intervention by the "West" was sanctioned by the United Nations. The other proxy war was in Vietnam (1955–75). Concerned about a possible domino effect (if one country "falls" to communism, others will follow), the USA, supported by Australia, New Zealand, Thailand, the Philippines and South Korea, poured ever-increasing resources and troops into defending South Vietnam against communist North Vietnam. Eventually, however, the futility of this became all too apparent and the USA and its allies withdrew in 1973. Saigon, the capital of South Vietnam, fell in April 1975, and hostilities were formally ended in November 1975. The casualties had been extensive. Somewhere between 1 and 3 million Vietnamese lost their lives, as did nearly 60,000 US military personnel. From the American point of view, all this must have seemed to no avail when Vietnam was united as a single (communist) country in 1976. Nevertheless, there was no domino effect.

The Korean War had been in effect the start of the cold war between the Soviet Union and the USA (with its capitalist allies), although the Berlin blockade of 1948 gave a strong hint of what was to come. The cold war did not end with the truce in Korea and continued with varying degrees of intensity for over three decades. For many of my readers it will have been a "real presence" during a significant proportion of their lives, which is perhaps difficult for younger readers to appreciate. It was marked by a proliferation of nuclear weapons on both sides. By 1953, the Soviet Union and the USA were about equal in terms of destructive nuclear power. Indeed, as the cold war went on, the nuclear powers, mainly the USA and Russia, but also including smaller nations such as the United Kingdom, accumulated total nuclear arsenals that were large enough to destroy the population of the world several times over.

It appeared from the Western side of the "fence" that the Soviet Union was determined to dominate the world and would use military force (including nuclear weapons) to do so. And yet the prevailing view inside the Soviet Union was that the USA and its allies were equally determined to dominate the world. The differences between the two sides had been dramatically emphasized in a standoff between the Soviet leader Nikita Khrushchev and President John F. Kennedy concerning, among other things, the status of Berlin. This led directly to the building of the Berlin Wall in 1961, a heavily guarded barrier to prevent movement from communist East Berlin to capitalist West Berlin.

These events, taken with the unsuccessful invasion of Cuba by USA-supported anti-communist Cuban exiles in 1961 (the "Bay of Pigs" incident) and the positioning of Soviet missiles in Cuba in 1962, brought the world as near to nuclear war as at any time during the cold war era. It is salutary to remind ourselves how quickly situations can escalate.

As a young graduate doing fieldwork in Bulgaria (a Soviet "satellite" country) in the mid 1960s (prior to returning to university to do my PhD), I was struck by the anti-American propaganda everywhere, in posters, in statements broadcast from loudspeakers in village squares, in school history books and so on. There was also a good deal of misinformation about Western (including UK) social conditions, with workers thought to be living in conditions of great privation, as in Dickensian times. And yet it seemed to me that the average Bulgarian enjoyed much less freedom than I did, and that was certainly the view of those citizens who were prepared to talk openly (but discreetly) about their situation. It had also been the view of the citizens of Hungary and of Poland who attempted to rise up against Soviet domination in 1956. These uprisings were ruthlessly crushed by Russia, and the same would happen again in Czechoslovakia in 1968. The people of Poland had another attempt at freeing themselves from Soviet rule in 1980–81. Following a visit to Poland of Pope John Paul II (Polish by birth), workers at the Gdansk shipyard went on strike in August 1980. This catalysed the formation of a trade union, Solidarność (Solidarity), led by an unemployed electrician, Lech Wałęsa. Solidarność membership reached several million (possibly up to 25 per cent of the population) and the union became a symbol of the struggle for freedom in Eastern Europe.[1] However, the Soviet Union regarded these developments as very dangerous and in December 1981 imposed martial law on Poland (this was lifted in 1983). The leaders of Solidarność, including Lech Wałęsa, were arrested and imprisoned, although most were released after a year. The rest of the world had clearly taken note of all this because in 1983 Wałęsa was awarded the Nobel Prize for Peace (an award much criticized in the Soviet Union).

But this time the seeds of freedom actually germinated. In 1985, Mikhail Gorbachev became head of the Soviet Union and immediately introduced reforms. Citizens were now free to express their opinions, including criticism of the government, without fear of reprisal. Many political prisoners were released and ordinary Soviet citizens were allowed to travel outside the country. However, Gorbachev is best remembered for his major role in ending the cold war.[2] He initiated a series of meetings ("summits") with the then (Republican) president of the USA, Ronald Reagan. Reagan was initially suspicious but came to understand that Gorbachev really wanted change. Both sides agreed that they should be at peace with each other; they stopped accumulating nuclear weapons and indeed started to reduce their arsenals.

In the view of many commentators, Gorbachev is one of the most significant figures of the late twentieth century. He has been praised by people as different as Margaret Thatcher and

Desmond Tutu,[3] and was awarded the Nobel Prize for Peace in 1990. The results of his policies are visible on a modern map of Europe. As the Soviet Union sought rapprochement with the West, so its grip on the satellite countries in Eastern Europe began to weaken. One by one, like a series of dominoes, governments fell and people were freed from communist rule. This started almost inevitably with Poland, where Solidarność came back into the open in 1988 and was recognized as a legitimate trade union in 1989. One of the most dramatic events was the fall of the Berlin Wall in November 1989. The East German government, realizing that the game was up, opened some of the crossing points. Immediately, crowds of people on both sides started to tear the wall down without any intervention from the police. I found it very moving. I had seen the wall from both sides during a professional visit to Berlin in 1987, viewing it with some despair as yet another "monument" to the "inhumanity of man to man" – and now it was gone. The Soviet Union itself collapsed in 1990 and Gorbachev resigned almost immediately afterwards, leaving a significant mark on history.

Finally, we need to consider the complex subject of Yugoslavia. From 1945 until his death from cancer in 1980, it had been headed by Marshall Josep Broz Tito, who was held in great affection as a war hero. The country was socialist/ communist but was not a member of the Warsaw Pact; it was part of the network of unaligned nations. Tito is best described as a benevolent dictator; certainly the people enjoyed more freedom than did those of the Soviet satellite countries. However, Yugoslavia felt under threat from the Soviet Union, and that is one of the factors that enabled Tito to hold together in one country a disparate group of regions/states with at least three languages, two alphabets and at least two religions. After Tito's death cracks began to appear, and this process accelerated as the peoples of the neighbouring Soviet satellite countries gained their freedom. Slovenia, Yugoslavia's most north-westerly state, and Macedonia in the south-east managed to secede relatively easily but the break-up of the rest of the country from 1991 onwards was a very violent affair, marked by horrendous atrocities and war crimes, including mass murders, "ethnic cleansings", genocides, indiscriminate bombing and forced mass expulsions. All this happened despite the best efforts of UN and NATO peacekeeping forces. Further, the conflicts were brought right into our living rooms because reporters and camera operators from all the main TV channels, plus reporters from newspapers and agencies, were present during the conflicts; some of these were "embedded" with the peacekeeping forces, but others were more independent. It was actually a very dangerous time for journalists, reporters and camera crew and several were killed.

Even after fighting had ceased, boundaries were fluid for some years as states organized and reorganized themselves within Yugoslavia's old boundaries. Eventually five stable countries emerged, namely Slovenia, Macedonia, Croatia, Serbia and Montenegro. The status of a sixth, Kosovo, is still uncertain since less than half of the nations in the UN have recognized it as an independent state (although nearly all EU members have done so). And the significance for us is that all this happened within Europe, right on the doorstep of the European Union, and yet we were unable to stop the fighting. Humankind was still involved in conflict.

3.3 ISRAEL AND PALESTINE

Another event that happened soon after World War II still has repercussions in the twenty-first century: the partitioning of Palestine between the Jews and the Palestinians. This too was a complex process but eventually, in 1948, the Jews declared the formation of the state of Israel. This occupied

78 per cent of the land and was followed by about 726,000 Palestinians becoming refugees, mainly in Egypt, Jordan, Lebanon and Syria. Arab villages were thus depopulated and even destroyed, with Jewish villages being built in their place. Israel further expanded its borders in 1967 in the Six-Day War, although much of the land it captured in Sinai was later restored to Egypt. Land grab goes on today, exemplified by the building of Jewish settlements on land taken from the Palestinians in the West Bank region. At present, a just settlement between Israel and the Palestinians seems out of reach. The Holy Land, the cradle of both Judaism and Christianity, is a land of conflict and political tension.

There were also knock-on effects outside of the borders of Israel/Palestine. One of the most dramatic was the civil war in Lebanon which started nearly three decades after the partitioning of Palestine. As mentioned above, many of the Palestinian refugees had settled in Lebanon. Many more arrived after the 1967 Arab–Israeli war (see above) and again after unrest in Jordan in 1970. Among the latter were Yasser Arafat and the Palestinian Liberation Organization (PLO). There was unease about the number of Palestinian refugees and at the same time, tensions between Lebanon's Christian and Muslim populations were growing. This situation exploded into a complex civil war in 1975 when a right-wing paramilitary organization, the Phalangists (who, incidentally, enjoyed the support of some of the Christians), massacred a bus-load of Palestinians in reprisal for the murder of four of its members. It is too simplistic to regard it as a war between Muslims and Christians (and I still shudder when I hear the term "Christian militiamen"), first because of the different factions associated with one side or the other, and secondly because of PLO hostility towards neighbouring Israel.

Israel invaded and occupied southern Lebanon in 1982 and drove out the PLO. However, this provoked the emergence of

Hezbollah, a militant Islamist organization (or a connected network of militant Islamist organizations) funded by Iran and Syria. Hezbollah engaged in hostage-taking on a large scale. A total of 96 people, mainly American or Western European, were kidnapped. Among them were journalists, academics, negotiators and peace envoys, including Terry Anderson, Terry Waite (the Archbishop of Canterbury's special envoy), John McCarthy and Brian Keenan. For many hostages, months of captivity dragged on into years before they were finally released. A small number of hostages were killed and some died because of lack of access to medical aid.

The civil war finally ended in 1990–91, by which time about 200,000 people had lost their lives and much of Lebanon's infrastructure had been destroyed.

3.4 THE EUROPEAN UNION[4]

By the middle of the twentieth century, Europe had come through two World Wars. There was a universal feeling that this must not happen again. On the worldwide stage, the United Nations was formed. On the European stage, countries agreed to collaborate together in such a way that armed conflict between them would be very difficult. This eventually led to the formation of the European Economic Community (EEC) in 1957 (the Treaty of Rome) to which Britain, together with Ireland and Denmark, was admitted in 1973. By 1992, there were closer economic, scientific, technological, political and even social ties between member states, leading to the establishment in the Treaty of Maastricht of the European Union. Several former Soviet satellite countries have since joined, as have some of the countries that once formed Yugoslavia. Member states cede some of their decision-making powers to the European Parliament and twelve of the countries have adopted a common currency, the Euro (although at the time of writing, the Eurozone is having problems). As in all big families, there are occasional squabbles but in general, the EU seems to me to be a force for good, conferring a good deal of stability to the region.

While all this was happening, the sun had indeed set on the British Empire, with its former colonies gaining independence but becoming a looser association of nations, the British Commonwealth. Immigration from those former colonies, especially from the West Indies and from the Indian subcontinent, has greatly enriched UK culture and has even had an effect on medical genetics, as I show in Chapter 5 (section 5.4.1).

3.5 THE 1960S

In Western Europe and North America (and to some extent Australia), the 1960s was a remarkable decade. Many long-held social norms were challenged and society underwent considerable change as a result. Thus, the American sociologist Peter L. Berger, writing in 1998,[5] stated:

> *The cultural situation in America today (and indeed in all Western societies) is determined by the cultural earthquake of the nineteen-sixties, the consequences of which are very much in evidence. What began as a counter-culture… has achieved dominance in elite culture and, from the bastions of the latter (in the educational system, the media, the higher reaches of the law, and key positions within government bureaucracy), has penetrated both popular culture and the corporate world.*

Bob Dylan was so right when he sang that times they are "a-changin'".

The challenge to long-held social norms was multi-pronged; here I will examine the main aspects.

Perhaps the overriding impression that we get is that it was a time when students and other young people challenged authority, but actually some of the "streams" within the general flow of the 1960s involved people of all ages. Authority and cohesion had been quite effective thus far; indeed in the 1940s it had been totally necessary in the Allies' war effort. But now it seemed that authority was in many cases being wielded for no good reason, or even to keep up appearances. Those subject to authority, especially the young people, had no say in making the rules. And thus, barricades were "manned", most famously at the Sorbonne in Paris (please excuse the gender-specific language, but "staffed" doesn't sound right), lecture halls occupied, offices stormed. However, although we carry these images, it was only a minority of students and young people who took this sort of action.

Expanding our view a little shows us that, in general, rules for the sake of rules were challenged and this included areas of personal morality. It was a time of increased sexual freedom (thanks partly to the contraceptive pill); there was widespread experimentation with drugs, partly encouraged by some of the rock songs popular during the era and also by writers such as Timothy Leary. One strand of the counter-culture rejected totally what Hans Rookmaaker (Free University of Amsterdam) called the bourgeois standards of the middle class. Many people, especially in the state of California, dropped out of "normal" society and formed communes, attempting to live self-sufficiently. This was nicely illustrated in the film *Easy Rider*, when, during their motorcycle odyssey (which was to end so violently), Peter Fonda and Dennis Hopper accepted hospitality from one such commune. One image that has stayed with me is of commune members giving thanks before a meal but not sure whom or what they were thanking.

My reference to the Sorbonne is a reminder that in different countries the unrest and protests took different forms. In France, the strikes and protests by university students and

staff in May 1968 were part of a much wider series of
protests against the government led by Charles de Gaulle.
The protests included wildcat general strikes involving up to
22 per cent of the population of France. De Gaulle eventually
dissolved the National Assembly and called a general election.
Ironically, his party won a landslide victory, soundly defeating
the socialist–communist alliance that had been at the centre
of the protest movement. Nevertheless, many commentators
believe that France came very close to another revolution in
May 1968.

There were several other specific strands or themes that
could be discerned in different countries. The first of these,
especially in the USA, was concerned with racial equality and
civil rights. In the 1950s, following non-violent protests by black
people, segregation laws in the Deep South were beginning
to be relaxed. The struggle by black people for equality,
including voting rights, was beginning to take effect. A young
black pastor, Martin Luther King Jnr, rose to prominence at
this time and in 1963 led a march of thousands of civil rights
campaigners (blacks, whites and Hispanics) to Washington,
"for jobs and freedom". It was at the end of this march that
King delivered his famous "I have a dream" speech from
the steps of the Lincoln Memorial. The broadcast and print
media in the northern states played a major role, with their
stark portrayal of the indignities and deprivation suffered
by black people in the southern states, and of segregationist
violence and harassment of civil rights workers and marchers.
The US government passed the Civil Rights Act in 1964
and the Voting Rights Act in 1965. I need to say, however,
that although laws were changed, it took much longer to
change people's attitudes. And enough attitudes have been
changed for Barak Obama, an "African American" in their
current politically correct terminology, to have been elected as
president[6] – a wonderfully inspiring event.

In 1964, Martin Luther King was awarded the Nobel Prize for Peace, at the time the youngest person to have ever won it (35 years old). He donated the prize money to the civil rights movement. On 4 April 1968 he was assassinated, one of three prominent "left of centre" leaders to suffer that fate in the 1960s (John F. Kennedy, Martin Luther King and Robert Kennedy).

In respect of women's rights, World War II had involved many women in the war effort, both in the forces (although not as combatants) and as civilians. After the war, many more women went out to work than had previously been the case. However, in many cases they were denied the better jobs, received lower pay and were discriminated against in the workplace. Further, there was growing anger at societal sexism and at violence, both physical and verbal, on the streets. What became known as the "pro-choice" movement, demanding that abortion be legalized, had started on both sides of the Atlantic. Thus another strand or stream that took its place in the movements of the 1960s was feminism, the battle for women's rights, including social equality. I am proud to call myself a Christian feminist and from that perspective I suggest that although women did win many of their battles in the 1960s, the war has not yet been completely won.[7] Even when laws on equality, for example on pay, have been introduced, people find ways of getting round them, while violence against women is still too common (see also Chapters 8, section 8.7.4 and 10, section 10.5).[8]

However, one area where victory did seem complete was in the legalization of abortion. I do not want here to comment on the morality or otherwise of abortion. I am sure that there are several different views on this among my readers, but for the women's rights movement this was a victory. Abortion was legalized in the UK in 1967, from where it spread across Western Europe.[9] Only in Ireland and Poland is abortion

illegal (both are strongly Roman Catholic countries and in
Poland, under the influence of the church, abortion became
illegal in the 1990s, having been legal since 1956). In the
USA, abortion was legalized in 1973, thereby following
Canada where legalization occurred in 1969 (thus catalysing
cross-border abortion tourism until 1973). However, both in
individual states and at national level, Republican politicians
in the USA are now attempting to restrict significantly the
availability of abortions (see Chapter 6, section 6.2.2).

The final strand to consider is the protest movement against
the masters of war, the governments that sent young people
to fight in far-away places and/or that stockpiled nuclear
weapons and, indeed, tested them from time to time. On the
American side of the Atlantic, protests were mainly against
the Vietnam War; on the European side, they concentrated
more on nuclear weapons and the possibility of nuclear war.
However, there was some crossover. In the UK, the protest
against nuclear weapons was spearheaded by the Campaign
for Nuclear Disarmament (CND). From 1959 to 1963 (and
sporadically since then) CND organized marches from the
Atomic Weapons Research Establishment at Aldermaston
in Berkshire to London, often attracting tens of thousands
of marchers. CND continued its protests in other ways after
1963, with demonstrations at air bases and acts of civil
disobedience, for which many were prepared to go to prison.
CND is rather less in the public eye since the end of the cold
war but still mounts protests against the UK's possession of
Trident missiles.

There is one final point to make about the 1960s. In Britain
and in other parts of northern Europe, two World Wars
had challenged ideals that people may have held about the
goodness of humankind and their faith in a loving God. If
there is a God, how could he allow humans to do this to each
other; how could he allow so many "innocent" people to be

killed? And so the breakage of the Christian consensus that I mentioned in the previous chapter continued. The 1960s saw a further twist in this tale. I have already mentioned the challenge to the bourgeois which includes doing things just to keep up appearances, just to appear respectable. Even though religious observance was on the decline by the beginning of the 1960s, there was still a lot of churchgoing: going to church because a person (e.g. a politician) needed to be seen there or because it was part of village life. For those caught up in the 1960s' ferment, it was legitimate to ask why people did this; what did they actually believe, if anything? And if they did not believe, was there really any point in dressing up and being bored for an hour every Sunday morning? Thus the fall in bourgeois or social churchgoing accelerated further in the 1960s, especially among younger people. Couples may have still wanted a church wedding for themselves or a church christening for their babies, but it was "ceremony" that they wanted and the church could still provide that. As a student during the 1960s I found this exciting rather than depressing. The church – that is, the followers of Jesus Christ – could shake off its cultural and social baggage and start to become truly Christian.

I also need to say that in the USA, this decline in religious observance did not happen in nearly such a dramatic way. A large proportion of the US population still call themselves Christians and, furthermore, most of those attend a place of worship, although I wonder how much of this is just "social" churchgoing.

3.6 NORTHERN IRELAND

I said in the previous chapter that the partitioning of Ireland in 1921–22 had echoes down the years, and this was especially true in the last 30 years of the twentieth century and into the early years of the twenty-first. The partitioning had left a minority of Roman Catholics in Northern Ireland, with political leanings towards the Republic, among the Protestant majority who definitely wanted to remain in union with Great Britain. In 1969, tensions between the two "sides" escalated into skirmishes and thence into ongoing conflict. The terms Catholic and Protestant were used as convenient labels to describe the two sides but actually we should use the terms Republican and Unionist. The Republican cause was largely fought politically by Sinn Fein and militarily by various factions of the Irish Republican Army (IRA), many based south of the border. On the Unionist side, a number of paramilitary groups were involved, especially the Ulster Defence Association and the Ulster Volunteer Force.

This conflict hung over the United Kingdom like a threatening shadow. On both sides, the paramilitary forces indulged in shootings, mass murders and bombings. The staff of the Europa Hotel in Belfast now talk humorously of working in the most frequently bombed premises in the United Kingdom, but it cannot have been funny living through it. The IRA also bombed mainland targets, stating that it was legitimate to bomb centres of economic activity on the British mainland.

Eventually, however, ordinary people who wanted to live in peace said that enough was enough and so on several occasions there were grassroots attempts to put an end to the violence.[10] During the 1990s, a desire for peace began to suppress the appetite for conflict. Further, both sides realized they could not "win" by continuing violence. Thus, in 1998, after long and protracted negotiations, the Good Friday Peace Agreement was signed. The Agreement was supported overwhelmingly in referenda held in Northern Ireland and the Republic. Violence ceased but there was still a long way to go; political enmity remained. However, in 2007 the process was finally completed. It had been a long time.

3.7 TERRORISM AND WAR

3.7.1 Hostages and hijacks

Human conflict runs like a thread through the history of our species; one of the most notable features of recent times has been the effectiveness of small groups of people in fighting for particular causes, not in the main area of conflict, but at places remote from it. For example, in 1972 a group of Palestinians representing an organization called Black September stormed the Israeli accommodation in the Olympic Village in Munich. They took eleven athletes and coaches hostage and eventually killed them; a West German police officer was also killed. Thinking back to section 3.3 in this chapter, it is interesting that the Palestinians called this operation *Ikrit and Biram*, the names of two Christian Arab villages in Palestine whose inhabitants had been expelled during the expansion of Israel.

One particularly effective way of drawing attention to a cause has been the hijacking of planes, often combined with taking the passengers hostage. An epidemic of plane hijacks started in the 1960s, accelerated in the 1970s and barely slowed down in the 1980s. Hijacks have occurred all over the world, including the USA. Many of them have been carried out in the name of political causes but some have been the work of criminals.

3.7.2 Gulf War I

In August 1990, Iraq, under the leadership of Saddam Hussein, invaded Kuwait, whose army was defeated in two days. Kuwait was annexed and declared to be the nineteenth province of Iraq. The action was universally condemned on the international scene and, formally, by a United Nations resolution. Saddam Hussein refused all attempts to negotiate; he would not give up the newly won land. So an international force, led by the USA, launched an attack, first gaining a foothold in Kuwait and then pushing the Iraqi army back into Iraq and on towards Baghdad. The war was over in a month. It was the first war to become effectively a TV show. Reporters and camera crew were in Kuwait and in Iraq, including Baghdad itself, the latter watching the rockets and bombing planes arriving.

While this was regarded with a great deal of pride and satisfaction, we should remind ourselves that the West and especially the USA had, in the 1980s, supported Iraq in its war with Iran. Some of the weapons used against the international force may well have actually come from the West in the first place! International relations can be very fickle.

3.7.3 Militant Islam

Bubbling in the background to all this was the rise of an extreme Islamist organization, al-Qaeda, led, organized and bankrolled by a very wealthy exiled Saudi, Osama Bin Laden, living in Afghanistan. Al-Qaeda declared jihad, holy war,[11] against the "infidels" of the West and especially the USA. The USA's ongoing support for Israel, running counter to many UN resolutions and perceived interference in the affairs of Islamic countries, including the presence of troops in some of those countries, especially Saudi Arabia, were among the factors provoking this declaration. It was almost as if the Crusades had been reversed. Jihad was carried to American targets such as the US embassies in Kenya and Tanzania, both of which were bombed on 7 August 1998. Above all, jihad led to one of those events that, for the majority of us, will be seared into our memories for ever. We can remember exactly where we were in the early afternoon (UK time) of 11 September 2001, now known universally as 9/11. Hijacked planes had been flown into both towers of the International Trade Center in Manhattan, both of which eventually collapsed. A third plane was flown into the Pentagon, and a fourth plane was unaccounted for. It had been intended to fly it into the White House, but the courageous passengers overcame the hijackers and crashed the plane in open countryside.

These events have had profound knock-on effects. Afghanistan was invaded in October 2001, under the terms of the UN Charter that permit self-defence. The fundamentalist Islamic Taliban, who were the country's government and the political allies of al-Qaeda, were removed from overall power but whether they have been defeated is another matter. Eleven years on, American and British troops are still there; Taliban guerrillas are still active, even though Bin Laden was captured and killed (in Pakistan) in 2011. Inter-tribal conflict continues. Lives are still being lost.

Following 9/11, President George W. Bush also decided to invade Iraq on the grounds that Saddam Hussein's government had and was prepared to use "weapons of mass destruction". We now know that this claim was untrue, and, indeed, the invasion was not mandated by the United Nations. In UN terms it was illegal, but the British Prime Minister Tony Blair supported Bush in this, with the *disapproval* of the majority of British citizens. Saddam Hussein was removed from power but conflicts between different Muslim groups led to car bombings and many deaths. Christians are now persecuted (which, somewhat ironically, did not happen under Saddam's rule) and many have fled the country. This surely was not an outcome that George W. Bush would have wished for.

It is interesting to note that the activities of al-Qaeda in Africa and in the USA seemed to give confidence to militant Islamists in general. Young British Muslim men became radicalized through the teaching of extremist Islamic teachers and went to training camps in Pakistan to learn the techniques of urban terrorism. Since 9/11, there have been a number of attempted terrorist attacks on UK and US targets but most have been foiled through the vigilance of the security services. However, on 7 July 2005 (7/7), a small group of suicide bombers succeeded with coordinated bombings of tube trains and a bus in London during the morning rush hour. Scores of people were killed or seriously injured; interestingly, and on a lighter note, one of the seriously injured, Martine Wright, who had her legs amputated, represented Great Britain at seated volleyball in the 2012 Paralympic Games – a brilliant example of courage and determination.[12]

Socially, there is no doubt that all these events have led, among some elements of our society, to prejudice against and even hatred of Muslims. This extends to anyone who looks or sounds at least vaguely Arabic or Pakistani. It has enabled extreme racist groups like the British National Party to stir up more racial or ethnic hatred. In the USA, this mindless prejudice has extended to other groups, including, for example, Sikhs. Indeed, in the summer of 2012, several Sikhs were killed when a right-wing extremist gunman stormed a Sikh temple and opened fire.

3.8 POWER BASES SHIFT AGAIN

For many, many years, financial power was located in the global north, with the USA being an especially big player. However, with the advent of globalization and especially the freeing up of international trade, there has been a movement away from the global north to the largest of what were the less-developed nations, namely China, India and Brazil. We are still in the early stages of the revolution, but already China is about to become the world's largest economy. It will be very interesting to see how the situation plays out over the next few years.

3.9 SCIENCE, RELIGION AND CULTURE

3.9.1 Modernism, modernity and postmodernism

In northern and Western Europe, the Enlightenment and/ or the establishment of the scientific method are taken as the beginning of modernity. There was confidence that science could uncover objective reality about the world, although recognizing that at any one time our knowledge of that reality is partial and provisional. Human intellect was held in great respect. The idea that "truths" about the world might simply be cultural or social constructs would have been laughable. Further, many of the early proponents of modernity, including scientists, had a faith in God; some were definitely Christian in their beliefs while others had a vaguer deist faith. Nevertheless, the main point was that there are discoverable truths that are of universal validity in both science and religion.

However, this is not true of postmodernism, a group of overlapping ideas that have their roots in the nineteenth century (or perhaps earlier) but came to prominence in the 1970s. One of the main thrusts of postmodernism is that truth is socially constructed. Thus truth becomes local or even personal; there is no such thing as "objective" truth, there are no big stories, no "metanarratives". It will be immediately obvious that there is no room for overarching religious beliefs or for absolute moral values in postmodernism. Furthermore, science is also under threat because it makes claims to be seeking verifiable truth about objective reality.

Where did such an idea come from? We can see strong hints of it in the work of Nietzsche and stronger hints in twentieth-century existentialism. They both lead to a position in which beliefs, values and morals are personally defined and thus socially constructed, strongly influenced by culture and therefore not necessarily relevant or even tenable in other cultures. The philosopher Wittgenstein insisted that words, including scientific terms, must be interpreted in their social context. While it is clear that culture will certainly affect the perceived meanings of words, a problem arises if we assume that this means there can be no underlying universal truth. We certainly see the latter conclusion in the work of writers such as Derrida and Foucault and in the deconstructionist school of literary criticism (there is also a deconstructionist or postmodern movement in architecture,[13] exemplified by the amazing Imperial War Museum at Salford Quays in Manchester).

At its most extreme, postmodernism would state that all things are relative. The statement is of course self-defeating; we cannot live by it. However, some postmodernists would argue that this in itself is a symptom of the absence of any overriding truths or principles, and an indication of the futility of trying to derive any.

There are indications that twenty-first-century academic philosophers and sociologists are moving away from postmodernism, but it has had a major influence on thinking in wider society. My estimate is that, because of its prevalence in the media, and especially the broadcast media, most people under the age of 60 in the UK and in Western Europe in general have been strongly influenced by postmodernism. The influence has perhaps been weaker in the USA but it is there nevertheless (see e.g. Chapter 4, section 4.3). We can see its influence in discussions where a non-expert's view is given the same weight as an expert's view. The media debates on the MMR controversy, on GM crops and on climate change have all been riddled with this type of approach. Above all we see the influence of postmodernism in attitudes to religion (see below) and to ethics, as discussed in the next chapter.

3.9.2 Science

Throughout the period I am discussing in this chapter, there has been extensive progress in all areas of science, from cosmology down to particle physics. In the latter sphere, the probable discovery of the elusive Higgs Boson in the Large Hadron Collider has been a real highlight. However, I do not want to present a catalogue of all the scientific discoveries of the past 70 years (however interesting that may be for me), neither do I have the time or space to do so. I simply want to present some of the major discoveries and developments that have made possible the medical biotechnologies that are discussed in subsequent chapters.[14]

In genetics, the identification of DNA as the genetic material had happened in 1944. The next big prize was to elucidate its structure in order to gain insights into how it worked. That prize went in 1953 to James Watson and Francis Crick, working in Cambridge, and Rosalind Franklin and Maurice Wilkins, working in London. The double helix, now an icon of the genetic age, was discovered. This quickly led to a general understanding (details are still being added) of how genes work and how DNA is replicated in order to pass on copies in cell division. This knowledge was applied to the development of genetic modification of bacteria in 1973, and soon afterwards of animal cells and then of whole animals (plant genetic modification was first achieved in 1983). Methods for sequencing DNA were invented in the late 1970s (and have since become very much more sophisticated), opening the way for elucidating the structure of individual genes and for genetic diagnosis and testing.

A combination of genetics and developmental biology helped us to understand how genes work in the development, growth and maintenance of living organisms and this led to the possibility of cloning. Mouse embryonic stem cells were discovered in 1998 (the existence of adult stem cells had already been known for some time), leading eventually to their being found in human embryos. This paved the way for the possible development of therapies based on embryonic stem cells.

We have also achieved a much greater understanding of the physiology, biochemistry and electro-chemistry of all types of cell and tissue in the body. This has enabled us to modify brain function, for example in depressive illness, and to intervene in malfunctioning biochemical pathways and physiological processes, leading to some of the developments discussed in Chapter 9 in relation to cognitive enhancement and ageing.

In general, science has been and continues to be a dynamic part of modern society. It receives large amounts of funding from the public purse, and many aspects of medical research are also funded by charities. All this is a long way from the situation in the seventeenth and eighteenth centuries when only a handful of scientists were paid for their work. I say a little more about this in Chapter 10.

3.9.3 Religion

As I noted earlier in discussing the 1960s, religious belief declined significantly in Britain in the 1960s, although perhaps less so around its Celtic fringes than in England. This has continued into the twenty-first century, as indicated in the quotation from Graham Tomlin at the head of this chapter, but the trend may actually now be reversing, albeit not dramatically.

In the past twenty years there has also been a rise in militant atheism, exemplified by the writing and verbal communication of academics such as Richard Dawkins and Peter Atkins, interpreted and popularized by celebrities such as Stephen Fry, Ricky Gervais and Jimmy Carr. Religion is put down as irrational; thus Dawkins states that we have evidence for evolution but not for the existence of a deity. This is curious for two reasons: first, it sets up evolution as a similar sort of thing to a deity (which may indicate something of Dawkins' thinking) and, secondly, it implies that people have faith in a deity for no reason at all (which is clearly untrue). Indeed, there is much about Dawkins' anti-religious stance that is curious. He states that he will accept nothing for which he has no scientific evidence. However, in real life he accepts many things for which the evidence is not "scientific". Further, he suggests that religion is a type of virus that affects memes, which are a kind of cultural unit of inheritance. Needless to say, there is no concrete evidence for memes, nor for meme viruses.

Nevertheless, militant atheism has had wide effects in society. Our society has definitely become more secular. Religion is regarded with suspicion or even hostility, not helped when militant adherents of religion resort to terrorism to further their cause or when fundamentalists deny the well-established findings of science.

Militant atheists may well be the "jihadists" of the non-religious ranks, but in general, religious observance has just gone into decline with little, if any, hostility being expressed towards religion itself. However, lack of religious observance does not necessarily imply lack of religious belief, as shown in Cole Morton's fascinating book *Is God Still an Englishman?* Although church attendance has declined dramatically, a large proportion of our population still believe in some sort of supreme being/god and/or regard themselves as spiritual, often exhibiting a "pick and mix" approach to belief. This was particularly evident in March 2012 when the young Bolton Wanderers footballer Fabrice Muamba suffered a cardiac arrest while playing in a cup match against Tottenham Hotspur. In the days following this, while he was in hospital with his life in the balance, footballers and football fans conducted, via Twitter, Facebook and slogans on T-shirts, a campaign to "Pray 4 Fabrice". I note in passing that Muamba himself is a Christian, but this has little to do with this extraordinary outpouring of "popular" spirituality. All this ties in with Graham Tomlin's observation that many people still seek spiritual enlightenment, but do not find it in conventional religion.

I need to say two more things about the decline of religious observance. First, the decline started very much later and has proceeded much more slowly in the USA. Thus, the percentage of the USA population calling themselves Christian had declined from 86 per cent in 1990 to 75 per cent in 2009. Against this slight fall, there has been an amazing rise in the number of Christians who call themselves evangelicals. Indeed, in some surveys, one in three Americans identify themselves as evangelicals. There has been a growing association between some elements of the evangelical churches and the right wing of the Republican Party, giving rise to the "religious right" and also a growth of Christian "fundamentalism", which challenges, among other things, an evolutionary view of creation.

The second point is relevant to our discussion of ethics. The atheist philosopher Julian Baggini has written that the decline in moral standards in the UK parallels the decline in respect for the authority of the church. Part of that decline has been a loss of community values and a rise in individualism, and in general levels of aggression. These are related to the way that society is organized, which I discuss in the next section.

3.10 HUMAN SOCIETY: FRAYING ROUND THE EDGES OR CRACKING DOWN THE MIDDLE?

One of the trends in industrialized societies has been the dispersal of families. Prior to the Industrial Revolution, families often lived in the same area for generations and thus members of one's extended family were in easy reach.

Further, although the Industrial Revolution led to greatly increased urbanization, the extended family pattern still held. Yes, members of individual generations moved into towns and cities, but often subsequent generations remained in the same areas of those towns and cities. Thus, in the middle years of the twentieth century, one could still encounter three generations of the same family living in the same part of a major city like Manchester or Nottingham, none of the two elder generations of which had ever been further than a few miles from home. However, the later years of the nineteenth century also saw the beginning of a trend for extended families to disperse, a trend that accelerated in the twentieth century; further, this trend exhibits quite a strong correlation with the level of education and so it accelerated again as more and more young people stayed longer in education. We thus came to regard the nuclear family – parents plus their children – as the basic family unit and when politicians speak grandly about "family values" it is the nuclear family that they have in mind.

Moving to the present day, it is clear that the situation has changed again. The frequency of marriage breakdown and divorce has increased, giving rise to "blended" families and "instant" families. The number of single-person households is also increasing, not just because of divorce or relationship breakdown but also because, on average, people are settling into long-term relationships later than they did 40 years ago (and indeed, increasing numbers avoid commitment altogether). In the UK, 34 per cent of households consist of one person. In Norway the figure is 40 per cent and in Sweden an amazing 47 per cent. In Germany and the Netherlands, the percentages of single-person households are intermediate between those in the UK and Scandinavia.[15] Further, as the level of industrialization of a country increases, so does the proportion of single-person households and thus numbers are growing fastest in China, India and Brazil. For tens of thousands of years, the human species has lived in families, groups and other forms of community. Now that is changing rapidly in the world's industrialized developed countries. It is often said that humans are social creatures, and yet large numbers of us are now living alone. Does this make a difference to the way we are as persons, to our humanity? Will this take us "beyond human"? Time will tell.

Associated with this trend of living alone is a strong tendency to individualism; indeed, individualism may be one of the drivers of the solo lifestyle. Thus human society consists not of a network of social or family groups but a network of individuals, with varying degrees of interconnectedness (or not – some individuals are very lonely). Furthermore, the division between the haves and the have-nots becomes ever more visible and, in the specific context of this book, bars many people from many of the benefits of modern technology. This will become clearer in subsequent chapters of the book, but in the meantime, let us consider the "haves".

The individualism to which I have already alluded is linked with the idea that *my* needs, *my* wants are the most important. Thus, even when it comes down to something like healthy eating, one supermarket chain brands its low-fat products as "Be Good to *Yourself*". And that leads to another aspect of this individualization of society, namely that the individual is defined as a *consumer*, provided of course that he or she is one of the "haves". It is instructive to flick through the pages of a glossy magazine or one of the weekend supplements that come with our daily papers. Advertisement after advertisement appeals to the idea that we want a certain product, so why not have it? Indeed, some advertisements even give the product in question a personal pronoun, telling the consumer, "You know you want me."

It even involves our bodies, or perhaps our images of our bodies. Our supposed physical inadequacies are made very clear by comparison with the airbrushed images of fit young men and women who are often used in advertising. But wait a minute, you *can* have the body you want: just join a gym, or undertake a particular exercise regime, or embark on a particular diet (often endorsed by a "celebrity"), or drink/eat a particular dietary product. And if all else fails, there is always surgery. "Cosmetic" surgery is the fastest growing area of "private" medicine in the UK.

The Harvard ethicist and philosopher Michael Sandel is very critical of the way market values have crept into so many areas of modern life. Thus the front cover of his most recent book carries the following statement:

> *In the past three decades, market values have crowded out non-market values in more and more areas of life – medicine, education, law, sport, art and even personal relations. We have sleep-walked… from having a market economy to being a market society.*[16]

We should have remembered all along that money can't buy me love.

In respect of the ethical systems that are discussed in the next chapter, this focus on the individual as a consumer whose needs/wants must be met is a long way from ethics of virtue to which that chapter points. Indeed, this type of individualism tends to *egoism*, where *my* needs and wishes become the standards by which the rightness or wrongness of actions is judged. It is a viewpoint that is widely criticized by communitarian and virtue ethicists (see next chapter). Further, in medical ethics it means that of all the principles which guide the ethical behaviour of medical practitioners, *autonomy* has become pre-eminent. This then leads me, in the next chapter, to consider ethics and medical ethics in more detail.

3.11 AFTER WORLD WAR II: A FINAL COMMENT

Millions and millions of people go about their lives in a peaceable way, getting on well with neighbours and colleagues and, from time to time, exhibiting care and compassion towards them. However, much of what I have discussed has concerned conflict, war and terrorism and the suffering caused by them. In that respect, modern society has shown no improvement on those early civilizations that I described in the previous chapter. Despite our best efforts to prevent war, it continues, but at least there are international peacekeeping organizations such as the United Nations. Without them, who knows how much worse the situation would be? Our human nature, our humanness, is too often worked out in aggression to our fellow-humans. Further, with the level of rapid and sophisticated communications available to us, we can become within a very short time aware of events happening on the other side of the world. It is just as predicted in Marshall McLuhan's 1967 concept of the Global Village: communications technology has indeed become an extension of our senses.

I know that against this background and even with the more aggressively individualistic atmosphere in twenty-first-century UK society, there are many, many examples of human behaviour at its best. But can we actually hang on to the words of Gandhi: "You must not lose faith in humanity. Humanity is an ocean; if a few drops of the ocean are dirty, the ocean does not become dirty?" I wonder.

NOTES

1. There was a certain irony in the way that right-wing politicians in the UK, so opposed to trade unions in their own country, were so fulsome in their praise of Solidarność.
2. In formal terms, this ended with the signing of a treaty at a summit meeting held in Malta in December 1989, but its end had been signalled at least two years earlier.
3. Desmond Tutu also stated that Gorbachev's policies were a factor in the fall of apartheid in South Africa.

4. I need to note in passing that during the period described in this section, three European countries changed from being led by fascist dictators or military juntas to being democracies: Greece (1974), Portugal (1974) and Spain (1975). All joined the EEC, now the EU.

5. From "The Culture of Liberty: An Agenda", published in *Society*, 1 January 1998.

6. In 2012, he was elected to a second term.

7. In sport, for example, women were finally admitted to membership of the prestigious Augusta National Golf Club (home of the US Masters' Championship) in 2012, twenty years after black male players were first allowed to become members.

8. And in many other parts of the world, women still do not enjoy anything like equal status with men. It is interesting that the 2012 Olympic Games were the first to which all countries had sent women competitors as some of the Islamic countries finally bowed to the pressure from the IOC. The applause for a Saudi Arabian female 800-metre runner coming in over half a minute later than the rest of the field was truly heart-warming.

9. Note that in some European countries, e.g. Sweden, abortion had already been legal for many years.

10. As early as 1976, Betty Williams and Mairead Corrigan Maguire founded the Northern Ireland Peace Movement and brought thousands of people from both sides to walk together in peaceful protests against the violence. For their work, the two women received the Nobel Prize for Peace. However, this glimmer of hope was snuffed out by those who could not put down their hatred of the other side and the violence continued.

11. The primary meaning of *jihad* in Islam is not actually "holy war". A typical definition would be "striving physically and spiritually to achieve an Islamic result", and many Muslims would argue that the true jihad is their own inner spiritual struggle against sin. Nevertheless, Islamic militants use the word to mean "holy war".

12. There were also several military personnel, seriously wounded in Iraq or Afghanistan, in the British Paralympic team in 2012.

13. But, of course, postmodern architects do abide by the overarching, non-socially-constructed laws of physics!

14. Note that the chapter on digital technology is self-contained in this respect – it carries its own history.

15. Please interpret these figures correctly; they are *not* the percentages of people living alone but the percentages of households in which only one person lives. The former is somewhat smaller than the latter.

16. Michael Sandel, *What Money Can't Buy: The Moral Limits of Markets*, London: Allen Lane, 2012.

4

MORALS, ETHICS AND COMPLEX ISSUES

Right is right, and wrong is wrong, and a body ain't got no business doing wrong when he ain't ignorant and knows better.
Mark Twain, in *The Adventures of Huckleberry Finn*, 1884

Sometimes our problems with knowing what is wrong and what is right arise because our world is changing so fast that we are constantly facing new situations that do not fit into our existing ways of thinking.
Margaret Killingray, in *Choices*, 2001

4.1 INTRODUCTION

Many of the situations and issues discussed in this book have ethical implications. In other words, decisions about them or outcomes from them – or the situations themselves – have a moral content, embodying the concepts of *right* and *wrong.* So how, when we are thinking or making decisions about them, do we decide what is right and wrong?

If I ask my students how they make ethical decisions, some will say, especially if they have absorbed postmodern ideas (see Chapter 3, section 3.9.1) to any extent, that they do what *feels* right – there is no actual framework for decision-making, and feelings become the main or even sole arbiter in deciding about right and wrong. Others, less influenced by postmodernism, may say, "I decide what is (morally) right and (morally) wrong and try to go with what I think is right." It may be that the distinction between thoughts and feelings is a little blurred but at least there is some analysis of the situation. So, how do my students – or indeed anyone – decide what is right and what is wrong?

In order to answer this question we need to think more generally about ethics and ethical decision-making. Ethicists and moral philosophers make a distinction between ethics and morals, defining ethic as *a (philosophical) study of the principles involved in making moral decisions*. We might say that *ethics* covers the theory and *morals* covers the practice.[1] However, in general usage, the words "ethics" and "morals" are often used interchangeably. We can speak of ethical decision-making or moral decision-making and most people would regard those terms as meaning the same thing.

4.2 ETHICAL SYSTEMS

The terms *ethics* and *morals* lead us to consider briefly the various ethical systems described by moral philosophers. The most straightforward ethical systems are those based on rules. Systems of ethics with clear "black and white" rules are known as *deontological* systems, from the Greek *deon*, duty. To obey a rule is morally right; to disobey a rule is morally wrong. In ancient times, Jewish society (the "Children of Israel") was governed by a system of rules known as the Ten Commandments, which is mostly a set of prohibitions. Some of the commandments would have been quite difficult to keep; "you shall not covet... anything that belongs to your neighbour" is a matter of internal attitudes and character, rather than actions. Nevertheless, the value of the Ten Commandments as a framework for moral behaviour is widely recognized; they certainly served the Jewish people well. However, problems arose when every aspect of life was brought within the framework of a set of rules which, as they increased in number and complexity, became more and more difficult to observe.

Nevertheless, other essentially deontological systems have been developed. In Islam, the whole of life is governed by shari'a law based on the Qur'an and the writings of the Prophet. In ancient Arabic, *shari'a* means "path to the water hole". The importance of such a path in an arid desert environment helps us to understand why the word is used to describe the governance of a complete lifestyle. In many of the countries where Muslims live, including the UK, some aspects of shari'a law conflict with the law of the land. In general, the law of the land prevails but in several Western countries there are Muslim enclaves where some elements of shari'a law are allowed to operate. Interestingly, there are some Muslim countries, exemplified by Brunei and Indonesia, which contain enclaves that enforce shari'a law while the rest of the country operates under a more moderate legal system.

Deontological frameworks are also seen outside the confines of strictly religious thinking. The philosopher Immanuel Kant (1724–1804) believed that our moral duty could be summed up in a series of overarching rules for conduct. He called these rules *imperatives*, typified by the categorical imperative "Act in such a way that you treat humanity, whether in your own person or in the person of any other, never merely as a means to an end...".[2] We might say now that other human beings are not to be used as mere instruments to fulfil our wishes or desires. Kant was clear that he regarded his imperatives as universally binding. Thus, everyone should tell the truth because if people tell lies, trust is lost and society cannot function.

In wider contexts, the laws that govern the workings of human society also form essentially deontological systems. Law and morals are not the same: the law may permit actions that are not acceptable to particular individuals (and vice versa). Sometimes the tension between private and public morality (the latter expressed through appropriate laws) is very strong and may lead to direct action by the individuals who are affected (or offended). Finally we can note that since the middle of the twentieth century, deontological ethics has often been framed in terms of rights (as in the United Nations Declaration of Human Rights). It is *my* duty not to transgress *your* rights (and vice versa). Indeed, much of today's moral discourse is conducted in terms of rights: "It is my right to..." However, the distinguished moral philosopher Mary Warnock is very critical of what she calls "the language of rights": "Why should we not prefer simply to talk about ways in which it would be right or wrong, good or bad, to treat our fellow human beings..." and "... there cannot be a morality *founded* on the concept of rights".[3]

Returning to the ancient world, Aristotle (384–322 BC) proposed an ethical system that has become known as *natural law*. This is the idea that what is right is that which enables humans (and other entities) to reach their natural potential or to flourish. Aristotle classified the different elements within nature in a hierarchy, going from totally inanimate objects such as stones, via plants, non-human animals and humans to God. Within this hierarchy, only humans and God were said to possess rationality. Each item within each level of the hierarchy had its own *telos*, its essential nature, its reason for being and it was morally wrong to prevent that *telos* from being expressed. In the thirteenth century, the writing of the theologian Thomas Aquinas (1226–74) also suggests a natural law approach to ethics. Natural law, in his view, arises from the wisdom with which God rules the created order and humans need to bring their thinking into line with this divine wisdom. Thus Aquinas believed that an action was right if it was consistent with (God-ordained) natural purpose.

Elements of natural law thinking, derived from Aquinas, are encountered today in the Roman Catholic prohibition of contraception: contraception is regarded as wrong because the "natural purpose" of sexual intercourse is procreation.

More informally, we also see a "mutant" version of natural law thinking in those who believe that "it's not natural" is a moral prohibition of any advance in science and technology. This is unworkable and goes far beyond the essential motivation of the natural law system of ethics.

Then there are the *consequentialist* systems, in which the main consideration of whether an action is right or wrong is what happens as a result of that action being taken. Are the consequences "good" or "bad" (noting that different individuals may have different ideas of right and wrong)? If the consequences are good, then the action is good. Consider telling a lie: under a deontological system, one never lies – Kant was very clear about this. Under a consequentialist system, lying may be regarded as acceptable, or even right, if the outcome is good. Telling a lie about someone's whereabouts in order to prevent their being found by people who might harm them would be morally acceptable. A number of different versions of consequentialism may be discerned, of which the most influential is *utilitarianism*, proposed by Jeremy Bentham (1748–1832) and John Stuart Mill (1806–73). In this system, good decisions promote the most (or most widespread) happiness or satisfaction (and in the late twentieth and early twenty-first centuries, happiness has frequently been interpreted in economic terms). Early proponents of utilitarianism believed it was a good antidote to what they perceived as the negativity of Christian ethics. At the other end of the scale to utilitarianism, if the decision-maker is considering the consequences only for themselves then they are exercising *(rational) egoism*, an ethical system arising from the ideas of Nietzsche and supported strongly by the Russian-American author and philosopher Ayn Rand (1905–82). She developed a philosophy known as *objectivism*, categorized altruism as evil and selfishness as a virtue, and declared that laissez-faire capitalism was the only socio-political system in which individuals could be truly free. She totally rejected all religion and especially Christianity, with its emphasis on love and community.

It is undoubtedly true that in secular Western society consequentialism in its various forms, tempered by deontology (e.g. obeying the law) and occasionally nuanced by a smattering of natural law, is the main ethical system used by most people in day-to-day moral decision-making (even if they do not analyse the means by which they reach such decisions). It is also the ethical system upon which much public policy is based. However, although consequentialist thinking is very widespread, these systems have their drawbacks. If only outcomes are considered, we may ignore at our peril the means of reaching those outcomes. Telling a lie to save someone's life is one thing; ending one life deliberately to save another is different. The ends do not always justify the means. Further, in utilitarianism there is the danger, in promoting the most widespread happiness or satisfaction, of ignoring the minority.

At this point we need to return to Aristotle. He argued that good moral decision-making in line with natural law involved applying virtue, including wisdom, courage and temperance (or moderation), to each decision. Thus we have *virtue ethics*: a person's character affects their decision-making, although in Aristotle's system, virtues such as charity (love) and humility seemed unknown. Indeed, Mary Warnock describes these latter two virtues as specifically Christian, even though many people who are not Christians also exhibit them. The virtue ethics system relates to the word *ethos*, the Greek word for character and the root of our modern word *ethics*. Overall we see this combination fitting well into the Platonic (Plato, 423–347 BC) concept of the ideal society in which morals, the arts and objective knowledge about the world (natural philosophy) were in balance, like the sides of an equilateral triangle.

The role of virtue in moral decision-making was picked up by Thomas Aquinas, who added to the list of virtues those ignored by or unknown to Aristotle, especially love (charity) and humility. He said that good ethical decision-making involves bringing our human wisdom into line with God's wisdom. We have already seen that in Aquinas's view, God's wisdom defines the natural law, but now we also see that human character has to grow or to be changed to fulfil that law. So character and virtue (including wisdom) contribute strongly to our decision-making.

For many years, several centuries indeed, virtue ethics had very little influence, at least in Western society. However, in the second half of the twentieth century there was a reawakening of interest in it, initiated by the writings of several philosophers, including Alasdair MacIntyre. In his 1981 book, *After Virtue*,[4] he discusses what he calls the dysfunctional quality of moral discourse within modern society (he is particularly critical of the rational egoism of Nietzsche and the existentialism of Sartre: see Chapter 2, sections 2.9 and 2.10) and suggests that we should rehabilitate the "forgotten alternative" of virtue ethics in the tradition of Aristotle and Thomas Aquinas. The comeback of virtue ethics continues to gather pace in the twenty-first century. It is seen in the global Charter for Compassion movement, headed by Karen Armstrong, and in the writing of several philosophers and theologians, including Stanley Hauerwas and Tom Wright. Wright insists that true Christian ethics, rather than being a negative legalistic system (as the early proponents of utilitarianism suggested), is a positive virtue ethics system.[5] The ethical teachings of Jesus are based on virtue. The apostle Paul, in a passage on Christian behaviour, lists nine qualities of Christian character and then comments, "Against such things there is no law."[6] Nevertheless it needs to be said that virtue ethicists do not disregard the law or throw away the rule book. After all, if I drive at 50 mph (80 kph) down my village street, I am hardly acting virtuously. Neither do they ignore the likely outcomes of their actions. Appropriate consideration of rules and consequences is part of a virtuous approach to moral decision-making.

The BBC website (www.bbc.co.uk) entitles one of its pages "Religion and Ethics", and there is a sense in which discussion of ethics leads to at least a mention of religion. Most of the major religions of the world have moral codes laid out in a set of rules and/or indicated in wide-ranging principles. Indeed, even in secularized societies such as twenty-first-century Britain we owe much to Judeo-Christian ethical codes. Further, it may be claimed that believers are empowered or enabled to act in a morally good way because of their relationship with or faith in God. In this context, the comment made in July 2012 by the atheist philosopher Julian Baggini is very interesting: "... the decline of morality... has paralleled the decline of respect for... the Church."[7] Nevertheless I do not hold the view that it is impossible to develop a moral code in the absence of religious belief. The Humanist movement, for example, has established a clear set of moral principles, while a recent book on virtue ethics barely mentions religion. Non-religious development of ethics is discussed at some length by Mary Warnock.[8] While acknowledging the specific contributions made by Christianity to our ethical thinking (especially in the area of virtue), she makes a very good case that secular societies, using human rationality, can and do develop ethical systems (and thus she draws heavily on a long line of philosophers, from Aristotle via Kant to modern scholars such as Wiggins). She argues that "the need for an ethical system is a fundamental need of human nature",[9] based on a personal sense of moral good and a tendency to altruism ("when someone begins to see he must postpone his immediate wishes for the sake of the good"[10]), notwithstanding the existence of a minority who do not seem to possess the sense of moral good, nor show any indication of altruism.

It may be argued that Warnock is too optimistic about human nature (see e.g. Chapter 10). After all, some secular and atheistic societies have perpetrated some very evil deeds. Yet we must also acknowledge that many people possess the qualities she describes and that their possession is not confined to those of religious faith. In the Judeo-Christian tradition this is interpreted as evidence of "being made in the image of God". However, we must admit that much wrong has been done in the name of religion, albeit in what most religious believers today would say were distortions of the real thing (see e.g. Chapter 3, section 3.7.3).

4.3 A BRIEF EXCURSION INTO POSTMODERNISM

The influence of postmodernism on ethical decision-making has been briefly mentioned. One of the many manifestations of postmodernism is moral relativism about many issues (see Chapter 3, section 3.9.1). Thus while most postmodern thinkers would agree with the proposition that murder, rape and child abuse are wrong, in respect of many less serious moral issues they would say, "What is right for me is right and what is right for you is right." As some of my students might have said, "If it feels right for me, it is right." The technical term for this is *emotivism*: moral statements are just statements of personal preference. Therefore the statement "It is good to contribute to famine relief" is of the same order as the statement "I like blue cars". In a very interesting recent study in the USA, 230 young adults (18–23 years old) were interviewed in depth about personal morals, moral decision-making and ethical dilemmas. The "default position" recorded by the researchers, to which most of their interviewees kept returning, is that moral choices are just a matter of individual taste. "It's personal," was a typical response – "It's up to the individual. Who am I to say?" One interviewee said: "I mean, I guess what makes something right is how I feel about it. But different people feel different ways, so I couldn't speak on behalf of anyone else as to what's right and wrong." Whether they knew it or not, these young people had been very much affected by the postmodern thinking prevalent in the last 30 years of the twentieth century and the first few years of the twenty-first, even though its influence has been less pervasive in the USA than in the UK.

Emotivism is not just the preserve of postmodern thinkers. The essentially modernist philosophy, logical positivism, reaches the same position. In logical positivism, only statements about things which can be quantified or measured are said to have meaning. Any statement which claims to make an objective judgement about an area which cannot be measured or quantified (e.g. that an action is good or bad) is meaningless, just an expression of opinion.

Whether emotivism arises via logical positivism or postmodernism, it has been strongly criticized by philosophers of other persuasions. MacIntyre, for example, devotes chapters 2 and 3 of *After Virtue* to an attack on emotivism, stating that the development of his own "thesis" must be set in the context of a "confrontation with emotivism". More specifically he says that "philosophy has allowed itself to be robbed of moral language... Moral reasoning has been undermined to the extent that words like *good*, *moral* and *useful*, although used frequently, have lost their meaning." Indeed, such was the extent and strength of this confrontation that some commentators have mistakenly regarded this as the only real theme of the book, rather than recognizing MacIntyre's very much more positive call for a return to virtue ethics.

4.4 APPLICATION OF ETHICS IN MEDICINE

After the excursion into postmodernism and emotivism I need to return to ethical decision-making and in particular its applications in the wider world. This section and the next thus provide some "tasters" of some of the issues discussed in subsequent chapters.

In general, ethical systems relate to ways that people treat each other, whether as individuals, groups or even whole societies. We speak of humans as having moral value or moral significance. It is our treatment of other humans that may be defined in terms of right or wrong, under whichever ethical system we operate. However, several of the issues discussed in subsequent chapters are more complex. They fall into the general category of biomedical science and so we may start to extend our ethical thinking by considering medical ethics.

Since the early formalization of medicine in ancient Greece, doctors have operated under clear ethical guidelines. For many hundreds of years, newly qualified doctors took or assented to the Hippocratic Oath, initiated by Hippocrates (460–370 BC), who taught and practised medicine on the island of Kos. Since World War II, the ethical framework under which doctors work has been updated. There is now the Declaration of Geneva (last updated in 2006), covering most elements of medical practice, and the Declaration of Helsinki (last updated in 2008) that covers the use of human subjects in medical research.

Although the issues with which doctors and other medical practitioners are presented may be complex, two American ethicists, Tom Beauchamp and James Childress, suggested that ethical decision-making in medicine should be guided by four main principles: *beneficence*, *non-maleficence*, *autonomy* and *justice*. The book in which they proposed this (*Principles of Biomedical Ethics*, New York: OUP-USA) was first published in 1979. It has become a "classic" in the field and the currently available edition, published in 2008, is the sixth. So, what do these principles mean?

- Beneficence: doing good or bringing benefit.

- Non-maleficence: not causing or inflicting harm.

- Autonomy: the patient is a person and their rights and wishes must be respected. A doctor may not undertake any medical intervention against the wishes of a competent individual.

- Justice: treating each patient as of equal value.

What sort of ethical system is this? I have previously suggested[11] that these four principles embody deontology, utilitarianism and virtue. However, a consideration of how these principles are applied leads me now to suggest that this is actually a virtue ethics system (as stated earlier, virtue ethicists do not ignore rules nor disregard outcomes; where appropriate, they factor them into their decision-making). The four principles are based on the virtues of charity (love) and empathy, which need to be applied with skill (a result of the doctor's training and experience), wisdom and often patience (which are also classical virtues). All four of the principles are open-ended. The doctor can never tick the box to say that they have completed the "task" of beneficence or justice. These are continuing requirements. Further, in many cases, the "weight" of one principle must be balanced against the weight of another. Some treatments that are beneficial for a patient suffering from a particular condition may also have unpleasant or even harmful side effects. Wisdom is needed to decide whether the good outweighs the harm. There is a real difficulty in treating patients equally when resources are scarce; how does a medical practitioner decide between patient A and patient B when the available resources will only permit treatment of one? The doctor will need to bring all their compassion, empathy and wisdom to work out what is just.

There are many more examples, some of them very complex, in discussing the application of the "four principles". Great care and wisdom are needed to decide what is right and wrong, with several factors to be considered very carefully. And if that is true for doctor–patient interactions, it is even more so of some of the wider applications of ethical decision-making.

4.5 EXTENDING THE ETHICAL VISION

Ethical treatment of other human beings is one of the indications that they have value; we ascribe value equally to all humans (or at least should do) in the same way that a doctor, in the narrower context of medical practice, treats all patients as of equal value. In terms of ethical theory or moral philosophy, we say that all humans are of *moral significance* – they all come within the boundaries of our moral community.

This raises the question as to how far these moral boundaries extend. In human development, for example, British law affords little protection to foetuses *in utero* and thus abortion is legalized, albeit with significant restrictions after the 24th week of pregnancy. But once a baby is born it has the full protection of the law. So, if the law were the sole determinant of our moral boundaries, foetuses would be outside those boundaries. However, as has been pointed out already, legal codes and moral codes do not necessarily coincide. Positions on abortion vary between the essentially deontological "Abortion is wrong" to the very permissive.[12]

The first position brings the foetus firmly within our moral boundaries, while the second tends to exclude it.

We can go back further in human development, to the very early embryo prior to implantation, and in doing so we begin to move from medical ethics to *bioethics*. British law concerning what can and cannot be done with these early embryos (in relation to *in vitro* fertilization [IVF], genetic selection and the use of embryonic stem cells) has developed from the Warnock Report, published in 1984. The moral significance of the embryo was a major focus of the Warnock Committee, leading them to state that "the early embryo is not yet a person but nevertheless should not be regarded as just a ball of cells... the embryo of the human species [should] be afforded some protection in law".[13] Some regard this as outrageously liberal because it effectively allowed the destruction of embryos. Indeed, some members of the Warnock Committee itself opposed the committee's majority view so strongly that they produced a minority report. There was also significant opposition in Parliament during the debates that led to the main points of the Warnock Report being enshrined in an Act of Parliament.[14]

However, even deciding what to include within and what to exclude from our moral boundaries only goes part of the way in dealing with ethical issues arising from modern science and technology and from other aspects of human activity. Some situations are so complex, involving the interaction of so many different factors, that it is hard to know what is right and what is wrong (under whichever ethical system one is operating) or even to define the relevant issues. Further, some technologies are so novel and/or so far-reaching that they raise unprecedented choices and problems. Whatever the net outcome of our deliberations, these situations need to be approached with wisdom and humility (and even moderation and charity, depending on which issue is under the spotlight). This immediately introduces the idea of a virtue ethics approach and, indeed, authors such as Celia Deane-Drummond have for several years promoted the use of a virtue ethics framework in dealing with biomedical and environmental issues.

I also lean strongly towards Christian-based virtue ethics and indeed believe that virtue ethics is the one ethical system that can effectively be applied to some of the issues discussed in later chapters. Nevertheless I recognize that deontology, consequentialism and natural law have all been brought to bear on one or more of these issues. However, perhaps the key point here is that whichever ethical system is used, the complexity of these issues must be acknowledged; answers to ethical questions may not come easily.

NOTES

1. The word "ethics" is derived from the Greek word *ethos*, meaning character; the word "morals" comes from the Latin word *moralis*, meaning manners, and was often used in Roman times to indicate the proper behaviour of people in society.

2. From *Groundwork for the Metaphysics of Morals* (1785).

3. In *An Intelligent Person's Guide to Ethics*, London: Duckworth, 1998, page 71.

4. First edition published in 1981 by University of Notre Dame Press, USA.

5. See e.g. Tom Wright, *Virtue Reborn*, London: SPCK, 2010.

6. Galatians 5:22–23, Today's New International Version.

7. "Why politicians are making morality fashionable again", *The Guardian*, 24 July 2012.

8. M. Warnock, *An Intelligent Person's Guide to Ethics*, London, Duckworth, 1998, pages 75–90.

9. *Ibid.*, page 90.

10. *Ibid.*, page 89.

11. John Bryant and John Searle, *Life in Our Hands*, Leicester: IVP, 2004.

12. In the UK, the current law is effectively based on rights (see earlier discussion): it is a woman's right to have an abortion if she wishes to do so. Similarly, the campaigns to legalize euthanasia and/or assisted suicide speak of a person's right to choose to end their life.

13. Report of the Committee of Inquiry into Human Fertilisation and Embryology, 1984 (usually referred to as The Warnock Report, 1984).

14. The Human Fertilisation and Embryology Act, 1990.

5

GENES, GENETICS AND HUMAN DISEASE

At birth, I was not expected to live much past my teens. Every day has been a battle to stay alive and defy the odds. My survival regime over the past 25 years has roughly consisted of swallowing 364,000 tablets, having 10,000 nebuliser sessions, 18,200 physiotherapy sessions, 50 IV treatments, 600 visits to the chemist and 250 visits to hospital.
Tim Wotton, in *The Guardian*, 15 February 2011

5.1 INTRODUCTION

In some current commentaries on the human condition we are said to be living in "the age of genetics". Human activity is expressed in terms of the outworkings of genes. Some aspects of medicine are becoming increasingly "geneticized" and, indeed, large claims have been made about the potential efficacy of genetically based personalized medicine. Knowing about our genetic make-up is said to tell us "who we are". Human identity is increasingly seen in genetic terms. Prospective parents are said to have "genetic choices". How and why did we arrive at this position? I want to deal with the history and development of medical genetics, including descriptions of genetic diseases, at some length in order to provide a complete picture. This is important. It is all too easy to reach conclusions based on limited understanding. This chapter will help us to avoid that and will prepare us for discussion of current applications and of the associated ethical and social issues in the next chapter.

5.2 EARLY UNDERSTANDING

The slow awakening of knowledge about genetics makes a fascinating story. Knowledge of it helps us to understand how we arrived at where we are today. Interest in what we would now call human genetic inheritance goes back many centuries, even though knowledge of genes is much more recent. Through history, we get glimpses of phenomena that are obviously related to genetics but which, to the observers of the time, were simply interesting or tragic or strange features of the human condition. Thus, the "father of modern medicine", Hippocrates, writing in about 400 BC, and the philosopher Aristotle (in about 350 BC) both recognized that certain physical characteristics ran in families. Aristotle further observed that sometimes children can look more like their grandparents than their parents.

Traits that run in human families were also noted by Jewish scholars. Thus, the geneticist Steve Jones recounts an incident in the life of Rabbi Judah the Patriarch (second century AD), who noted that a baby boy bled to death after circumcision. When a second boy born into the same family also bled to death, the rabbi realized that something was amiss. He therefore granted exemption from circumcision to other boys (including cousins) in that family.[1] Moving forward to the end of the tenth century, an Arabian doctor, Al Zahrawi-Albucasis, made a more detailed study of this condition, including its pattern of inheritance (although he did not call it that) via women and its appearance in male children. However, he remained completely ignorant of its cause. The condition (or disease) in question was of course *sex-linked haemophilia* which, from a medical geneticist's view point, is a particularly interesting example of an inherited disease.

By the nineteenth century this understanding of the inheritance of particular traits was becoming more formalized, with more extensive and reliable observations on, for example, the repeated occurrence of particular diseases in particular families. The occurrence of haemophilia among the relatives of Queen Victoria was an especially interesting example, highlighting again the passage of the trait through the female line (although it is very unlikely that Victorian doctors knew of the work of Al Zahrawi-Albucasis). How traits were passed on from generation to generation, whether conventionally or maternally, was still unknown. One common view was that these traits were "in the blood"[2] and that parental "bloodlines" were mingled during reproduction to give a sort of average. In respect of children who inherited a specific feature from one parent rather than the other it was suggested that some traits were stronger or more dominant[3] than others. However, the discovery of genes completely revolutionized our understanding of heritable traits.

It was a Czechoslovakian monk, Gregor Mendel, who discovered, from his work on pea plants, that patterns of inheritance were best explained by the passage from generation to generation of actual physical entities or factors. Further, some of these factors were dominant while others were recessive. The latter feature means that particular heritable traits might be hidden in a particular generation, only to surface later. We are thus reminded of Aristotle's observation about children's resemblance to parents and grandparents.

5.3 GENES AND MEDICINE: THE EARLY YEARS

Mendel published his findings in 1865 but it was not until his paper was rediscovered in 1900 (by Hugo de Vries, Karl Correns and Erich von Tschermark) that its significance was appreciated. Indeed, this rediscovery was a major turning point in the history of biology and medicine. It quickly became apparent that Mendel's work was as applicable to animals as to plants. His "factors" were first called genes by the Danish biologist, Wilhelm Johannsen, early in the twentieth century.[4] The scene was thus set for a more informed study of inheritance in humans and in particular of heritable diseases. The diseases that were obviously heritable provided clear-cut examples of genetic variation that could be tracked through families. This led to knowledge of a growing list of "single-gene" disorders – disorders that are attributable to a change in a single gene. It was also possible, by study of the distribution of the commoner mutations within families, to determine whether particular mutations were dominant or recessive. However, with a few exceptions, it was not possible in the first half of the twentieth century to map human genes to particular chromosomes. The exceptions were those diseases, such as haemophilia, and other conditions, such as colour blindness, for which the genes are carried on the X chromosome, i.e. the sex-linked conditions. Examination of chromosomes under the microscope to elucidate the "karyotype"[5] had quickly established that human females have two X chromosomes and that human males have one X and one Y chromosome. The maintenance of particular traits in females, albeit hidden, and the overt appearance of these conditions in males led to the surmise, later confirmed to be correct, that the mutations were recessive and that the genes were on the X chromosome. Females could thus carry one mutant copy without showing the condition itself; a recessive mutation on one X chromosome would be hidden because of a non-mutant ("wild-type") copy of the gene on the other X chromosome. Males with a mutant copy on their one X chromosome have no wild-type version to override the mutation. This information would later be used in prenatal testing (see below).

Study of the human karyotype also revealed that not everyone possessed a conventional set of chromosomes. For example there are several variations in the number of sex chromosomes. These include:

- *Klinefelter syndrome*, the possession by a male of an extra X chromosome (the XXY karyotype), occurs at a frequency of about 1 in 1,000 but the effects are very variable. Some Klinefelter males develop apparently normally (in such males, the condition is likely to go undetected unless the chromosomes are looked at for some other reason); however, in others the testicles do not fully develop and the man is sterile.

- *Turner syndrome*, the possession by a female of just one X chromosome (the XO karyotype), occurs with frequencies of between 1 in 2,000 and 1 in 5,000 in different parts of the world; the woman is of short stature and is nearly always sterile.

- *Trisomy X*, the possession by a female of an extra X chromosome (the XXX karyotype), occurs at a frequency of about 1 in 1,000. In general, a woman with the XXX karyotype will be taller than average and this may be the only visible symptom; however, in a minority of cases the woman exhibits learning difficulties, is sub-fertile and may undergo early ovarian failure.

What these syndromes tell us is that having the wrong total number of a particular chromosome (and thus the wrong total number of the genes on that chromosome) can have a profound effect on the development and the life of individuals. This is also true of numerical imbalances among the non-sex chromosomes (often called autosomes). I will focus on just one of these, trisomy 21, the possession of an extra copy of chromosome 21. A Victorian doctor, John

Langdon Down (1828–96), was very interested in the welfare of people with what we now call learning difficulties.[6] This led him to describe in detail (in 1866) one relatively common syndrome that is now named after him, namely *Down syndrome*. Jumping forward nearly 100 years, it was observed that Down syndrome was invariably associated with trisomy 21. This led to the development of prenatal tests for the condition and thus became a model for a wider range of chromosomal and genetic tests applied during pregnancy.

Prenatal testing, via sampling of the amniotic fluid, amniocentesis, was first performed in the mid 1950s in order to detect Rhesus-type blood-group incompatibility between the mother and the foetus.[7] In the 1960s, testing was extended to include detection of the sex of the foetus. This was offered to mothers who, based on their family history, were at risk of passing on serious X-linked conditions such as haemophilia or Duchenne muscular dystrophy to male offspring: if the mother is a carrier, each male child has a 50–50 risk of being affected. We note that the test did not reveal whether a foetus was in possession of the mutated gene. It merely indicated the sex; what was offered was termination of pregnancy if the foetus was male. This was permitted under UK law even before the 1967 Abortion Act.

The precedent was thus established that termination of pregnancy was appropriate if the foetus was at high risk of being affected by a serious genetic condition. In other words, in the UK, the consensus was that it was preferable to prevent the birth of individuals who, if born, would suffer from a serious genetic disease. This was a significant step in genetic medicine. And so we move on to 1968, the year in which prenatal testing for Down syndrome was introduced. Over the years, the test has become more sophisticated, combining the determination of karyotype with an analysis of particular proteins and with ultrasound scans. The condition is much more frequent if the mother is over 35, but in both the USA and UK it is recommended that the test be offered to all pregnant women. It is not "compulsory" to take the test and many refuse it. If the test is taken and gives a positive result, in the UK in the early part of the twenty-first century the prospective parents opt for termination of pregnancy in 90 per cent of cases. Even so, about 750 Down babies are born in the UK each year (to mothers who have not taken the prenatal test or who have refused a termination of pregnancy after a positive result). What we have then is a general outcome based on a mix of available technology, medical advice and individual attitudes to the seriousness (or otherwise) of congenital conditions and to termination of pregnancy. The tensions between different elements in this mix have increased in step with our increasing knowledge of genetics, as will become apparent in later sections of this chapter.

5.4 THE NEW GENETIC REVOLUTION

Publication in 1973 of the paper describing the first successful genetic modification (GM) experiment was greeted enthusiastically by the scientific community. The obvious application was of course the transfer of specific genes between living organisms, an application quickly and widely adopted by the pharmaceutical industry. However, GM plus an array of associated techniques and innovations led to a hitherto undreamed of ability to investigate genes. Indeed, I have often described this application of GM techniques as like the hidden 90 per cent of an iceberg. Until this time, analysis of individual genes had been confined to the tiny handful that, because of their particular biological activity, were more accessible to researchers. The idea that it would be possible to analyse the structure and activity of almost any individual gene was just a dream – and yet that is precisely what GM and associated techniques enabled us to do.

Applying this to medical genetics, it led to mapping onto specific chromosomes of the genes associated with genetic disease and knowledge of the specific genetic changes that lead to those diseases (see Chapter 7, section 7.4.1).

A further acceleration of progress occurred during the Human Genome Project (HGP).[8] This project, initiated in the USA but incorporating human genetic research around the world, aimed at sequencing the whole human genome, i.e. determining the order of the building blocks ("bases") in each human chromosome. The genetic content of an individual chromosome lies within a single, long DNA molecule. In the complete set of 23 chromosomes, the lengths of the DNA molecules add up to about 3,000 million (3×10^9) bases (the chromosome set containing the X chromosome is slightly bigger than the set containing the Y chromosome). In 1990 when the project started, the projected finishing date of 2005 was regarded as very ambitious. However, rapid technical advances, especially in the automation of the sequencing process, meant that progress was much more rapid than expected, such that a first draft was published in mid 2000, four and a half years before the official end of the project, while a "final" version was published in 2003. With sequencing methods becoming ever faster, researchers were then able to carry out several more passes over particular regions in order to increase the accuracy and detail of the analysis; this was completed in 2006.

Of course it is not really a final version. At the start of the HGP it was said that it may take fifteen years to get a sequence but it will take a century to understand it. Thus, research goes on, investigating the genetic differences between people, looking at the correlates of those differences (such as the incidence of genetic disease) and characterizing the mutations and other changes associated with genetic disease or with susceptibility to disease. There is also a lot of basic science to be done. The discovery that we have only about 25,000 genes was a really big shock. Based on our complexity and on all the activities that cells perform, estimates of gene numbers prior to the HGP were generally around 100,000. So, as we are beginning to discover, significant numbers of genes have multiple functions, with the different functions being differentially regulated. Many genes are much more versatile than we previously thought, a fact that excites me and my fellow-biologists. Alongside this, we are learning a lot about comparative genetics and evolution as the number of organisms, ranging from bacteria to mammals, in which the complete genome has been sequenced grows by the week and is now numbered in the hundreds.

The announcement of the first draft of a human genome sequence in 2000 was accompanied by much publicity and a transatlantic press conference featuring the then UK prime minister Tony Blair and the then US president Bill Clinton. In his speech, Bill Clinton suggested that because of this new genetic knowledge many people could look forward to living to an age of 100 or more. Leaving aside the fact that average life expectancy in parts of Africa is little over 40, and that the latter fact has little to do with lack of genetic knowledge, Clinton had accepted the idea that the new genetics would lead to significant changes in Western medicine and hence in our longevity. Indeed it was widely stated in the early years of this century that we were witnessing a revolution in medical genetics, leading to more effective treatment for a range of diseases. However, despite the hyperbole, the revolution has not occurred. Nevertheless, similar claims continue to be made, for example by Francis Collins, former US director of the HGP and now, at the time of writing, director of the USA's National Institutes of Health (appointed by President Obama). Collins is an active Christian and desires to see scientific knowledge used for the good of humankind. I share both his faith and that desire but, along with many biologists, I fear that the "revolution in personalised medicine" about which he writes[9] is still a long way in the future (see section 5.5.2). So, what applications have emerged from our rapidly expanding knowledge of human genetics?

5.5 SCIENCE, SEQUENCES AND SICKNESS

5.5.1 Genetic diseases: some examples

As mentioned already we have far fewer genes than expected and indeed far fewer than are able to account for our functional and developmental complexity. Scientifically this is very interesting and challenges us to try and find out how this can be. Even before this discovery we knew of genes with multiple functions and genes which although exhibiting individual function also have functions that rely on cooperation with other genes. The known number of such situations continues to grow and certainly adds complexity to the interpretation of some aspects of genetic knowledge. Despite this, there are also many instances in which we can ascribe a specific function to a gene and further to analyse the outcomes of malfunctions in such genes.[10] Three examples will help to illustrate this and will also help us to understand what it is like to suffer from such illnesses, thus providing useful background for later sections of the chapter.

The first example is the colloquially named *cystic fibrosis* gene,[11] which features significantly in genetic testing, as discussed later in this chapter. Mutations in this gene are recessive and it is estimated that in the white population of north-west Europe, about 1 in 25 people possess a mutated copy; among people of Celtic lineage this frequency rises to 1 in 22. The gene codes for a protein[12] that regulates the ion and water balance in tissues that produce mucus, including the intestine, the lungs and nasal passages. In people with two mutated copies of the gene, the mucus secretions are sticky and non-free-flowing. This causes problems in any mucus-producing tissues but especially in the intestines and lungs. Forty years ago, most people with cystic fibrosis (CF) died in their teens or twenties, but as treatment and management of the disease has improved, so has life expectancy. Thus in 2011, *average* life expectancy in the UK was 38 years; we note in passing that the increased lifespan means that CF sufferers are now much more likely to have children and thus to maintain the mutant gene in the population.

To try to understand what it is like to live with such a condition I turned to the experience of one British CF sufferer, Tim Wotton:[13]

> *For most people turning 40 is a shock, but for me it will be a revelation. I have cystic fibrosis (CF), and reaching this age was always unlikely. Life expectancy is currently set at 38 years for CF sufferers – though for a long time it was fixed at 30. Reaching my 30s often seemed unachievable, while 40 felt impossible. Not many people with CF in the UK make it this far. It always feels inspirational when someone hits this milestone.*
>
> *When people look at me, they see a married 39-year-old with a gorgeous three-year-old son, Felix. I work in London as a communications consultant and play sport regularly. What they don't see is my illness, which is one of the UK's most common life-threatening inherited diseases. Cystic fibrosis clogs up your lungs and digestive system with a thick sticky mucus. It makes it hard to breathe, exercise and digest food. It is relentless and unforgiving – like having a heavy chest cold every day of your life. There is no cure.*
>
> *At birth, I was not expected to live much past my teens. Every day has been a battle to stay alive and defy the odds. My survival regime over the past 25 years has roughly consisted*

of swallowing 364,000 tablets, having 10,000 nebuliser
sessions, 18,200 physiotherapy sessions, 50 IV treatments,
600 visits to the chemist and 250 visits to hospital.

The second example is *sickle-cell anaemia*. This occupies
a special place in the history of genetic medicine, both
scientifically and socially. The gene involved here is the one
that codes for haemoglobin, the blood's oxygen carrier. This
was the first genetic disease in which the difference between
the normal ("wild-type") protein and the mutant protein
was identified (in 1956) using very painstaking analysis
techniques long before the modern rapid techniques were
available. Identifying the change in the mutant haemoglobin
enabled scientists to predict the corresponding change in
the code carried by the haemoglobin gene, but it was over
twenty years before this could be confirmed. It is all too easy
to forget, in these days of automated sequencing, how much
hard work it used to take to obtain data of this type.

The mutant form of haemoglobin is somewhat less
efficient as an oxygen carrier; more importantly, it also tends
to form aggregates within the red blood cells, causing them
to become sickle-shaped and rather stiff, hence the name
of the disease. These malformed blood cells do not move
very well in the circulating blood, leading to blockages in
the capillaries. This causes painful swellings and also reduces
dramatically the oxygen supply to the tissues served by those
capillaries. Indeed, it is this feature that is the most important
element of sickle-cell anaemia, although the reduced
oxygen-carrying capacity is also significant. Unlike cystic
fibrosis, a cure (in the form of a bone marrow transplant) is
theoretically possible. However, this rarely happens and, in
general, treatment consists of alleviating and/or managing
the symptoms. This has led to improvements in quality of life
for sickle-cell patients along with increased life expectancy

(average around 44–48 years in 1994 increasing to 56–60 in 2011).

The disease is very common in areas where malaria is endemic, and the reason for this is a nice example of natural selection. Although the mutant gene is technically recessive, possession of one mutant copy (the "heterozygous state") does lead to the formation of some faulty haemoglobin. This in turn has some effect on the shape of the red blood cells, not severe enough to cause full-blown sickle-cell anaemia, but enough to prevent entry into the cells of the malaria parasite, *Plasmodium*. Possession of one mutant copy of the gene thus protects the carrier against malaria (an example of "heterozygote advantage").The gene is thus maintained at surprisingly high levels in populations living in areas such as sub-Saharan Africa and the Indian subcontinent. We can also see this when we look at African Americans who are mainly descended from slaves brought over from West Africa. The frequency of carriers (people with one mutant copy of the gene) in the general population of the USA is about 1 in 150. Among African Americans it is somewhere between 1 in 11 and 1 in 12, giving a birth frequency of about 1 in 500. However, these frequencies, although high, are much lower than we see today in sub-Saharan Africa and parts of the Indian subcontinent, where up to 1 in 3 people may be carriers. The reason for the lower carrier frequency among African Americans compared to actual Africans is not clear. It has been suggested that slaves without the mutant gene were more likely to survive the terrible conditions of the journey and thus the frequency of carriers was reduced. Another possibility is that the absence of malaria in the USA has removed the heterozygote advantage and thus the frequency of the mutated gene is decreasing.

Whatever the reason, the effects of the much higher frequencies in countries where malaria is still a problem are plain to see in the UK. There has been extensive immigration into the UK from these regions, adding to the earlier waves of immigration from the Caribbean. Although these groups make up a relatively small proportion of the population, sickle-cell anaemia has become the most frequent of the serious genetic illnesses in the UK (birth frequency is about 1 in 2,000), pushing cystic fibrosis into second place. There are three main reasons for this. The first is the high sickle-cell carrier frequencies (up to 1 in 3 in those of African or Indian subcontinent lineages; about 1 in 12 for those of Caribbean lineage); the second is the tendency to have larger families than the "white" population; and the third is the frequency of cousin marriages in some of these communities, increasing the likelihood of inheriting two mutant copies of the gene.

The third example is *Huntington's disease*, which at any one time affects about 7,500 people in the UK. The first symptom to appear is usually loss of memory of recent events, followed by confusion, personality changes and mood swings, in some cases leading to aggressive and antisocial behaviour. As the disease progresses, the sufferer exhibits clumsiness or uncontrolled muscle movements and rigidity. Dementia slowly takes over, indicated by poor concentration and loss of rational thought. Other later symptoms include involuntary movements, difficulties with speaking and swallowing, seizures, depression and anxiety. Essentially, then, Huntington's disease is a neurodegenerative condition leading to a slow lingering death: the patient may live for fifteen to twenty years after the first clear-cut symptoms appear. Perhaps even more tragically, this is mostly a late-onset condition (but see below), appearing after the affected person may have had children. He or she then knows that each of their children has a 50 per cent chance of inheriting the condition (it is caused by a dominant mutation).

In order to understand the significance for families of this illness, we need to look at the science slightly more closely. The mutation is a strange one. It consists of the insertion of repeated copies of a "triplet" (CAG) of bases (the building blocks that make up DNA) into the relevant gene. This in turn causes a malfunction of a brain protein called huntingtin. The number of CAG copies is important. Up to 28 copies have no detrimental effects at all. People with between 29 and 35 copies are also normal but have an increased chance of passing on the disease to their children, as will become apparent. People with 36 to 40 CAG copies are partially affected (have a milder form of the disease), whereas more than 40 copies will always cause the full syndrome of Huntington's disease.

In the formation of gametes, the number of CAG copies tends to increase, and this is much more marked in sperm formation than in egg formation. Thus Huntington's disease inherited via male parents is likely to become more severe with each generation. However, increased CAG copy number also leads to a decrease in the age of onset of the disease. Thus, one case that I came across was a man whose father had shown first signs of Huntington's disease in his 50s, whereas the man himself began to exhibit symptoms at the age of 34. At the extreme end of this age spectrum, some patients as young as seven have been observed. Obviously such young patients, even if they live for another twenty years, are very unlikely to have children and the mutation will die out at that point in the lineage.

I have discussed these three diseases at some length because they encapsulate some of the major dilemmas in discussions of genetic diseases. In respect of cystic fibrosis and sickle-cell anaemia, as we understand more of the diseases themselves, treatment and symptomatic relief improve, leading to extended life expectancy. Yet this increases the burden on the healthcare system, not forgetting the burden on parents when the sufferers from these conditions are too young to look after themselves. One answer to this, as mentioned in passing earlier, is that "society" should try to prevent the birth of babies with serious genetic illnesses; in later sections of this chapter various ways of achieving this are discussed. In the meantime, it is worth noting again the words of Tim Wotton that I quoted earlier. Although CF has had a profound effect on his life, there is no hint in the quotation, nor indeed in the rest of the article, that he wishes he had not been born. He lives life as fully as his condition allows.

The three genetic diseases that we looked at in some detail are just a tiny proportion of the 4,500 or so disorders that we can attribute to malfunctioning genes. Most of these are rarer than any of the three discussed above and some are very rare indeed. The conditions range in seriousness, from metabolic disorders such as phenylketonuria, which can be managed within a relatively normal lifestyle, to very serious malfunctions that lead to death in infancy or childhood. Many, probably the majority, are recessive, and most people who are carriers of one malfunctioning copy of the relevant gene are completely unaware of the fact. Indeed, it is estimated that most humans are heterozygous for (i.e. carry one copy of) mutations which in the homozygous state (i.e. when both copies are mutated) would be lethal.

As with cystic fibrosis and sickle-cell anaemia, several of these diseases are associated with particular population groups. For example, the carrier frequency of Tay-Sachs disease is between 1 in 25 and 1 in 30 among Ashkenazi Jews,[14] giving expected birth frequencies of between 1 in 2,500 and 1 in 3,600 (see Chapter 6, section 6.1.2), but only 1 in 300 in most other populations. It is a disease that affects the nervous system; the first symptom is a loss of motor skills, which often begins in infants as young as three to six months of age. The nervous system continues to degenerate, the child suffers frequent seizures, blindness sets in and death usually occurs before the age of four. It is undoubtedly a heart-breaking experience for the parents.

Another recessive genetic disease more common in Ashkenazi Jews is Fanconi anaemia.[15] This is genetically more complex than Tay-Sachs and exhibits a range of severity according to which mutation is involved. In most populations, the carrier frequency is between 1 in 180 and 1 in 300, so it is a rare disease. However, among Ashkenazi Jews, the carrier frequency is 1 in 90 (birth frequency of 1 in 32,400) and the mutation they carry leads to the most severe form of the disease. As is implied by the name, Fanconi anaemia is considered to be mainly a disease of the bone marrow. Bone marrow failure may set in as early as the age of three or four in severe cases, although in less severe cases may not occur until the teenage years or even later. Bone marrow failure may be cured by a bone marrow transplant from a compatible donor, as discussed in the next chapter. However, although this procedure, if successful, rectifies the bone marrow malfunction, it does not deal with the problems that occur later. In particular, patients who survive into young adulthood develop a range of cancers, often more than one type in any one patient. The median survival age is currently about 25; patients with the milder forms may survive into their 40s or even 50s, while those with the severe forms may die in their teens or earlier (although these short lifespans are extended following successful bone marrow transplants, as again discussed in the next chapter).

Alongside these diseases are those in which the mutation does not lead inevitably to the disease but nevertheless makes occurrence of the disease very likely. The dominant mutations *BRCA1* and *BRCA2* each give an 80 per cent lifetime probability of getting breast cancer (although between them these two genes account for only about 10 per cent of breast cancer cases). Similarly, dominant mutations in one of the *HNPCC* genes give a 70 per cent lifetime probability of getting cancer of the colon or rectum. A dominant mutation in the *APC* gene on the other hand gives a nearly 100 per cent probability of getting colon cancer before the age of 40. However, genetically caused colon cancer is rare. The *HNPCC* and *APC* genes account between them for only about 5 per cent of cases. Diet and lifestyle are much more frequently implicated.

Finally, as we find out more about human genetics, we are discovering more and more instances in which genetic variations (which may be as small as a difference in one of the bases that make up the DNA chain – a single nucleotide polymorphism or SNP) have some correlation with the occurrence of a particular condition, including some mental illnesses. Thus, a particular SNP may give an increased susceptibility to a particular condition but that susceptibility only turns into actuality in relation to particular environments or lifestyles or even genetic backgrounds. Thus a person may be told that they possess a genetic variation that is associated with an n per cent increased probability of having condition X, whatever X may be. In respect of this type of situation, the former director of the Human Genome Project, Francis Collins, has suggested that all illness has some genetic component. Thus, for example, differing susceptibility to common viruses may be associated with genetic variability in the effectiveness of the immune system.

5.5.2 The human genome: in sickness and in health

As already indicated, much of the earlier interest in human genetics centred on the inheritance of disorders. That is not to say that there was no interest in non-medical genetics because there certainly was – and obviously still is. However, the "human interest" stories around human genetics mostly concern health and disease and, even more to the point, research activity tends to follow the money, much of which is allocated to medical research. This was true before the start of the Human Genome Project and has remained true through the operation of the Project and on to the present day. One of the results of this is that we have detailed information on approaching 3,000 mutations that cause or are involved in or are correlated to varying extents with heritable conditions. But has this helped in treatment of those conditions?

One of the questions posed by Francis Collins during his term as director of the HGP was: "Will we successfully shepherd new genetic tests from research into clinical practice?"[16] However, to date, the impact of the HGP on the cure of genetic conditions has been only slight. Cure involves completely removing or permanently preventing the lesion that results from the genetic mutation. We have seen already that the bone marrow defect in Fanconi anaemia can be cured by a bone marrow transplant but that other facets of the illness still continue. For some, albeit very few, genetic diseases it has been possible to override the faulty gene through gene therapy, as discussed in the next chapter. Actual cures for most genetic diseases remain a pipe dream, as does the "revolution in personalised medicine" to which I referred in section 5.4. Nevertheless, there has been some improvement in treatment of symptoms for some genetic diseases. Understanding the specific mutation in the gene helps to understand the reason why the mutation leads to a specific range of symptoms and this in turn can lead to better control of those symptoms. However, the major impact of genetic sequence information has been not on cure or treatment but on testing and diagnosis, and it is to those topics that we turn in the next chapter.

NOTES

1. Circumcision "on the eighth day" is the rite by which male babies are incorporated into the Jewish community; the rite dates back to the time of the Jewish patriarch Abraham, about 3,700 years ago.

2. This terminology remains with us in, for example, describing racehorses as being of good bloodstock.

3. This term is still used in modern genetics.

4. Different authorities give dates between 1902 and 1911. The word is based on the Greek *genea* (generation or race).

5. The karyotype is effectively the array of chromosomes, suitably stained, as seen under the microscope.

6. He was also a strong supporter of higher education for women and of the abolition of slavery; he argued strongly that no "race" was inferior to any other. Indeed, he regarded racial differences as being trivial and superficial, a view that is upheld by our current knowledge of human genetics.

7. Rhesus incompatibility and its treatment is clearly described at http:// anthro.palomar.edu/blood/Rh_system.htm.

8. I have described the background to the HGP more fully elsewhere: J. Bryant and P. Turnpenny, "Genetics and Genetic Modification of Humans: Principles, Practice and Possibilities", in *Brave New World?*, ed. C. Deane-Drummond, London: T. & T. Clark, 2003; J. Bryant and J. Searle, *Life in Our Hands*, Nottingham: IVP, 2004; J. Bryant, L.B. la Velle, and J. Searle, *Introduction to Bioethics*, Chichester: Wiley, 2005.

9. F. Collins, *The Language of Life: DNA and the Revolution in Personalised Medicine*, London: Profile Books, 2010.

10. Malfunctions include mutations in which the code in the gene has been changed in some way but also include deletions of whole genes and malfunctions in the tracts of DNA involved in controlling genes.

11. Its full name is *cystic fibrosis transmembrane conductance regulator* (CFTR).

12. "Codes for a protein": the genetic code embodied in the gene leads to production of a particular protein. This is how most genes work.

13. http://www.guardian.co.uk/lifeandstyle/2011/feb/15/how-have-i-cheated-death-cystic-fibrosis.

14. Jewish people of Middle and East European origin. Many emigrated to the USA in the twentieth century. Millions were murdered in the Holocaust.

15. See my article "Learning to Play God", in *Third Way*, January 2012, available online at http://www.thirdwaymagazine.co.uk/editions/janfeb-2012/features/learning-to-play-god.aspx.

16. See his article, "The Human Genome Project: Tool of Atheistic Reductionism or Embodiment of the Christian Mandate to Heal?", in *Science and Christian Belief* 11 (1999), 99–111, available online at http://www.scienceandchristianbelief.org/download_pdf_free. php?filename=SCB+11-2+Collins.pdf.

6

GENETIC TESTING AND DIAGNOSIS: THE GOOD, THE BAD AND THE MUDDLY

Because the prospective child is deliberately selected on qualitative, genetic grounds out of a pool of possible embryonic siblings, PGD risks normalizing the idea that a child's particular genetic make-up is quite properly a province of parental reproductive choice, or the idea that entrance into the world depends on meeting certain genetic criteria.
The President's Council on Bioethics, Washington DC, in *Reproduction and Responsibility*, 2004

... we should be more concerned with broader cultural trends that elevate liberalism to such an extent that children become rights that can be purchased according to parental desires and wishes.
Celia Deane-Drummond, in *Genetics and Christian Ethics*, 2007

6.1 GENETIC TESTING AND DIAGNOSIS

6.1.1 Introduction

In a relatively short period of time, beginning with the invention of genetic modification techniques in the 1970s,

DNA has become a very powerful diagnostic tool for a wide range of conditions. Indeed, DNA testing is now widely available commercially as well as via clinical practitioners. For those genetic diseases in which the relationship between the mutated gene and the disorder is clear, and in which the specific mutation in the gene has been identified, very reliable diagnoses can be obtained. A test based on DNA does not rely on symptoms, although such tests are often used to confirm diagnoses initially based on symptoms. Thus DNA testing can provide a diagnosis of a condition in which the symptoms have not yet appeared but which will appear later, as for example in Huntington's disease. Further, since DNA testing can be applied at any stage of life from adult right back to the pre-implantation embryo, a diagnosis can be obtained as early as nine months before birth. Testing at any stage can and often does raise personal, social and ethical dilemmas, some of which we now examine.

6.1.2 Testing of adults and children

Adults

The number of genetic conditions or disorders for which there is a direct test now approaches 3,000. However, the implications of such tests are not always straightforward, because, as mentioned in the previous chapter, some of these tests indicate a somewhat raised probability of having a particular disorder rather than a definite *Yes* or *No*. The other factors affecting the expression of such genetic changes are difficult to ascertain. The extent to which the effects of a gene are expressed may vary from person to person. Even for the many diseases for which DNA-based diagnosis is reliable, the actual course of the disease and therefore the prognosis may be uncertain. Nevertheless, there are some positive sides to genetic testing of adults. Where treatment is available, it can be started early in the course of the disease. For late-onset conditions such as *BRCA1*- and *BRCA2*-related breast cancer or *HNPCC*-related colon cancer, the person concerned and/or his/her medical advisers will be looking for the first signs of clinical symptoms so that treatment can be initiated as soon as possible.

In many other conditions the results of testing may bring huge disappointment or even despair, as there may be little or no treatment for the particular disease which has been diagnosed. Huntington's disease (discussed earlier) and the heritable version of Alzheimer's disease are examples of this. Thus advice about testing should always be realistic, measured and compassionate, exploring carefully why a particular person may or may not want to be tested. We might assume that the burden of knowing that one will suffer from an incurable degenerative disease would deter people from being tested. Indeed, in 2007, several years after the test for Huntington's disease first became available in the UK, there was evidence that the number asking for tests was a very small proportion of those who were at risk. This situation is slowly changing, and one reason for this is a greater awareness of genetics in general but in particular of genetics in relation to having children. For some, it is very important to know whether or not they could pass on an incurable condition to any children they might have; it is preferable to live with the burden of waiting for the symptoms to appear than it is to pass on unwittingly the mutant gene to the next generation. Nevertheless, we must not underplay the weight of that burden. In one tragic case, a young person with a 50 per cent risk of inheriting Huntington's disease became emotionally convinced that she had indeed inherited it; she did not ask for the test but committed suicide. A post-mortem genetic test showed that she had not inherited the disease; had she subjected herself to the test she would have known this. This is, sadly, unlikely to be an isolated case because the high frequency of suicidal thoughts among those at risk of inheriting Huntington's disease is well documented. Interestingly, the frequency decreases after both positive and negative test results. Nevertheless, it shows us again that the emotional and mental burden can be very heavy.

Children

Turning now to genetic testing of children, there may again be beneficial outcomes. First, of course, it is a huge relief when testing shows that a child does not have the disease when it was a possibility that they might. Secondly, when the diagnosis is positive, if treatment is available it can be started early in the course of the disease, as already discussed in respect of adults. Even if no treatment is available, it helps the parents to know that a child has a particular disease. They can then start to find the appropriate support in education and through social benefits and support groups. It also aids parents in helping their children to understand what is wrong with them. It enables the future to be faced and for informed decisions to be made about their reproductive life in adulthood. However, a positive test in a child raises other problems: Will the knowledge alter family dynamics? At what age should the child be told?

The genetic testing of children raises the issue of consent. In English law, parents may make decisions about diagnostic testing and treatment for their children who are minors. It is accepted that small children particularly lack competence in giving informed consent, but it is assumed that as the child gets older so he/she may be involved increasingly in discussions about testing and treatment. So, at what age should a child be told of their condition and what if, on reaching the age at which they can give consent, the child decides that they actually would have preferred not to know?

Where a disease is present in childhood or will develop in later life and the prognosis is poor, a very considerable burden is placed on the child and the family, and the knowledge may well alter family dynamics, despite the best intentions of the parents. A huge amount of pastoral care and support may be needed over a long period of time. The major burden for this usually falls on the parents and this has implications for other family members, especially siblings of the affected child.

Newborns

In the UK, testing of newborn babies for the metabolic disorder phenylketonuria was introduced in 1969. A drop of blood taken from the baby's heel was tested biochemically for evidence of the condition. If phenylketonuria is detected, a strict dietary management programme is initiated, which avoids the effects of failing to metabolize properly the amino acid phenylalanine (the genetic defect causes a toxic metabolic by-product to build up, leading to brain damage, mental retardation and seizures). More recently, six more inherited diseases have been included in the routine screening of newborn babies, always with the aim of starting treatment or management programmes as soon as possible. These added conditions thus include cystic fibrosis, sickle-cell anaemia and a particular defect in lipid metabolism. Tests for thalassaemia (a condition in which functional haemoglobin is not made) are included for babies born to Greek Cypriots. This genetic screening programme for newborns has been described as quite conservative in comparison with what happens in some other countries. In the USA, for example, 29 conditions are tested for routinely, while another 25 are optionally available.

Tay-Sachs disease: an interesting case

In respect of children affected by genetic disease, we discussed Tay-Sachs disease in Chapter 5, and I want to further consider it here because it occupies a special place in the genetic testing arena. In the large Ashkenazi Jewish populations in the USA, the birth frequency of Tay-Sachs disease is very much lower than expected because of a system of genetic testing that was initiated by Rabbi Joseph Ekstein in New York, once the specific mutation had been identified. The religious authorities organize the testing for Tay-Sachs carrier status of every member of the community and keep the results of those tests in coded form. If two young people fall in love and plan to marry (or even, in very traditional families, are brought together by the matchmaker), they obtain their test results and if both are carriers, they are advised not to marry or, if they do marry, to consider very carefully as to whether they should have children. That advice, tough though it may seem, is nearly always accepted and has resulted in new cases of Tay-Sachs being virtually eliminated from those communities,[1] without recourse to termination of pregnancy. Among the Ashkenazi Jews the programme is called in Hebrew *Dor Yeshorim*, meaning "the generation of the righteous", and more widely known as "eugenics with a smiling face".

Whether this practice will continue to be used so widely among Ashkenazi Jews is a matter for debate. The advent of pre-implantation genetic diagnosis (see below) has certainly led some at-risk couples to adopt that method for avoiding birth of a child with Tay-Sachs disease. Nevertheless, the efficacy of *Dor Yeshorim* should not be underestimated.

6.1.3 Knowing and not knowing

It is clear that for some people ignorance is bliss. For any genetic test that becomes available there are always some who are at risk who do not take the test, albeit, based on experience with Huntington's disease, the proportion of such people may be decreasing. Nevertheless, the dilemmas posed by the availability of genetic testing and the burden of genetic knowledge are very real. However, these are not the only issues raised by a positive test. People affected by genetic disease and people who are healthy carriers of recessive conditions have to decide who else, in addition to their medical advisers, should be told. Of course, they cannot actually be forced to tell anyone, but we might justifiably argue that those who themselves are now known to be at risk should be informed. This will certainly include children (when they are old enough to know), siblings and, for some situations, cousins.

It might seem obvious that a spouse/partner should be informed of the test result, because they have to live with the affected person. However, it is clear that this does not always happen. Thus in one couple that I encountered, the wife of a person affected by a genetic condition had not been informed and became very puzzled about changes in his behaviour until he was eventually persuaded to tell her.

Finally, should the knowledge go outside the family, for example to employers and to insurance companies? Do they have the right to know? For some genetic conditions it may not be possible to continue to do a particular job, whether for reasons of safety or increasing incapacity. Nevertheless, the possibility of uninformed discrimination, not just with regard to employment but also to insurance, is very real. In the UK, there is an agreement between insurers and the government that there will be no discrimination on genetic grounds, except for very large life insurance policies. In the USA, it is currently illegal for insurers to discriminate against people for genetic reasons except for life insurance and for long-term care. However, as is illustrated by an increasing numbers of cases, insurers are very ready to use the latter let-out in order to refuse insurance.[2] In 1999, Francis Collins asked: "Will we solve the problem of genetic discrimination?"[3] Based on current evidence, at least in the USA, it seems that the problem is far from solved, and we can understand the reluctance of any person affected by a genetic disorder to inform people or organizations outside the family.

6.1.4 Prenatal and pre-implantation testing

Prenatal genetic testing

Prenatal testing of foetuses growing in the womb was first performed in the 1950s, and by 1968 had been applied to detection of Down syndrome. It was thus inevitable that when direct tests for genetic conditions started to become available in the 1980s they would be used in prenatal diagnosis. This was originally done at about the fifteenth or sixteenth week of pregnancy by examining foetal cells from the amniotic fluid which surrounds the baby in the uterus. Nowadays a technique known as chorionic villus sampling is used, in which cells are examined from the edge of the placenta. This can be done as early as the eleventh or twelfth weeks of a pregnancy.

In the early days, tests for only a handful of genes were available, but that number has grown hugely in the past 25 years or so. However, of the approximately 3,000 gene tests that are available, only about 200 are used in prenatal diagnosis in the UK. Prenatal tests are generally carried out, by parental choice, where the family history indicates that the foetus may be at risk of having a particular genetic disease (noting that the test itself carries a small risk of causing a miscarriage). If the foetus is found to have the disease, should the pregnancy be terminated (i.e. should the mother have an abortion)? Many people feel more comfortable about an abortion at 12 weeks than at 16 weeks, but timing is not the only factor that influences the decision.

If we look at the incidence of births of cystic fibrosis and sickle-cell anaemia, it is clear that many at-risk couples do have children with the disease. This suggests that significant numbers of such couples do not opt for a prenatal test or, having received a positive diagnosis, do not opt for a termination of pregnancy. Surveys in the USA suggest that both occur. Added to this is the suspicion that many African Americans have a negative attitude towards genetic testing for sickle-cell anaemia because of past examples of discrimination by the US government against people with the sickle-cell trait and the belief that the tests are part of a discriminatory eugenic programme.

So, what are the factors that influence the decision to terminate a pregnancy for genetic reasons?[4] The first is the severity of the condition. There is a clear indication that the more severe the genetic disease diagnosed before birth, the easier it is to make the decision to terminate the pregnancy, on the grounds that severe suffering is prevented. Conditions that involve neuro-degeneration and death in early childhood are, for example, very likely to elicit a decision to terminate the pregnancy.

Situations also arise where parents did not know that they were both carriers of a recessive condition and thus birth of an affected child was unexpected; or perhaps they already knew their genetic risk but went ahead with the pregnancy (as discussed above). In either case, the reality of caring for a sick child leads to the avoidance of having any more with the same condition, even if this means termination of pregnancy.

Pre-implantation genetic diagnosis

The rapid development in the 1980s of DNA testing procedures and the ever-increasing ability to handle embryos in the laboratory led to a very powerful "marriage" between *in vitro* fertilization (IVF: see Chapter 7, section 7.2) and genetics. Embryos at the eight-cell stage survive, without harm, the removal of one cell. The use of DNA amplification techniques makes possible the use of this single cell for genetic testing in a procedure known as pre-implantation genetic diagnosis (PGD). Thus a couple who are at risk of having a child with a genetic disorder may opt for IVF and PGD. Only embryos that are free from the mutant gene will be implanted in order to start a pregnancy. Some couples find it more acceptable ethically to reject an eight-cell embryo than to terminate a pregnancy at 11 or 12 weeks. This is discussed more fully in the next section.

In both the UK and the USA, the first births following PGD were in 1990. In the USA the first case involved cystic fibrosis, while in the UK it was used for sex selection to avoid an X-linked condition; cystic fibrosis followed shortly after. In the UK, the Human Fertilisation and Embryology Authority has approved the use of PGD for about 200 genetic disorders. These include the more serious illnesses, some of which I have discussed earlier in this chapter but also some more manageable conditions such as phenylketonuria. However, despite this range of available tests, PGD has not yet made a significant impact on the birth frequency of many common genetic conditions. Comparison between the UK and the USA is interesting. In the UK, births resulting from IVF account for about 1.75 per cent of all births; PGD is involved in about 1.6 per cent of these. In the USA, births resulting from IVF make up about 1 per cent of the total, but PGD is involved in up to 10 per cent of these. This suggests that in the USA a greater proportion of IVF treatments are undertaken specifically in order to use PGD. In both countries, the number of babies being born following PGD is much lower than might be expected from the number of prospective parents known to be at risk. Some of the discrepancy arises from limitations on availability (see below). However, it is also clear that the physiological and emotional stresses imposed by IVF-PGD lead many prospective parents either to undergo prenatal testing, followed by abortion (if the foetus is affected), or to "let nature take its course" and risk having an affected child.

In both countries there are issues of availability. In the UK, up to two cycles of IVF are in theory available under the National Health Service for women who satisfy certain criteria (see next chapter). The need to include PGD does not entitle a couple to extra cycles and, indeed, some Primary Care Trusts do not fund PGD at all. For many couples it therefore comes down to whether they can afford it. This is even more pronounced in the USA where healthcare provision is funded by insurance (for those who can afford insurance). It then becomes a question of whether insurance companies will fund IVF and PGD and this seems to vary between insurance companies and/or policies. This reminds us of another of Francis Collins's challenges to society (see Chapter 5, section 5.4.2): "How will we ensure equality of access to treatments based on the new genetic knowledge?"[5]

6.2 PRENATAL AND PRE-IMPLANTATION TESTING: WIDER ETHICAL ISSUES

6.2.1 Introduction

Some of the problems associated with genetic testing and diagnosis have been mentioned already, including ambiguity of test results, possible difficulties in decision-making, the possible burden of genetic knowledge and the fairness or otherwise of availability. However, there are broader, more generic, issues that are raised by genetic testing.

6.2.2 The moral status of the foetus and of the pre-implantation embryo

In Chapter 4, I considered the question of how far our "moral boundaries" extend and I revisit this question here. Adherents of the majority of religions, philosophies and moral codes believe that killing another human is wrong, and

many use the term *the sanctity of [human] life*. Even so, many
of these, although certainly not all, accept the possibility that
other humans may be killed under specified conditions (such
as "just war"). But does this general prohibition of killing
extend to foetuses and to very early embryos, or, to revert
to earlier terminology, are foetuses and pre-implantation
embryos within our moral boundaries? To put it another way,
are foetuses and early embryos human persons? Indeed, this
is the real meaning of the question "When does human life
begin?". When do we start treating a developing human as if
they were already a fully fledged person? The law is somewhat
ambiguous. In countries where attention has been paid to this
issue, the developing foetus has no "human rights" until it
is born. Further, in many countries, including of course the
UK and the USA, abortion has been legalized. However,
time limits are set such that, except under well-defined
medical circumstances, abortions cannot be performed after
a particular time in pregnancy, even if human rights are not
granted until birth. Thus the law certainly permits abortion
on the grounds of genetic disease, even though some, whose
views are often described as "pro-life", oppose abortion on
all grounds.

So, if the law does not treat the foetus as an entity with
an absolute "right to life", we may surmise that the law
would not invest the pre-implantation embryo with human
personhood. That assumption is correct and thus allows the
creation of spare embryos and, relevant for this chapter, the
discarding of embryos with the "wrong" genes. However, in
the UK it took a great deal of discussion by the Warnock
Committee (see Chapter 4, section 4.5 and Chapter 7, section
7.2) and then in Parliament to reach that conclusion. One of
the factors that helped this decision-making was the biology
of the early embryo. In natural fertilizations, only 20–30 per
cent of early embryos implant into the lining of the uterus

to start a pregnancy. Implantation is a significant event in mammalian, including human, development. Nevertheless, some are opposed to discarding early embryos on any grounds, pointing out that, although implantation is a sort of "pause and evaluate" point in reproduction, any born human being has a genetic continuity with the one-cell embryo, the fertilized egg from whence it developed. They suggest that even if we do not or cannot invest the early embryo with human personhood, its potential to become a human person should lead us to protect it.

Indeed, conservative political groups in the USA have introduced proposals to define all embryos, from fertilization onwards, and all foetuses as human persons (the "personhood amendment"). Several states have voted on this already, but none has yet approved the measure; had they done so, several acts would be reclassified as murder, including abortion at any stage, use of the "morning-after" pill and, significantly, any deliberate rejection/destruction of very early embryos. This is a far cry from current legislation in the UK and USA in which, as noted above, human rights are not enjoyed until the baby is born. Although genetic testing of foetuses would be allowed, subsequent termination of pregnancy would be prohibited. As for any form of IVF, whether or not involving PGD, the practice of creating "spare" embryos or of discarding embryos with the wrong genotype would also be prohibited.

6.2.3 Saviour siblings: a special case?

As indicated earlier, PGD may be used by couples who know they are at risk of having a child with a genetic illness. However, there are couples who discover that they are both carriers of a recessive mutation only when they have a child with the condition caused by the mutated gene. Such was the case with Jack and Lisa Nash, in Denver, Colorado, whose first child, Molly, was born with Fanconi anaemia (described in the previous chapter). The main component of the syndrome, failure of the bone marrow, could be cured by a bone marrow stem cell transplant from a compatible donor. No compatible donors were available. However, the Nashes were eventually offered PGD to select not only for a child free from Fanconi anaemia but also one who could donate stem cells to Molly. After several attempts, a baby boy, Adam, was born and Molly, already very ill, received stem cells from Adam's umbilical cord.[6] This saved her life and at the time of writing she is 18 and Adam is 12.

There are several other conditions for which a stem cell donation from a compatible donor is an appropriate treatment and thus has arisen the concept of *saviour siblings*: children selected via PGD in order to save the life of a pre-existing child. There are many questions we can ask about this, several of which were explored by Jodi Picoult in her novel *My Sister's Keeper*. We can ask "what if…". What if the initial stem cell donation did not work, what else would be expected of Adam? What if, in the end, Molly had died from her condition? How would Adam feel?

The news of Adam Nash's birth unleashed a storm of criticism, much of it from people who were unaware of all the facts. Nevertheless, we can appreciate the concern of those who place a very high moral status on the early embryo. Not only did embryo selection occur but healthy embryos (i.e. without the Fanconi mutation) were rejected because they were not potential stem cell donors. This leads on to another deep question: Is a saviour sibling brought into the world as a commodity or will he or she be loved in their own right? While it is true that couples have children for many reasons, saviour siblings are specifically selected so that their cells can be useful. Does this run counter to ideas about the equality and dignity of every human being? I leave the reader to decide.

6.2.4 What is normal?

Although in terms of our DNA we humans are remarkably similar to each other (two individuals will differ, on average, by between 0.1 and 0.5 per cent), nevertheless, what appears to be quite limited genetic variation gives rise to a beautifully wide range of phenotypes, i.e. how we actually turn out. Some of that variation is in appearance, but much of it is hidden in the form of subtle and not so subtle differences in metabolism and physiology, in susceptibility to illness and so on. This variation is for many of us a glorious feature of the human species and yet the range of variation that we have regarded as normal for so long may be under threat from genetic testing. What is the evidence for this?

It may well be true that pre-implantation and prenatal genetic testing are carried out in order to lessen the burden of human suffering, but how far should that motivation carry us? Several people with high profiles in the worlds of medicine and medical law have suggested that it should be regarded as immoral or even illegal for parents to deliberately bring into the world a child with a serious and non-treatable genetic condition. Thus, several years ago, Robert Edwards of IVF fame (Chapter 7, section 7.2) stated that "... it will be the sin of the parents to have a child who carries the heavy burden of genetic disease".[7] This reflects a concern I have expressed in other publications, that with an increasing emphasis on genetics in medicine, some members of the medical community have adopted a "search and destroy" policy in respect of heritable diseases.

This leads us to refocus on the criteria for rejection of embryos (in PGD) and termination of pregnancy (in prenatal testing). How serious does a genetic condition need to be before these courses of action are taken? The range of tests available includes conditions such as phenylketonuria that are dealt with by a managed lifestyle and in which those with the condition can lead fulfilled and successful lives. In offering tests for such conditions, are we on a slippery slope to selection for any trait for which a test might be possible? Even without this possibility, is there already a shrinking of our concept of what is normal? Do current practices discriminate against disabled people because we try to prevent the birth of people who may be disabled because of a genetic condition? This is certainly the view held by Professor Tom Shakespeare of the Newcastle Life Centre. That view is backed up by data from a recent UK survey where, despite current emphasis on "diversity" and "inclusiveness", there is increasing discrimination against and, in the worst-case scenarios, hostility towards disabled people.[8] Whether this can be attributed to a narrowing of our idea of normality is open to discussion, but, even if not, the trend is worrying. Such attitudes are a long way from the Christian imperative to "love your neighbour as yourself" or the Victorian Golden Rule: "Do unto others as you would be done by."

6.2.5 Parental choice and designer babies

The number of genetic variations for which we can identify some sort of effect increases by the day. Some of these effects are rather vague, such as slight but measurable increases in risk of particular illnesses. Others may be one of a large number of genes involved in features such as height or in a smaller group involved in characters such as eye colour. Further, the interactions of genes with environmental factors and with each other often make the outcome of some genetic variations very difficult to predict. However, with other variants the outcome is clearer. This raises the possibility of testing for traits that are not related to medical conditions.

The emphasis on parental choice and autonomy already means that in the UK we allow parents to select or reject embryos on the basis of genetic make-up when the genes concerned are associated with medical conditions. Depending on our view of the early embryo, we may or may not regard this as a good thing. However, we have already noted concerns that this facility is now offered for some conditions that, although life-threatening if no action is taken, can actually be managed, for example by a controlled diet within a careful lifestyle. What then are the criteria for offering a genetic test? Where is the line drawn? In the UK, the line is drawn between medical and non-medical applications so that, for example, testing for genes involved in the make-up of muscle fibres (in relation to athletic performance) is not permitted (see Chapter 9, section 9.2.1). Nevertheless there are some "genetic libertarians", such as Professor John Harris of Manchester University, who believe that we should permit the testing of embryos for any trait that prospective parents wish, provided they are prepared to pay for it. This libertarian attitude is also seen in parts of the USA, including the state of California where it has been suggested that testing for eye colour (which is quite complex genetically) and other non-medically related traits should be made available as soon as the state of scientific knowledge permits. This would indeed mean "open house" on genetic selection, with the market determining what is offered and what is not.

We need to pause to consider the implications of all this. First, it would mean that embryos would be rejected not because they carried a genetic variation that would lead to (serious) illness but because the prospective parents did not wish to have a child with a particular non-medically related trait. For many, even among those who do not ascribe personhood to the early embryo, this would be a morally unacceptable development that turns the child into a commodity whose genetic make-up is, at least to some extent, the result of parental wishes. This seems to many of us an indication that too much emphasis is being placed on the principles of autonomy and rights rather than asking whether this is the virtuous or wise thing to do. Biologist-turned-theologian Celia Deane-Drummond expresses the same concern in a slightly different way: "... we should be... concerned with broader cultural trends that elevate liberalism to such an extent that children become rights that can be purchased according to parental desires and wishes".[9]

Secondly, this does not mean that "designer babies" are just round the corner (unless we mean by "designer baby" a baby for whom one or a few genetic traits have been selected). The term "designer baby" is generally taken to mean a baby in which a wide range of traits, including aspects of physical appearance and perhaps even aspects of intelligence,[10] has been selected for. However, as noted already, many of the traits in which parents may be interested are very complex and not amenable to a simple genetic test. Taking facial features as an example, we do not understand how a particular group of genes "collaborate" together to form a particular face. Even more mysterious is the way in which that set of genes may travel through a family lineage so that children may resemble very closely one parent or the other. More puzzling still is the observation first noted by Aristotle that particular facial features may be hidden for a generation. This results in a close resemblance of a child not to one of their parents but to one of their grandparents, a situation that I see regularly in a family who live in the same road as me. Thus, literally "designing" a baby within the constraints of the parental genes possessed by the embryo is not feasible and may never be.

Thirdly, even with the limitations just described, although some parents may undertake genetic selection of embryos for non-medical reasons, this is unlikely to become "mass technology". Genetic selection of embryos involves IVF, which itself is not an easy procedure, especially for the woman. So, although commentators such as Gregory Stock in California believe that some prospective parents will avail themselves of these tests, my own view is that the number would be small. The need for IVF will surely deter most prospective parents, leaving only a small number who are desperate to have a child with a particular genetic trait and who are prepared to pay for it.

6.2.6 Genetic selection and eugenics

In the minds of some people, the term "human genetics" is still closely associated with eugenics, a word that may be translated as "well born" or "good breeding". Plato and Aristotle over 2,000 years ago both believed that society could be improved by members of the elite classes having more children than less "worthy" people. Jumping forward to the nineteenth century, this idea was put in more formal terms by Charles Darwin's cousin, Francis Galton, who wanted to apply the new evolutionary theory to British society, again believing that society would be improved if the "lower classes" had fewer children and the middle and upper classes had more. We need to say that the idea was based on erroneous ideas about genetic inheritance but nevertheless it caught on. Indeed, in the first part of the twentieth century, eugenic ideas were espoused by many we would tend to describe as members of the liberal intelligentsia.

However, it was in other countries that eugenics really took hold. In the USA there was even a "colony" set up by a group of eugenic enthusiasts in which an experimental breeding programme was started. In the 1920s and 1930s, many states of the union incorporated into their laws eugenic policies that involved sterilization of the "morally feeble" and of "imbeciles". There was in addition often a strong racial element, with particular "races" being regarded at that time as inferior to others. Overall, it is estimated that at least 30,000 people were sterilized for eugenic reasons in the USA in the 1920s and 1930s, and some very tragic stories have emerged from investigations of that era. Fewer sterilizations took place after World War II, and the practice had ceased in the USA by the 1950s.

Eugenic policies were also adopted in Canada and in several European countries, most notably in Nazi Germany, where sterilization (probably involving at least 400,000 people), experiments on humans, compulsory euthanasia and some enforced breeding experiments were all part of the programme, in addition to the extermination of millions of Jewish people in the name of racial purity. It is this aspect of eugenics that has lodged in people's minds, especially in Germany where there is still a quite widespread concern about modern genetic research, especially as related to humans. However, other countries also introduced compulsory sterilization on eugenic grounds; in Canada and Switzerland, eugenic sterilizations continued until the 1960s and in Sweden until the 1970s.

So, is there any element of eugenics in the "new genetics"; are PGD and prenatal (and, among Ashkenazi Jews, pre-marital) genetic testing, eugenic practices? Well, in a limited way they are. Their purpose is to avoid "faulty" genes being passed on, thus improving the genetic health of particular family lines. However, it is not being used for social engineering but to avoid human suffering and thus, as mentioned earlier, these applications of genetic testing have been described as "eugenics with a smiling face". That does not mean we can be complacent. In discussion of what is normal in section 6.2.4, I noted a worrying trend to narrow our perceptions of normality and also noted an increase in discrimination against the disabled. If genetic selection contributes to these trends, then the eugenic element embedded within it will have lost any smiling face it may have had.

6.3 A GENE FOR THIS AND A GENE FOR THAT

6.3.1 Iconic DNA

With all the publicity (and even hyperbole) surrounding the Human Genome Project and with the media hailing every discovery of another "disease gene" as a major breakthrough, DNA has come out of the lab and become embedded in public awareness as never before. DNA and "the gene" have become icons in late twentieth- and early twenty-first-century Western society. Like icons, they are revered and even worshipped. The double helix, with the links between the two halves being described as steps, has become our stairway to heaven, a heaven in which the gene is god. So, for some people, genes provide a universal explanation of who we are, what we do and under whose control we operate. They have also become commercial items that may be paid for, as already noted in connection with selection of embryos, in order to gain some advantage that may be conferred by a particular tract of DNA. What are the implications of all this, both for medicine and for wider society?

6.3.2 Genes, genomes and genetic medicine

One of the promises held out during and following the Human Genome Project was that new genetic knowledge would usher in a new era of personalized medicine based on an individual's genetic make-up or aspects thereof. This would be more effective, more efficient and more cost-effective than the more general approaches to disease, illness and other conditions that we now use. To this end, there has been extensive research in which whole genomes are sequenced and links between common variants (known as single nucleotide polymorphisms – SNPs) and individual traits are analysed. More recently, an individual's DNA is mapped against an extensive library of several thousand SNPs in a technique known as micro-array analysis. The individual's particular pattern or array can then be analysed in respect of his or her known traits and can be compared with similar micro-arrays from many other individuals, again searching for particular patterns of SNPs in relation to known traits. These investigations are known as genome-wide associative studies, and the hope is that they will eventually provide predictive tools enabling a clinician to be aware of what conditions a person might be vulnerable to. Unfortunately, except for situations in which we already know that a particular SNP is directly associated with a particular condition (sickle-cell anaemia is a good example of this) the results are usually less clear-cut. They often just provide percentage increased or decreased risk of having or getting a particular illness compared with the population average. This increase or decrease may or may not be significant (in the non-statistical sense of that word). Thus a 15 per cent greater risk of succumbing to a condition where the population average was 1 in every 10,000 would not be especially worrying; on the other hand it might be more concerning if the population average was 1 in 100. However, even that may not be helpful because with very few exceptions we do not know what other factors are operating that may turn a risk into an actuality.

So, in the late 1990s, personalized genetic medicine was held to be just around the corner but we find in 2013 that we still have not reached the corner. However, the promise is still made, and currently faith is being placed in new DNA sequencing methods. One of the outcomes of the Human Genome Project and associated genetic research was a huge improvement in DNA sequencing methods coupled with a huge reduction in the cost. So while it took years and $3,000 million to complete an "average" human genome sequence during the HGP itself, the time to sequence an individual genome dropped to a few weeks and the price to around

$10–20,000. And that trend has continued: in mid-2012, a USA company, Life Technologies, launched a sequencer that analyses an individual human genome in one to two days, prompting one commercial sequencing company to offer a full sequence for $1,000 – a far cry from several years and $3,000 million. Now, it is said, we can sequence the genome of every newborn baby (or even of every foetus), to provide us with the information to personalize their healthcare. Time will tell whether this is yet one more "just round the corner" promise or whether it actually comes to fruition. If it does, there will need to be tight ethical oversight of the use of that information, not least to prevent genetic discrimination (as discussed earlier).

However, although increased knowledge of human genetics is very welcome, its increased emphasis in some areas of medical practice has drawn attention away from other factors that affect health. It is true to say that in general we can still get a better picture of someone's overall health from the postcode of where they live than from their genome sequence or SNP array. Environmental and social factors such as air quality, housing, diet, access to services, and unemployment are still hugely important in the health of an individual.

6.3.3 Genes, genomes and the general public

As the costs of DNA sequencing have come down, the number of companies offering direct-to-customer genome analysis has gone up, especially in the USA. The customer sends a sample (in the form of saliva collected in a small tube) and a few weeks later back come the results. Until recently, very few of these companies have offered full genome analysis, it being too expensive for most customers to think worth the cost. However, this will change now that full genome sequencing can be done in a day or two. What most companies offer is analysis of the informative parts of the genome. For some customers who are just interested in ancestry, this might be confined to the X or Y chromosomes but most want more than that. Thus the American company 23andMe[11] sequences the parts of the genome that are expressed (the exons) for $299 (price in mid-2012). This, the company states on its website, will enable the customer to connect with their past by learning about their ancestry, be "on the lookout now" because of knowledge of their genetic health risks, and plan for their future by learning whether they are carriers of any recessive trait that might be passed on to children. In respect of the genetic risks, the company claims to be able to provide information on between 100 and 200 conditions. I have discussed above the limited use of risk data but, nevertheless, the company claims on its website that "knowing your health risks will help you and your doctor figure out health areas to keep an eye on" and that the customer can plan personalized healthcare with their doctor.

The promised benefits for health certainly appeal to the "worried well", a distinct subset of people in wealthy Western society for whom life is generally comfortable. It is almost as if they need something to worry about. Further, these are the type of people who, having been told that their risk of disease x is a few per cent higher than the population average, will look for and indeed imagine they find symptoms of disease x. I therefore wonder whether the doctors will be as ready to work with someone who comes in armed with their sequence data as is implied by company advertising copy.

Other customers may have specific family reasons for wanting the analysis, while others are motivated by general interest. However, in addition to this, the company appeals to customers' altruism by asking them to participate in research so that they are "part of new genetic discoveries that can benefit us all".[12] To this end, each customer completes a questionnaire about a range of their own traits and also permits their data to be stored in the company's database for future reference. They are therefore paying to be a subject of research, a state of affairs that should cause us to raise an ethical eyebrow.

6.3.4 Just a set of genes?

The installation of DNA and "the gene" as icons and the increasing "geneticization" of some areas of medicine are symptoms of a wider trend to attribute too much to genes. There are many symptoms of this. James Watson, one of the discoverers of the structure of DNA, stated that sequencing the human genome would tell us who we really are. Many customers of the commercial DNA sequencing services make similar comments and, indeed, the name of one of the companies, 23andMe, implies that the knowledge is about the customer's personhood. Too often we also see simplistic statements in the media about a gene for this and a gene for that. These statements are usually, at best, gross over-simplifications or distortions of scientific data or, at worst, just plain wrong. The problems with the media are twofold. First, it is easier to present a straightforward over-simplistic view because it is more readily presented to readers, viewers or listeners. Secondly, this view resonates with a philosophy that has permeated much of our media, and that philosophy is genetic reductionism or genetic essentialism – i.e. that our individual personhood can be reduced to or lies entirely in our genes or that our "essence" can be completely ascribed to our genetic make-up. Richard Dawkins is one of the loudest and most influential proponents of this view, typified by his statement that "… DNA neither cares nor knows. DNA just is. And we dance to its music."[13]

This is quite a bleak view of humankind and is one that Dawkins himself cannot actually live with; he has also written that, although we are genetically determined, it is our privilege as humans to overcome the deterministic activity of our genes. This brings us to another of the questions that Francis Collins, while he was director of the HGP, posed about the new genetic knowledge: "How will we counter the tendency to genetic reductionism/determinism – the belief that 'it is all in our genes'?"[14] The straightforward answer is, despite the strident comments of Dawkins and others, that the data simply do not support this view. Study after study has revealed very little evidence indeed for one-to-one links between genes and particular behaviours. Even our biological development is not totally determined by genes, neither is the wiring and rewiring in the brain as we learn new things and have different experiences. Identical twins with identical genotypes are different people. Thus writers as diverse as the atheist philosopher John Dupré and the Christian doctor John Wyatt have rejected totally the reductionist/essentialist position, as do I. We can never define a person by the sequence of their genome. Many aspects of our personhood, including our spirituality, are not written in our DNA.

6.4 CONCLUDING REMARKS

This chapter has interwoven our increased knowledge of genetics with applications in genetic testing and diagnosis. We have seen how knowledge of a specific genetic mutation that leads to a disease enables us to test for that disease at all stages of life, from pre-implantation embryos to adults. We have also seen that testing can be extended to other specific genetic traits, enabling prospective parents, should they wish to undergo the rigours of IVF, if not to design their babies at least to select for traits which have no medical relevance. Genetic testing can also be taken a stage further. Instead of looking for specific individual genes, individuals' whole genomes or particular features of those genomes can now be sequenced, providing people with information, albeit not always very clear, about their risks of having particular illnesses or diseases.

I have considered some of the ethical and social issues raised by these diagnostic and analytical techniques. Here I want to focus on just one, namely their availability. Even PGD carried out to detect a serious genetic condition is not universally available in state-funded (i.e. NHS) medicine in the UK or in insurance-funded medicine in the USA. This means that those who wish to use PGD may have to fund it themselves. Then, when we go on to consider those "non-medical" traits, in those countries that allow testing for these, it is market forces that will determine whether or not tests are offered. That leads us to the "direct-to-consumer" genome analysis. This is certainly a commercial enterprise and is thus available to those who can afford it. Overall then, it is clear that money will buy a whole range of genetic services, and that many will not be able to afford them. This theme of "haves and have-nots" also surfaces from time to time in the next chapter, where we consider the use of increasingly sophisticated technology (including further aspects of genetics) at different points in the lives of individuals.

NOTES

1. See the article by Walter Truett Anderson posted on the excellent Genethics website: http://www.genethics.ca/.
2. Added to which we note that at least 50 million people in the USA cannot afford health insurance.
3. In "The Human Genome Project: Tool of Atheistic Reductionism or Embodiment of the Christian Mandate to Heal?", *Science and Christian Belief* 11 (1999), 99–111, available online at http://www.scienceandchristianbelief.org/download_pdf_free. php?filename=SCB+11-2+Collins.pdf.
4. I note that the same problem is faced by couples when a routine ultrasound scan reveals an abnormality.
5. In "The Human Genome Project".

6. The full story is told in "Learning to Play God", in *Third Way*, January 2012, available online at http://www.thirdwaymagazine.co.uk/editions/janfeb-2012/features/learning-to-play-god.aspx.

7. In a talk at an international fertility conference in France, reported in *The Sunday Times*, 4 July 1999.

8. The brilliant wheelchair athlete Tanni Grey-Thompson recalls being spat at in the street and being called a "scrounger".

9. In *Genetics and Christian Ethics*, Cambridge: Cambridge University Press, 2007, page 8.

10. As pointed out by geneticist Steve Jones (in, for example, *In the Blood: God, Genes and Destiny*, London: HarperCollins, 1996), intelligence is itself a complex multifaceted feature and even for one facet many genes contribute. Neither should we forget complex environmental influences ("nurture"). So, even if a single gene were to be selected, it is likely to have only a very small effect on overall intelligence.

11. https://www.23andme.com/.

12. See company website: https://www.23andme.com/.

13. In *River Out of Eden*, London: Phoenix, 1995, page 155.

14. In "The Human Genome Project".

MEDICAL TECHNOLOGY: FROM GAMETE TO GRAVE

There are two ways to live your life. One is as though nothing is a miracle. The other is as though everything is a miracle.
Albert Einstein, quoted by Des MacHale in
***Wisdom*, 2002**

Dúirt mé leat go raibh mé breoite
Irish Gaelic inscription on Spike Milligan's headstone; it translates as "I told you I was ill"[1]

7.1 INTRODUCTION

In the previous chapter we saw that the very rapid increase in knowledge of human genes has led to a range of genetic diagnostic techniques that can be applied at any stage of life, right back to the pre-implantation embryo. However, it is not just in genetics that rapid development of new techniques, methods and medical interventions has occurred. In the developed countries of what is now often referred to as the "global north" there are sophisticated diagnostic techniques and equally sophisticated treatments that are available for the whole of an individual's life, from before birth right up to death. This is something that we have come to expect, almost as a right. I am not at this stage suggesting that this is on the one hand wrong or, on the other, just as it should be. Rather, I want to discuss specific examples of this "gamete to grave" provision of healthcare and the huge commitment of resources that is involved. These may cause us to marvel at human ingenuity and inventiveness while some examples raise social and ethical issues, which are also discussed.

7.2 THE ART OF REPRODUCTION: FROM DONOR INSEMINATION TO TEST-TUBE BABIES

In the UK about 15 per cent of those who wish to have a baby have significant difficulty in doing so. However, sub-fertility and infertility have come to be regarded as medical conditions and thus appropriate for medical treatment. We devote considerable resources to overcoming fertility problems in individual couples, which may seem ironic considering that during the writing of this book the human population of the world passed the 7,000 million mark, but that is indeed what happens. Assisted reproductive technologies (ART) are becoming ever more sophisticated and indeed may challenge some people's views about family structure and about who should and should not have babies.

The first recorded successful use of artificial insemination is credited to a Scottish doctor, John Hunter, who, in 1790, impregnated a woman with her husband's sperm. This led to pregnancy and the birth of a baby. This pre-dates by 76 years the claim, often seen in American texts, that the first successful artificial insemination with a husband's sperm was carried out by Marion Sims in 1866. However, no confusion about dates exists for the first recorded successful use of insemination with donor sperm. In 1884, Dr William Pancoast, a professor in the Jefferson Medical College, Philadelphia, was treating an infertile couple. The couple had assumed that the wife was infertile, but it turned out that it was the husband. Without informing the couple of this, Pancoast anaesthetized the wife in order to "treat her condition" and, again without informing the couple, inseminated her with sperm from one of his medical students. Nine months later a baby, which the couple assumed was theirs, was born. This case raises many ethical issues around informed consent and medical deception, and it was only many years later that the truth came to light when the medical student donor, by then well established in his career, owned up to what had happened.[2]

Although the ethics of Pancoast's treatment were dubious, the procedure paved the way for donor insemination (DI) as a means of dealing with male infertility. Thus by the 1930s, DI (or AID – artificial insemination by donor – as it was then known) was practised in several places in the UK. It is now widely available, and about 500 babies are born each year in the UK following this procedure. Egg donation is of course less straightforward and has only become available more recently (and even now there is a shortage of eggs). For both sperm and egg donation it is clear that the couple need to accept that half of the child's genetic make-up originates outside the couple. This is one of the factors that leads very conservative commentators, especially in the Roman Catholic Church, to suggest that acceptance of donated gametes is equivalent to adultery.

Moving on from gamete donation, I want to concentrate now on the more "technological" methods of assisted reproduction. The birth in 1978 of the world's first "test-tube baby", Louise Brown, was a major surprise to the public and to the majority of the scientific community, but actually it was the culmination of several years of research. That research involved collaboration between a scientist, Dr Robert Edwards, and an obstetrician, Patrick Steptoe, and of course Louise's parents, John and Lesley Brown. The latter are often forgotten in the discussion, but their willingness (and especially that of Lesley) to try *in vitro* fertilization was a key part of this success.

Responses were immediate and mixed. Many were of course delighted for the Browns and pleased that a new treatment had been developed. However, there were also negative responses; indeed there were expressions of dismay that this technique had even been considered. Let alone used. The Pope, speaking for the Roman Catholic Church, condemned IVF outright. It separated sexual intercourse from procreation, it involved masturbation and it replaced an act of physical union with a technological procedure. This last point was also made by several non-RC commentators, some of whom went as far as to say that this may affect parental attitudes to IVF children (although subsequent sociological research has not supported this view).

IVF also made surrogate motherhood possible: couples could elect to have embryos created by IVF and then "outsource" the pregnancy to another woman. This might happen because it is medically risky or just plain inconvenient for the female partner in the IVF procedure to become pregnant. The embryo is implanted into the second woman, who undergoes the pregnancy, gives birth to the baby and then gives it to the couple.[3] This was clearly even more of a departure from the natural way of having children and led people to ask whether IVF threatened "family values" (whatever those are).

And then of course there are the embryos themselves. It was in the context of IVF alone that their status was first considered. PGD (see previous chapter) followed later, but IVF itself raises the topic of spare embryos. Several years after Louise Brown's birth, by which time IVF had been accepted as an appropriate treatment for sub-fertility, a committee was convened under the chairmanship of the philosopher Mary Warnock to make recommendations on all aspects of IVF. I mentioned this in Chapter 4, but that was many pages ago, so I take this opportunity to note again a key statement in the committee's report, as shown in Text Box 7.1. With some justification we may feel that this statement walks an ethical tightrope. Nevertheless it has been enshrined in the Human Fertilisation and Embryology (HFE) Act (1990) and remains the basis for current practice concerning work with the pre-implantation embryo.

> ### TEXT BOX 7.1
> The Warnock Committee's summary of the ethical status of the early human embryo:
>
> *... the early embryo is not yet a person but nevertheless should not be regarded as just a ball of cells. Thus the embryo of the human species [should] be afforded some protection in law.*
> **Report of the Committee of Inquiry into Human Fertilisation and Embryology, 1984 (usually referred to as The Warnock Report, 1984)**

In the meantime, the technique had moved on. Louise Brown's sister Melanie, born in 1982, was only the world's 40th IVF baby but the annual total slowly grew from there. In the UK, for the past several years there have been about 12,000 IVF births (some of which are births of twins) annually. The procedure has certainly become more efficient, but there has also been the invention of more complex techniques to deal with more difficult problems. Three examples will be sufficient to show the degree of effort that has gone into and still goes into this area of medicine. The first is about dealing with very low sperm counts or with sperm of impaired motility. In such cases, one sperm is injected directly into the egg in a process known as ICSI (intra-cytoplasmic sperm injection). This bypasses the need for sperm to be able to swim and also the need to have about 100,000 functional sperm cells in order to effect the entry of just one of them into the egg.

The second example is more complex and relates to the inheritance of sub-cellular particles or organelles called mitochondria. These are vital for life because of their involvement in converting the energy in our food into a form that our bodies can use. These organelles possess a small number of genes, amounting to less than 0.2 per cent of our total gene set; these are inherited via the mother. A woman who knows that she has a malfunction in one of these genes can use a variant of IVF that enables her to avoid passing the malfunctioning gene to her offspring. Discussion of the technical details is not needed here, except to note that the embryos resulting from this form of IVF will have a normal complement of genes from the father, a normal complement of the main set of genes from the mother, plus "healthy" mitochondria from a second woman. This technique, which has only just become available, leads to a child having three "genetic parents", albeit that one of them has only contributed a very small number of the total gene complement. Inevitably, the reactions varied from dismay (usually along the lines of blurring family boundaries) to delight (another example of our technological expertise solving a complex medical problem, even if the problem is actually quite rare).

The third example I call reproduction without sex: use of stem cells to make gametes, followed by IVF, then pregnancy outside the body. It sounds very far-fetched but these procedures are being discussed. I pick up that discussion in Chapter 9.

Despite the increasing sophistication of IVF techniques, there remain some couples for whom it is not successful, raising the question of how much further we should go and how many more resources we should expend in treating this condition. The figure of 12,000 IVF births per year in the UK may be set against the number of abortions, approximately 200,000, over the same period; only a small proportion of these are carried out for strictly medical or genetic reasons. It is certainly true that some couples who cannot have children of their own are devastated by their condition, describing it as mourning for someone who never existed. And this is not a modern phenomenon. Similar distress is recorded in both the Old and New Testaments of the Bible in relation to wives such as Sarah, Hannah and Elizabeth, who were "barren". From those times right up to the present day, many women/couples who are unable to have children experience deep distress about their condition. Some of the couples who experience this will probably not want to adopt (adoption does not fulfil the yearning to have one's "own" child) but others may.

All this raises that well-worn question: "Does everyone have a right to a child?" Different commentators respond to the question in different ways. The philosopher John Harris, for example, would adopt quite extreme measures, including reproductive cloning (see Chapter 9), to support the right to a child (or what he calls procreative autonomy), while others do not think it is at all helpful to consider having a child as being one of the inalienable human rights. The question is brought into particular focus by IVF for post-menopausal women and lesbian couples. In respect of the former, the guidelines laid down by the UK's Human Fertilisation and Embryology Authority (HFEA) do not permit IVF for any woman who is past her natural child-bearing age. However, there are many countries where such guidelines do not operate. Thus several women well into their 60s have borne children after IVF and appropriate hormonal support. In respect of lesbian couples, it has always been open to them to ask a male friend to provide sperm for artificial insemination, and a good number of such couples have followed this route, with one of them electing to be the birth mother. However, with the increasing liberalization of attitudes (and in the UK of the HFEA's guidelines), IVF has been available to lesbian couples for several years. So, whatever we think about "the right to a child", we have reached a position where, if I regard it as my right, then I expect the healthcare system to enable me to enjoy that right.

Nevertheless, in the UK, where healthcare is mostly funded by the state, availability of IVF is not universal. As already mentioned, the HFEA guidelines exclude post-menopausal women but do permit IVF to be offered to pre-menopausal women up to the age of 50. In practice, only private clinics offer IVF to women in their mid to late 40s, and even some of them will not do so because the success rates are relatively low – and the success rates of course affect the reputation of the clinic. For state (i.e. NHS) funding of IVF, women over the age of 42 are excluded (this upper limit was recently raised from 40) but even lower limits, down to 34, are imposed by some Primary Care Trusts. Providers of fertility treatment are also increasingly likely to refuse IVF to obese women, firstly because of the health risks for mother and foetus during pregnancy and secondly because there are now data showing that IVF is significantly less successful if the woman is obese. In a randomized trial in Australia, obese women who followed a strict diet (losing on average 6.6 kg) were significantly more likely to conceive after IVF than women who did not follow the diet.

Smoking is another factor that is taken into account, with up to 25 per cent of Primary Care Trusts refusing IVF treatment to smokers. This is argued on health grounds, again relating to both mother and foetus. Thus, although the state does fund IVF (under the guidelines already mentioned), there is certainly rationing based on lifestyle choices. While the Primary Care Trusts involved support their actions with arguments based on health, there is the suspicion among some commentators that these restrictions are in place in order to save money. Whichever way we look at it, "a right to a child" does not enter the discussion.

7.3 GENE THERAPY

The increasing ability to handle and manipulate embryos in the laboratory and clinic, as detailed above and in the previous chapter, means that in principle it is possible to carry out GM on human embryos. Indeed, this is permitted in research on human fertility, on early embryo development and on genetic diseases, provided the embryos are destroyed at fourteen days after fertilization. This of course raises those issues that we have discussed previously, namely "spare" embryos and human embryos as commodities. However, what is not permitted is to use a GM embryo to start a pregnancy because that would allow the genetic modification to be passed on to subsequent generations: germ-line genetic modification (as it is technically known) of humans is against the law.

Nevertheless, genetic modification of cells in an existing human person is permitted and is carried out in a process called gene therapy. Some genetic disorders affect particular cells or cell lineages into which it is relatively straightforward to insert a properly functioning version of the gene in question. Initial targets for this were the mucous membranes of the nose and lungs in cystic fibrosis patients and the bone marrow in children with severe combined immune-deficiency disease (SCID). For several reasons, gene therapy for cystic fibrosis has met with very little success, but it is still the subject of a well-funded research effort. However, it is a different story with SCID. In this disorder, the child's immune system is non-functional and children with the condition need to be protected from infective agents – hence the disease is sometimes called "boy in a bubble syndrome" because of the protective clear plastic bubble sometimes used to isolate the child. The disease may be cured by inserting the correctly functioning gene into the bone marrow, and in three of the main centres in which this work has been done – London, Paris and Boston (USA) – success rates have been very high. Indeed, it is a measure of the efficacy of the treatment that the children can live a normal life, exposed to all the infective agents that we all encounter. However, the procedure is not risk-free. Some of the children cured of SCID went on to develop leukaemia because the GM procedure activated an oncogene (a gene that, when active at the wrong time, causes cancer) in the bone marrow. A further course of treatment, this time for the leukaemia, thus had to follow the treatment for SCID.

Nevertheless, encouraged by the success with SCID, the biomedical research community has turned its attention to more common inherited diseases that affect formation of blood cells in the bone marrow. In early trials, a small number of patients have been cured of thalassaemia (inability to produce functional haemoglobin) while, at the time of writing, a trial of gene therapy for sickle-cell anaemia is proposed. Other disease targets will doubtless follow as we learn how to deliver effectively a functioning gene to the cells affected by a particular genetic disorder. Thus, for example, the retina and the cornea are considered likely targets in using gene therapy to deal with some forms of blindness.

Gene therapy is not just being used for heritable gene malfunction. A whole range of conditions involve genes that become active in the wrong place (such as cancer) or genes that stop functioning properly (as in some degenerative diseases and in some forms of cancer). These too have become targets for gene therapy. There has been some success in switching off genes that are active when they should not be and, more recently, in a very small trial of Parkinson's disease patients, in replacing with active copies a gene that has become inactive in the brain.

The use of gene therapy, whether to replace a faulty gene that has been inherited or to deal with a gene that has become malfunctional in some way during life, raises another possibility. The procedure could also be used for enhancement; that is, to improve the functioning of a "normal" individual. It has often been discussed, for example, in relation to improving athletic performance, where the term "gene doping" is used.[4] In general, public opinion is very supportive of genetic research in relation to medical therapy but opposes the use of genetic knowledge in enhancement. Indeed, this is the position that I hold, but I also acknowledge, with several other commentators, that the distinction between the two may be very blurred. For example, we may define as therapeutic a procedure that restores a person to within the range regarded as normal. However (as was discussed in Chapter 6, section 6.2.4), definition of "normal" may be very difficult and thus the distinction between therapy and enhancement may be equally difficult. This difficulty may be illustrated by examples from non-genetic medicine. Is limb lengthening surgery undertaken in order to make a young woman tall enough to follow a chosen career, treatment or enhancement? What about surgery for breast enlargement or reduction, sex change operations for gender identity disorder and "pure" cosmetic surgery? The problem here is that one person's enhancement is another person's treatment. For example, some may have psychological problems (and therefore need "therapy") because of short stature, while others do not. We may regard it as therapy to provide growth hormone to children who are under-producing it, but do we think the same about children who are of somewhat below mean stature for other reasons? Self-image/body image, peer pressure and the cultural norms of a society are all important factors in determining individual perception of enhancement versus treatment.

Returning to gene therapy, we may perhaps define therapy as being directed at specific genetic or physiological malfunctions, while enhancement is a change in a non-disease-causing genetic feature. However, even these definitions have problems.[5] How, for example, would we regard a genetic modification that led to an increased resistance to disease-causing agents such as viruses or bacteria ("genetic immunization")? Some would class this as therapy but others may think that it elevates the individual above the norm and that it therefore should be classified as enhancement.

7.4 REPAIR, REPLACEMENT AND RENEWAL

7.4.1 Introduction

Cells, tissues and organs may stop functioning properly for various reasons, including disease, accident and ageing. Indeed, increased lifespan in the developed countries of the global north has been accompanied by an increased incidence of degenerative conditions. A small number of these conditions may eventually prove suitable for gene therapy, but most will not. Functional degeneration of whole organs or of tissues such as bone marrow may be cured by a transplant. Transplant surgery has progressed hugely over the past few decades, and transplants of kidneys, hearts, livers, corneas, heart–lung combinations and even ovarian tissues are now routine (although the frequency of these transplants varies markedly between the different organs in the list). Less routine are the more recent (and for some controversial) transplants of hands and faces. However, there are other approaches to the problem of dealing with degenerating or damaged (or even missing) tissues and organs, as becomes apparent in the next few pages.

7.4.2 Stem cells

Stem cells are cells that are firstly self-renewing – populations of them are maintained at different sites within the body, for example in the bone marrow – and secondly they give rise, by a process of differentiation, to a range of specialized types of cell. Their role is to provide cells to replace those lost by damage and by natural turnover. For example, the average healthy adult replaces about 2 million red blood cells and 100,000 white blood cells per second, while the surface layer of the skin[6] is replaced every two to three weeks in a young person but rather more slowly in elderly people.

In the examples given immediately above, the stem cells give rise to a limited range of cell types. However, there exists transiently in the early embryo, at the blastocyst stage (about seven days after fertilization), a population of stem cells that will, if a pregnancy is established, become the source of all the different types of cell in the human body. Based on this fact, it has been suggested that these embryonic stem cells (ES cells) may be used in tissue and organ repair – a process known as regenerative medicine. Developmental biologists have had some success in persuading these embryonic stem cells to grow into a limited range of cell types in the laboratory. Indeed, as long ago as 1999, this work was awarded the title of "Breakthrough of the Year" by the leading American research journal *Science*. Embryonic stem cells, perhaps from "spare" embryos generated by IVF, may be a source of tissues and even organs.

In the UK the 1990 HFE Act was amended in 2001 to legalize the use of early embryos for research on ES cells, including embryos created by cloning (see below). In 2008, the original 1990 Act was replaced by a new HFE Act. There were several major changes, some of which further extended the provision for research on early embryos, including the use of "admixed" or "cybrid" embryos (see below).

Why was there a need to include cloned embryos and admixed embryos in these changes to the law? With tissue and organ transplants, rejection is a major issue. This is no less true of replacement tissues generated from stem cells than of conventional organ and tissue transplants. However, if the replacement tissue arises from ES cells genetically identical to the patient, the rejection problem is avoided. This would mean the use of a cloning procedure (somatic cell nuclear transfer) – the genetic material, the nuclear DNA, from one of the patient's cells would be inserted into a human egg from which the nuclear DNA had been previously removed. This is the procedure that led to the birth of Dolly the sheep in 1996, but for regenerative medicine, development of the clone would proceed only to the blastocyst stage in order to generate the ES cells. This procedure is known as *therapeutic cloning* (contrasted with reproductive cloning, which is forbidden under UK law). But this immediately raises a further practical problem: from where will the human eggs be obtained? We have already noted the shortage of eggs for fertility treatment, and obtaining eggs for therapeutic cloning is not likely to be any easier. This is where admixed or cybrid embryos come in. A cybrid embryo is one in which an egg cell is obtained from another mammal, generally a cow or a rabbit; its nuclear DNA is removed and nuclear DNA from a human cell is inserted. It has been described as using cow or rabbit cells as vehicles for human genes. The cybrid embryos are again allowed to develop up to the blastocyst stage.

I will comment on ethical responses to these developments a little later, but before that it is helpful to evaluate progress in their actual use in regenerative medicine. At the time of writing, clinical trials are under way in the UK and the USA in which cells derived from ES cells are being used in attempts to repair the retinas of patients with macular dystrophy. A few months ago, a small-scale trial in the USA in which ES cells were injected into the spinal cords of patients with spinal injuries was discontinued suddenly. The company involved in the work announced that it was opting out completely from stem cell research because it is too expensive. Thus, medical applications have been far from extensive, although in the research lab, several different types of differentiated cell have been generated from human ES cells, raising hopes that further medical uses may follow.

In respect of therapeutic cloning, it has certainly proved possible, although far from easy, to generate embryos by nuclear transfer. However, most do not survive until the blastocyst stage and even if they do, it has proved very difficult indeed to establish stem cell lines from them.[7] The one recent positive report turned out to be not quite as it seemed: although genetic material from an adult cell had been inserted successfully into the egg, the egg's own genetic material had not been removed. The embryo and the stem cells obtained from it thus had three sets of chromosomes and would be totally unsuitable for actual clinical use.

It is almost inevitable then that opponents of the use of ES cells point out that thirteen years or so of intensive and expensive research has yielded very little that is of use in medicine. This brings us to the debate about the ethics of this work. Before both the 2001 amendments to the HFE Act and the new Act in 2008, there was public consultation which, needless to say, generated some controversy. Supporters of the changes included groups and societies representing the interests of patients with degenerative diseases and many clinicians and medical researchers. MORI polls have indicated that research on and use of human ES cells is acceptable to 70–80 per cent of the British public. Indeed, in a general survey of attitudes to science, Ipsos-MORI report that "many considered it more immoral not to develop treatments for patients with serious diseases when stem cell research offered

the potential to do this".[8] Further, the more liberal attitude
to this science (and actually, in the 2008 Act, to several other
aspects of IVF) very much reflects the zeitgeist of the early
twenty-first century in the UK. There is often a widespread,
more aggressive secularism, in the media at least, mixed in
with a strong dose of postmodernism. There are changes in
perception about what constitutes a family, with arrangements
previously regarded as unconventional now being more
widely accepted. The ethical decision-making leading to
these changes is strongly utilitarian, with an undercurrent of
rights-based thinking (see Chapter 4).

On the other side of the argument, there were strong
objections from groups representing people who see human
life as sacred from fertilization onwards (i.e. unlike the
Warnock Committee), and who believe that early embryos
should be treated as if they are human persons. If it was bad
enough to use embryos for research, it was even worse to
create them (by cloning) specifically to use them as sources
of stem cells. Human embryos would just be commodities.
Therapeutic cloning is seen as the start of a slippery slope:
if today therapeutic cloning is allowed, tomorrow we will
surely see reproductive cloning. The formation of admixed
or cybrid embryos is seen as an affront to human dignity.
Creating hybrid embryos has been described as making
monsters, even though they are only to be used in research
on the development of ES cells. Further, opponents of work
on human ES cells pointed out (and continue to point out)
that more progress had been made using other sources of
stem cells (see below) and therefore that attention should be
focused on these.

Interestingly, the adherence to the opposing viewpoints
does not map clearly onto religious views. The 20 per cent
of the UK public who specifically oppose work with human
ES cells represents more people than those who are active

adherents of Christianity, Judaism and Islam combined. Further, although some Christian organizations in the UK, such as CARE and the Roman Catholic Church, strongly oppose this work, others, such as Christians in Science, are generally supportive. There is a similar situation in the USA, where, although many members of the "religious right" have vigorously opposed research on human ES cells, other Christians have supported it.[9]

However, the claims that ES cells would revolutionize genetic medicine have yet to be realized. In this respect we see parallels to genetic medicine as discussed in Chapter 5, section 5.5.2. But what about other types of stem cell? As indicated already, the body contains several populations of stem cells involved in cellular turnover, wound healing and repair. These are often called adult stem cells, but that is a misnomer. More correctly they are called post-embryonic cells because they are laid down during foetal development. However, I will use the term *adult stem cell* because it is widely accepted and understood. In the body, each population has a limited role; thus, as already discussed, bone marrow stem cells give rise to blood cells. Because of their limited role, adult stem cells had not been thought of as having a wide potential in regenerative medicine. However, it is now known that under some circumstances these cells will *transdifferentiate*; that is, they will go down a different developmental pathway to the one they normally follow in the body. However, the topic remains scientifically controversial because the extent to which transdifferentiation observed in the laboratory occurs in the human body seems very variable. Nevertheless, several early stage clinical trials (and a handful of phase II trials) are under way in the USA and Europe, including the UK. However, perhaps the most spectacular example has been the transdifferentiation of bone marrow stem cells into the cells that produce cartilage, enabling scientists to grow them on an artificial frame to make a replacement trachea – a remarkable achievement. It has also proved possible to stimulate populations of adult stem cells to be more active than usual. The stem cells in the periosteum, for example, have been stimulated to enable a Cleveland surgeon to use them to lengthen a patient's bone, a process that would not happen naturally in an adult.

These examples certainly indicate that research on using adult stem cells is worth pursuing further. Nevertheless, we need to beware of exaggerated claims. Several of the organizations that campaign against research on human ES cells have claimed that adult stem cells are being used in over 100 different therapies. This is very misleading. Most of the "different therapies" are applications of bone marrow transplantation (a technique first used successfully in 1968) plus the clinical trials and occasional individual treatments mentioned above. Neither have proponents of ES research been modest in their claims. Some of the statements made during the run-up to the 2001 modification of the HFE Act suggested strongly that ES-cell-based treatments were just around the corner. Indeed, medical scientist and TV broadcaster Robert Winston, in his 2005 presidential address to the British Science Association, said:

> *Both in Britain and America, huge publicity has been given to stem cells, particularly embryonic stem cells, and the potential they offer. Of course, the study of stem cells is one of the most exciting areas in biology but I think it is unlikely that embryonic stem cells are likely to be useful in healthcare for a long time... I was concerned that parliamentarians have been convinced that it was just a matter of a few years before we would be able to transplant stem cells and cure a lot of neurological disorders.*[10]

Ethical debate is not helped by unrealistic claims, from whichever side of the debate they come.

The ethical debate received a fresh impetus in December 2006/January 2007 when scientists succeeded in persuading mouse skin fibroblasts (cells that produce collagen) apparently to behave like embryonic stem cells. These cells are known as *induced pluripotent stem cells* (iPS cells), and the trick to get them to behave this way is to use a GM technique to switch back on four genes (or to add extra copies of the four genes) that regulate ES cell activity. Opponents of ES research immediately claimed that if the technique could be applied to human cells (which was in fact first reported later in 2007) there was no need for research on ES cells. This view was further strengthened when it was shown that, in the laboratory, iPS cells could be induced to differentiate into other types of cell. Opponents of the use of human ES cells immediately referred to these iPS cells as "ethical stem cells" in a manner that implied that this was the only possible view of the matter. This was one of the lines of argument used in the run-up to the 2008 HFE Act. Further, it was pointed out, these cells would obviate the need for cloning. If a patient needed stem cell treatment, his or her own fibroblasts would be used to make the iPS cells, and those cells would automatically be immunologically compatible with the patient.

Thus it was suggested that iPS cells would make it totally unnecessary to use ES cells, and perhaps this is still the perception among those members of the wider public who think about these things. However, the scientific community have reservations about this, reservations that grow as we find out more about how iPS cells work. First, having switched on four genes that ensure the "youthful" cellular behaviour of iPS cells, there is a worry that these genes remain active such that they could cause cancer if the cells were used therapeutically. Even though a method has been developed to reactivate the cells without using GM techniques, this problem remains. Further, the cells do not actually become completely like ES cells. In particular, there may be some residual activity of the genes that were working before the cells were induced. The genetic programming that led them to become, for example, fibroblasts is difficult to reverse totally; we might say that the cells have a molecular memory of what they were. Scientific debate thus continues, as does work on ES cells, iPS cells and adult stem cells. The work is very much less in the public consciousness than it was but the ethical issues that concern perhaps as many as 20 per cent of the adult population have not actually gone away.

7.4.3 *The blind receive their sight, the lame walk*

Some readers will recognize that the words heading this section are actually taken from the Bible, in fact from Luke's Gospel. They were spoken by Jesus when he was asked (by some of John the Baptist's friends) whether he was "the one who was to come". Jesus was of course referring, among other things, to miracles of healing. This leads us to consider some aspects of reparative medicine – enabling people to walk, enabling the blind to see and so on – which although not "supernatural" nevertheless strike us as almost miraculous. Whereas the stem cell approach to regenerative medicine utilizes knowledge of developmental biology, we are now in an area where biomechanics, micro-engineering, electronics and computer technology interact, with neuroscience also starting to play a role. I will discuss three examples: prosthetic limbs, dealing with paralysis and dealing with blindness.

Prosthetic limbs

Mechanical–biological interfaces have been around for many centuries. It is easy to conjure up the traditional image of the seafaring man with a wooden leg, as with Robert Louis

Stevenson's character Long John Silver. Mechanical prostheses, replacing limbs lost in accidents or as a result of developmental defects or illness, have progressed a long way since the simple wooden leg. Nevertheless, even as we are about to consider the very latest in prosthetic limbs, it is good to remind ourselves that simple technology can be very effective. One example of this is the Jaipur limb, which is an artificial leg, developed at the Mahaveer hospital in Jaipur, India.[11] The foot is particularly innovative, made of a clever combination of wood and various densities of vulcanized rubber shaped into a realistic looking foot, coloured in a suitable shade of brown. So many people in India and Africa have lost limbs because of illness, snake bites, accidents and (in some African countries) landmines that there is a need for a simple and hard-wearing artificial leg. The Jaipur leg, costing only £25 to make, fits the bill perfectly and has restored mobility to thousands of people.

However, we return to consider the much more sophisticated devices available in more developed countries. Progress has been especially rapid over the past ten years and much of this progress has been a result of war. The wars in Iraq and Afghanistan have resulted in many combatants losing limbs, leading to pressure to improve artificial limbs. We may be sad that war becomes a driving force for medical progress but at the same time be pleased that others can benefit from this technology. These modern prosthetic limbs are much lighter and much less cumbersome to wear. They are mostly made from strong, light materials, including newer plastics and carbon fibre. They are engineered to mimic as closely as is practical, the biomechanics of the human limb, giving a lot more flexibility. Internal sensors linked to microprocessors mean that the limbs are more controllable, being able to sense their own motion thus making tasks such as walking up stairs or gripping much more efficient. Further, some are able to respond to muscle movements in the stump of the wearer's limb.

Most modern prosthetic limbs are shaped to resemble natural limbs. However, there is a major exception to this. Amputees, especially but not exclusively those who have had below-knee leg amputations, may opt for sprung carbon prostheses that look like curved blades. They are especially favoured by amputees who wish to run, as exemplified by the wonderful South African sprinter Oscar Pistorius.[12] For a while it was thought that his blades gave him an advantage over able-bodied athletes and he was banned from regular athletics meetings. However, the ban was lifted in May 2008. Nevertheless, he did not compete in the 2008 Olympic Games in Beijing but won three gold medals in the Paralympics. He ran as an able-bodied athlete in the 2011 World Championships and then, in 2012, competed in both the Olympic and Paralympic Games in London. In the former, he reached the semi-finals of the 400 metres and, in the latter, won silver in the 200 metres and gold in the 400 metres. He was not the first person to compete in both games but certainly the first leg amputee to do so as a track athlete.

One of the hopes of developers of prosthetic limbs is that one day it will be possible to make a direct interface between the wearer's nervous system and the microprocessors that regulate movements of the limb. If that can be done, it may be that, for example, walking with a prosthetic leg becomes as "unconscious" as walking naturally. There are, however, several problems to be solved, of which the most demanding is that human nerves are much more fragile than microprocessor components. Nevertheless, the prosthetic limb designers may take hope from some of the developments that have occurred recently in relation to paralysis and blindness.

Dealing with paralysis

Many paralysed people speak of being trapped in a body that will not work. Thought processes are still normal but because of damage to the nervous system, a thought is not "father to the deed" (to misquote an old proverb). However, let us suppose that we can use that brain power to engender movement, probably not in the paralysed body but in some device capable of responding to an external signal. It may sound a little far-fetched, but there are now enough examples to suggest that this may become, if not routine, then at least a feasible course of action. As long ago as 1990, functional connections were made between mammalian neurones and transistors, first raising the possibility of communication between the nervous system and an external device. Professor Kevin Warwick then showed that via a silicon chip implanted into his wrist he could not only open code-protected doors but also operate an artificial hand that was separate from him, indicating the feasibility of trying something similar for paralysed people. There was also the amazing demonstration that patients with locked-in syndrome[13] were able to use their thought processes to control a cursor on a computer screen. This was achieved via brain implants which provided an interface between the patients' brains and the computer software.

Thus the technology does indeed work with paralysed people and more recently this has been taken a little further. During the writing of this book, a woman who is paralysed from the neck down was able, by thinking about it, to get an artificial arm and hand, separate from herself, to pick up a drinking flask and bring it up to her mouth so that she could drink from it through a straw. This was achieved via a set of micro-electrodes implanted through her skull onto the motor-control part of the brain. These sensed the changes associated with thinking about an action and transmitted them to sensors in the arm–hand device, which then did as she wished it to do. Even though relatively simple, this is a huge achievement and opens up the prospects for more complex movements.

While the examples given already show that a paralysed person can move an external device, there are also developments that enable paralysed people to actually move, albeit not always in a conventional manner. First there is the case of Rob Summers, in Oregon, USA, who was paralysed from the chest down after being hit by a car. In 2011 he received a small spinal implant that sends signals to his legs to control movements (these signals would normally come from the brain). He can now stand and is learning to walk on a treadmill while being supported by a special harness. This development has come after 30 years' research, a figure that will surely bring hope to the stem cell community (see above), but of course we now need to find out how widely applicable it will be.

Finally, in several countries, "bionic" walking suits have been developed. These enable people with lower-limb paralysis to stand, walk, go up and down stairs and sit down. In the version used by Claire Lomas to walk (very slowly) the London Marathon course in 2012,[14] there is a single motion sensor (some versions have two). Leaning forward activates the sensor, which in turn starts the robotic motors moving, thus setting the legs in motion. Movement is maintained by continued forward propulsion of the wearer's legs in response to shifts in balance and body weight. Walking is not fast; even the speediest user of one of these suits has not managed more than about 3 km per hour (and that not for very long). It is also very tiring for the wearer: Claire Lomas could not manage more than 3 km per day (and often less) and thus took sixteen days to complete the 42.2 km of the London Marathon course. This was a remarkable achievement but more sophisticated "walking suits" are already in development. These can pick up electrical signals from the nerves which before paralysis "told" limbs to move, and convert those signals into instructions for the suit.

Dealing with blindness

Blindness may result from a wide variety of causes. We have already noted in passing corneal transplants and also the experimental trials of gene therapy and stem cell technology to repair particular retinal problems. It is estimated that across the world some 15 million people suffer from conditions that cause deterioration and eventually loss of sight with increasing age. Many of these conditions involve retinal damage and degeneration. Just one of these retinal conditions, retinitis pigmentosa, in which the eye's light receptors cease to function, affects about 200,000 people worldwide.

Since 2010, a number of variations of sub-retinal implantation of light receptors have been tried out in different countries. This positioning of the implant relates well to the normal position of the eye's light-receptive cells and allows more direct transmission and processing of the light signals (albeit that processing may require a very small electronic device to be attached to the skull). Even so, this type of retinal implant is much more convenient than earlier types of implant, which required the user to wear an external camera as well as the processor. First trialled in Germany in 2010, the sub-retinal implants enabled blind people to see shapes and objects within three days of receiving the implants. Indeed, one of the subjects could find and identify objects on a table, walk around a room without assistance, and even read a clock face. Between 2010 and spring 2012 about 65 more people received sub-retinal implants in Europe (including the UK) and the USA. The effectiveness of the implants varies between people but in general the implant systems are improving all the time as they become more sophisticated.

7.4.4 Fair shares for all?

In the previous sections we have looked at some very clever ways of dealing with a whole variety of losses of function of the human body. Some of the progress in regenerative and reparative medicine has indeed been spectacular. There may be questions about the use of resources when more basic or widespread problems remain unsolved, but it is difficult not to be impressed by some of the advances described here. The science and the technology involved are in many ways beautiful and invite a justified admiration of human ingenuity and inventiveness. For me, these are expressions of our God-given talents. Even for those who do not share my faith, I am sure there is a desire that human talents should be harnessed wherever possible for the flourishing of humankind. What we have in the examples are highly resourced solutions to particular problems. It may be that some of them, such as stem cell therapies, will eventually become more widely available, but it is difficult to see how others, such as some of the very "high-tech" approaches to blindness, loss of limbs, or paralysis, could possibly be so. Comparison of some of the prosthetic limbs available in the USA to the Jaipur limb highlights this (and that is not to decry the effectiveness of the Jaipur limb). Will these very high-tech solutions be available to just a privileged few who have the means to pay for them? Will they ever be available in less-developed countries?

7.4.5 Repair and regeneration or enhancement?

Whether or not these high-tech solutions become more widely available, other ethical questions arise. They are the same questions that were raised in relation to gene therapy, namely should we or should we not allow these techniques to be used for enhancement as well as therapy and if we think not, where do we draw the line between the two? These questions are discussed in the next chapter. In the meantime, we return to our theme of gamete to grave medical care.

7.5 THREE SCORE YEARS AND THEN

In the King James version (sometimes known as the Authorized Version) of the Bible, verse 10 of Psalm 90 states: "The days of our years are threescore years and ten; and if by reason of strength they be fourscore years, yet is their strength labour and sorrow." So, in biblical times, normal life expectancy was 70 years (although we recognize that this number was not a calculated average but a general observation). This is a much longer lifespan than pertained in northern Europe for much of the past 2,000 years. Average lifespans were strongly skewed by the high number of deaths in infancy or childhood so that in the Middle Ages, the average lifespan in Britain was 35 years. However, people who survived into young adulthood had a good chance of living into their early 60s, while some people lived into their 70s or even 80s. During the first part of the twentieth century, death in childhood became much less common so that by 1930, average life expectancy for a male at birth was 60. By 1971, the figure for males was 68 and for females 71. These figures have continued to rise so that our average life expectancies are now around the psalmist's upper limit: 79 for men and 83 for women, although there are clear variations correlated with locality and region. In the more deprived parts of Glasgow, for example, average life expectancy is notoriously low (54 years in Calton, compared with 82 years in more affluent areas such as Lenzie[15]).

Neither is this trend to higher life expectancy confined to the UK or to northern Europe. It has been calculated recently that across the world lifespans are increasing *each day* by an average of two hours. Of course, some nations start from a much lower baseline and may therefore be changing faster. These gross inequalities in current expectancies, symptomatic of a wider range of inequalities, are highlighted

by the data in Table 7.1. Even so, this average rate of increase
is astonishing. So, we are living longer, and in general this is
regarded as a good thing. This has financial and sociological
implications, which, despite their importance, lie outside the
scope of this book. However, the question I pose here (and
also in the next chapter) is whether an increased lifespan is
accompanied by maintenance of an acceptable quality of
life. The quotation from the Psalms with which I started this
section implies that a few extra years may not always be a good
thing: "and if by reason of strength they be fourscore years, yet
is their strength labour and sorrow". Being "strong" enough
to live to 80 did not necessarily bring joy. And that is mirrored
in our own experience. While many people living into their
80s and 90s in the richer nations of the world do enjoy a good
quality of life, it is equally true that as the population ages so
we see a higher incidence of degenerative conditions. From
the late nineteenth century onwards, clean water supply,[16]
antibiotics and improved healthcare have contributed to the
increased life expectancy, and many of the diseases that killed
our recent ancestors no longer kill us. We see instead higher
frequencies of late-onset conditions including some types of
arthritis (cases of which are predicted to double in number by
2050), impairment of eyesight (for example, through macular
degeneration of the retina), some types of cancer and, perhaps
saddest of all, different forms of mental deterioration and
dementia. The words of UK rock band The Who, expressing
a desire to die before they got old,[17] sound prophetic when we
consider these things.

Watching dementia take hold of someone is often described
as watching the person disintegrate, as we lose the person that
we have known. Dementia is the saddest of the age-related
conditions for partners, friends and relatives. The frequency
of its diagnosis is increasing and, while some of this may be
ascribed to greater awareness of the condition, much is due

Table 7.1 Life expectancies, in a selection of countries, of people born in 2012*

Country	Average life expectancy, years
Monaco	89.7
Singapore	83.8
Switzerland	81.2
Denmark	78.8
USA	78.5
Sri Lanka	75.9
Jamaica	73.4
India	67.1
Kenya	63.1
Botswana	55.7
Zambia	52.6
Swaziland	49.4
Republic of South Africa	49.4

Source: CIA World Fact Book

*Notes: (1) There is a general correlation between wealth and life expectancy. (2) In many of the poorer countries, the average is lowered by the higher rates of death in childhood. (3) In many African countries, deaths from HIV/AIDS also contribute to the lower averages.

to the increasing age of the population. For example, the incidence of Alzheimer's disease (which, at 60 per cent of the total, is the commonest form of dementia) in the USA is 3 to 5 per cent in the under-65s but the incidence doubles for every five years over 65. The situation is similar in the UK, as shown in Table 7.2. Data for the UK for 2012 show that of the 820,000 cases of dementia (all forms included), only 17,000 were among people under 65.

Table 7.2 Frequencies of dementia in the UK, 2012

Age range	Frequency of dementia
40–64	1 in 1,400
65–69	1 in 100
70–79	1 in 25
Over 80	1 in 6

Dementia is thus a serious problem in relation to health and social care, and the UK government has recently announced a doubling of funds devoted to research on Alzheimer's disease. For Alzheimer's disease we actually know the specific brain lesion associated with the condition, and for the early-onset version of the disease a specific dominant mutation (see Chapter 5) was identified as long ago as 1995, partly based on research with a family in Nottingham, UK. Since then two other mutations, in different genes, have also shown to lead to the early-onset disease. For the much more widespread age-related condition, one of the current lines of research is on the *ApoE* gene family and especially on *ApoE4*. Some variants of this gene, known to be correlated with Alzheimer's disease, cause "leakiness" of the brain's blood vessels, allowing harmful substances to cross the blood–brain barrier. However, it is a long way from this discovery to developing any therapies, despite the optimistic tone of the Alzheimer's Research UK website.[18]

Increases in lifespan bring a range of health and social problems, but there is a general wish to preserve life and to expect the medical profession to provide life-saving treatments. Hospital doctors report anecdotally that if a very seriously ill person dies in hospital then the patient's family and friends often blame the clinical team, and there is an increasing use of litigation to claim compensation. Such is the emphasis on the autonomy principle that I think it is my right that my relative (or I, for that matter) is cured of whatever condition.

7.6 ... AND THEN: WHEN AM I DEAD AND WHEN MAY I DIE?

One thing that medical care of patients *in extremis* has done is to make death more difficult to define. It used to be easy: when the heart had stopped beating and breathing had ceased, the person had died. Since 1976 in the UK, cessation of brain stem function has also been taken as an indication of death. However, with our increased understanding of the relationship between heart, lung and brain function and our technological ability to provide replacements for at least some of those functions, defining death has become more difficult, and this has led in turn to cases in which deciding about continuing or stopping treatment is very problematic.

The condition known as permanent vegetative state (PVS) typifies these dilemmas, as illustrated very well by the case of Tony Bland, a victim of the 1989 disaster at Sheffield Wednesday FC's stadium, Hillsborough. The case has been extensively reviewed elsewhere, but I summarize it here because it highlights our ethical dilemmas. Tony Bland's brain stem was still alive but the higher centres of the brain had been destroyed; there was no evidence of cognitive function. This is a condition known as permanent vegetative state (PVS), and by 1992 Bland had been in this condition for three years, with absolutely no sign of change or improvement. In PVS, sleep–wake patterns and the spinal reflex responses are normal. However, people in PVS cannot swallow and have to be fed and hydrated through a tube passed into the stomach through the nose. With expert nursing care, people with PVS can remain in this state for years.

We need to note here the important difference between PVS and brain stem death. If the brain stem is damaged irreversibly, spontaneous breathing cannot occur – hence the need for a ventilator ("life support machine"). Furthermore, no information can pass through the brain stem, without which the higher centre – the cerebral cortex – cannot function. In most cases of brain stem death, clinicians and the patient's family members can usually reach a decision that the ventilator should be switched off.

In making decisions about treating people with PVS, two important questions need to be considered. First, is someone in PVS alive in any normally accepted sense of the word? Certainly there is a human body that breathes, but with higher brain function destroyed is it still possible to ascribe to them human personhood? Put more starkly, do we just have a body but no person? Secondly, is feeding through a tube an *artificial* means of support (and therefore a medical treatment) or a provision of basic needs? If it is a medical treatment, is it in the patient's best interests? In other words, is treatment futile, doing the patient no good at all (as would be the case of keeping the ventilator switched on for a brain-stem-dead patient). In Tony Bland's case, the courts decided that artificial feeding was a treatment and was indeed futile and thus, with his family's permission, artificial feeding was eventually withdrawn (in February 1993).[19] He died a few days later, and is often known as the 97th victim of Hillsborough.[20] That is not to say that the decision in this high-profile case was universally welcomed. Many Christians, including the Roman Catholic Church, objected strongly, as did the Royal College of Nursing and significant numbers of doctors. They had no objection to the concept of futile treatment, but in Tony Bland's case they maintained that artificial feeding was provision of basic needs to someone who is still alive. Indeed, some of the more vehement protestors suggested that withdrawing his artificial feeding was nothing less than judicially approved murder.

PVS remains a very contentious issue. Between the Bland case and the end of 2011, a further 43 patients with PVS died in the UK following the withdrawal of artificial feeding. In all these cases, the courts were involved in making the decision. However, most decisions about futile treatment are much easier to make. So, while some doctors like to carry out "heroic" medicine, giving treatment when it is clearly doing no good, and may indeed be lessening significantly the patient's quality of life, most do not think that a treatment should be given just because it is available. Instead, decisions about withdrawing or not starting treatment in the later stages of terminal conditions need to be taken after discussion with the patient (not always possible), their family and carers and with the healthcare professionals involved in the case. A key point here is that it is often more compassionate not to continue treatment than to continue it. Further, it is possible in the UK for anyone to draw up a legally binding document, the Advance Directive, requesting that, if the person suffers a terminal illness and becomes incapable of rational thought and discussion (i.e. lacks capacity), particular treatments should be withdrawn or withheld under specific circumstances. Indeed, it is the patient's right to refuse treatment at any stage of life and in respect of any condition, not just in terminal illnesses, and although the doctor might try to persuade the patient to have the treatment, they cannot, except in certain very rare cases, enforce the treatment.[21]

The Advance Directive (colloquially called the "living will") is a symptom of the value we place today on autonomy in medical ethics. However, one area in which patient autonomy cannot be exercised in the UK is the area of euthanasia and assisted suicide. If I am terminally ill and in great pain and/ or distress, the argument goes, I should be allowed to choose when to die. This may be a case of voluntary euthanasia (the doctor directly hastens the end of life at the patient's request) or assisted suicide (getting someone to assist in ending the patient's life). Both are illegal in the UK, although they are legal, with strict provisos, in Belgium, Luxemburg and the Netherlands. Assisted suicide is legal in Switzerland, and there has been a steady trickle of British patients travelling to the Dignitas clinic in Zurich in order to undergo assisted suicide. Among the most poignant of these cases was that of Daniel James, a 23-year-old rugby player who became paralysed from the neck down after a training accident. After sixteen months in this condition, he came to the conclusion that life was no longer worth living; his parents (one imagines very reluctantly) supported him in this and took him to Zurich so that he could end his life at the Dignitas clinic. Mr and Mrs James had actually broken UK law in providing this assistance but were not prosecuted.

The arguments for and against legalizing euthanasia and/ or assisted suicide have been rehearsed extensively and frequently[22] and will continue to be so. It is not my intention to go over them again in detail here. Instead I want to make three points. First, the four principles of medical ethics (doing good, not doing harm, autonomy and justice – see Chapter 4) are used directly or by implication, but with different weightings, by those on both sides of the debate. Opinion polls among the general public suggest that between 65 and 80 per cent (depending on exactly how the questions were asked) would accept and even welcome the legalization of both euthanasia and assisted suicide. These data are often cited in the campaigns that are conducted every few years, asking for a change in the law. At the time of writing (2012), the British author Terry Pratchett, who is in the early stages of Alzheimer's disease (although still very lucid and articulate), is a high-profile spokesperson and "figurehead" for a current campaign. Two other cases also made the headlines in 2012. Both concerned relatively young men who had become extensively paralysed. Both wanted their doctors to give them a lethal injection, but this was refused. I will focus on one of these men, Tony Nicklinson. In 2005, at the age of 51, he became totally paralysed as a result of a stroke. He was only able to communicate by eye movements. He requested several times that doctors give him a lethal injection. The medical profession would not agree to this direct and active euthanasia so Nicklinson took his case to the courts – and eventually to the High Court – claiming that it is a basic human right to decide when to die (although the Declaration of Human Rights does not include this). *The Times*, perhaps the most "weighty" of the "serious" newspapers, also took up the case, with headlines suggesting that Nicklinson was being "condemned to life".[23] The High Court eventually (in August 2012) rejected Nicklinson's case, but he actually died a few days after the decision. He had started to refuse food and fluids and when he contracted pneumonia, he also refused antibiotics. His widow, Jane Nicklinson, has stated that the fight to change the law goes on and she has extensive public support. However, despite the apparent strength of public opinion, a majority (60–65 per cent) of the medical profession oppose any change in the law.

Secondly, in the Abrahamic faiths – Christianity, Judaism and Islam – life is regarded as a gift from God, and it is wrong to take human life, whether our own or anyone else's. As might be expected, the Roman Catholic Church has produced the strongest statement:

> ... *nothing and no one can in any way permit the killing of an innocent human being, whether a foetus or an embryo, an infant or an adult, an old person, or one suffering from an incurable disease, or a person who is dying. Furthermore, no one is permitted to ask for this act of killing, either for himself or herself or for another person entrusted to his or her*

> *care… For it is a question of the violation of the divine law,*
> *an offense against the dignity of the human person, a crime*
> *against life, and an attack on humanity.*[24]

The Church of England's statement is slightly less strident, but nevertheless clear:

> *The Church believes God has given people life, and as such*
> *they have no right to take it away themselves. Although it*
> *accepts that the matter of life and death is very much a*
> *personal decision, the problem is that changes to the law may*
> *encourage society to adopt unhealthy attitudes towards the*
> *sick, elderly, terminally ill and even death itself. There is a*
> *real possibility that terminally ill people may feel pressured*
> *to ask for an early death to avoid feeling a burden to their*
> *family or the health system.*[25]

Nevertheless, there are significant numbers of Christians who support voluntary euthanasia and/or assisted suicide. One of the clearest statements was made by the late Dr Leslie Weatherhead:

> *I sincerely believe that those who come after us will wonder*
> *why on earth we kept a human being alive against his*
> *will, when all the dignity, beauty and meaning of life had*
> *vanished; when any gain to anyone was clearly impossible,*
> *and when we should have been punished by the state if we*
> *had kept alive an animal in similar conditions.*[26]

These quotations, and indeed the whole debate, show that even if we hold to clear ethical principles and even when those principles are held within the framework of a religious faith, it is not always easy to work out how to apply them.

Thirdly, the UK has a very good record on palliative care.

The first purpose-built hospice, St Christopher's Hospice, was opened in London in 1967, following the initiative and fund-raising efforts of a Christian social worker and doctor, Dame Cicely Saunders. From there the UK's hospice movement has grown and spread. The aims are to provide adequate pain control and as high a quality of life as possible, ensuring patients' dignity in the last days of their lives. All this happens within a caring and peaceful environment, free from the noise and bustle that often characterizes conventional hospitals. In general, hospices succeed in their aims and requests for voluntary euthanasia from patients in hospices are very rare indeed. It is thus interesting that the three European countries in which voluntary euthanasia is legal do not have this tradition in palliative care.

7.7 WHATEVER NEXT?

In this survey of medical provision from gamete to grave I have picked on what I see to be some of the key developments that have added or have the potential to add to our "conventional" medical practice. Some of these developments are still very much in the category of "work in progress", while others are now well embedded and (relatively) widely available. This question of availability will, however, continue to be of concern. Some of the developments are very sophisticated and very expensive. Many thousands could in theory benefit but so far only a handful have done so. Who will decide who gets what? Sadly, it seems unrealistic to expect some of the very expensive developments to become widely available. Does that mean that their use will be confined to a rich few in the richer countries of the world? And finally, will the rich be able to or be allowed to use some of these technologies for enhancement; that is, to elevate their levels of ability, performance or health above the human norm? This controversial question is discussed in Chapters 9 and 10.

NOTES

1. The Diocese of Chichester would not allow the English version to be inscribed.

2. I am very grateful to Dr Anna Smajdor for drawing my attention to this case.

3. Interestingly, with the wider acceptance of surrogate motherhood, it has also become a way of donating eggs. A couple in which the woman does not produce viable eggs may arrange for the man to fertilize eggs of another woman, usually by artificial insemination but sometimes by IVF. The other woman becomes pregnant and when the baby is born, hands it over to the couple.

4. In principle, this is a feasible proposition but whether any athlete would want to undergo the procedure or whether any parent would want to put their child through the procedure is another matter, even when "Olympic gold" might be involved.

5. This topic is discussed more fully in Robert Song's *Human Genetics Fabricating the Future*, London: Darton, Longman and Todd, 2002.

6. It is quite difficult conceptually to regard skin as an organ but actually it is one – indeed, it is the largest organ in the human body.

7. Some expansive claims made by a research team in South Korea in 2004 were shown later to be untrue.

8. Ipsos-MORI, *Public Attitudes to Science*, 2011, page 16.

9. For an example of such support, see Ted Peters, Karen Lebacqz and Gaymon Bennett, *Sacred Cells? Why Christians Should Support Stem Cell Research*, Lanham, MD: Rowman & Littlefield, 2008.

10. Reported on the BBC News Channel, 5 September 2005: http://news.bbc.co.uk/1/hi/sci/tech/4213566.stm.

11. See http://www.rotaryjaipurlimb.co.uk/.

12. Like other "blade runners", Pistorius uses more sophisticated "conventional" prosthetic limbs when he is not running.

13. In this rare condition, the patient's mental abilities and processes continue to function, but they are unable to communicate or move because of damage to a specific part of the brain.

14. http://www.get-claire-walking.co.uk/.

15. WHO report, cited by BBC Scotland: http://news.bbc.co.uk/1/hi/scotland/glasgow_and_west/7584450.stm.

16. Provision of clean water is often a key element in improving health in communities in less-developed countries – and it does not require huge resources to do this.

17. From their seminal 1965 song "My Generation" (and I admit that the

context is different but nevertheless the words seem very relevant to the problems that many face in old age).

18. http://www.alzheimersresearchuk.org/home/

19. Sir Stephen Brown, the president of the High Court's Family Division, ruled that food and fluids could lawfully be withdrawn. There was an appeal but on 9 December the verdict was upheld by three judges in the Appeal Court. The case then went to the House of Lords, and on Thursday 4 February 1993, five Law Lords also rejected the appeal.

20. There were 96 who died on the day itself, or very shortly after.

21. The rare cases mostly involve minors whose parents, for whatever reason, are refusing to allow worthwhile, non-futile treatments. The child can be made a ward of court and the court will then permit treatment.

22. See, for example, J. Bryant, L.B. la Velle and J. Searle *Introduction to Bioethics*, Chichester: Wiley, 2005.

23. For example, "Why should Tony Nicklinson be condemned to live?", *The Times*, 21 June 2012.

24. Sacred Congregation for the Doctrine of the Faith, *Declaration on Euthanasia*, Vatican City, 1980.

25. Cited in *Christian Attitudes to Euthanasia, Part 2*, http://www.thatreligiousstudieswebsite.com/Ethics/Applied_Ethics/Euthanasia/euthanasia_christian2.php.

26. Very widely cited by pro-euthanasia organizations, but originally from Weatherhead's *Christian Agnostic*, London: Hodder & Stoughton, 1965.

8

CHIPS WITH EVERYTHING: COMPUTERS, INFORMATION AND COMMUNICATIONS TECHNOLOGIES[1]

Hyperbolvids of wondrous Light
Rolling for aye through Space and Time
Harbour those Waves which somehow Might
Play out God's holy pantomime
Alan Turing, 1954[2]

… more and more people are having less contact with
human beings. We spend all day with machines; all
night with machines…
Kate Bush, 1989[3]

8.1 INTRODUCTION

In this chapter, I am going to move away temporarily from discussion of advances in biomedicine to consider computing and other digital technologies. There are good reasons for this. In the previous chapter we noted the use of computer technology in prosthetic limbs, in "walking suits" for the paralysed, in helping blind people to see and so on. However, these high-profile examples are just the tip of the iceberg in respect of the way that computer technology is embedded in many, many aspects of modern life. It is important therefore to consider computing and digital communications systems. In some ways these technologies are having and will continue to have more widespread effects on our society than do the biomedical technologies. Indeed, the use of computer technology is so widespread that we take it for granted and indeed often use it, unaware that we are doing so. How did this happen? In this chapter I will trace very briefly the history of computing and then explore some of the social implications.

8.2 ALAN TURING AND THE DAWN OF THE COMPUTER AGE

I am writing this a few days before the 100th anniversary of the birth of the brilliant British mathematician, Dr Alan Turing, and just a few days after the 58th anniversary of his untimely death (see below). Turing was a real genius. His "Turing machine", invented in 1936, was effectively the ancestor of all modern computers.[4] In the early 1940s, he was a key member of the team that constructed a machine for decryption of Germany's Enigma code, thus having a dramatic effect on the progress of World War II.[5] After the war, he returned to the development of computers, and 1949 saw the first serious mathematical application of one of Turing's machines. He was honoured by the British government with the award of an OBE (Order of the British Empire); his scientific brilliance and his contribution to the development of computers were recognized by his election in 1951 as a Fellow of the Royal Society.

As well as being a mathematical genius, Alan Turing was a keen runner and for several years after World War II was a member of Walton Athletic Club in Surrey. His best time for the marathon was 2h 46min 03s, achieved at Loughborough in 1947. This was a very good time indeed for a club runner at a time when the world record was 2h 25min 39s, and even today (when the men's world record stands at 2h 03min 38s) many a good club runner would be delighted with Turing's time (I write from personal experience here). However, there was also a good deal of sadness in his life. Most of those who knew him, including his clubmates at Walton AC, were unaware that Turing's sexual orientation was homosexual. There were good reasons for his secrecy. Being "out" as homosexual was dangerous, because homosexual acts were at that time illegal. This is in marked contrast to the current situation in which homosexual couples may enjoy legal "civil partnerships" (and possibly soon actual marriages). In 1952 Turing was arrested, charged with performing an "act of gross indecency", and found guilty. He accepted "chemical castration" (i.e. injection with female hormones) as an alternative to prison. Although he continued to be active in research, his clearance to work on sensitive government-funded projects was withdrawn, and he started to turn his attention to mathematical biology. In June 1954 he committed suicide by taking cyanide, a sad end for a man who had contributed so much.

I have given these details of Alan Turing's life, not just to indicate his major role in the development of computers but also as a stark reminder of how much society has changed in the past 60 years. In addition to the changes in social attitudes about many things, including sexual orientation, there have also been major changes in technology that can be traced back directly to Turing's work. Sadly, he was not here to see the dawn of the "computer age" in the late 1970s, and I wonder whether he could have forecast the extent to which computers in various forms are embedded in our daily lives. For Turing, computers were machines capable of solving mathematical and logic problems much faster than the human brain was able to do so. He wondered how far this development of "artificial intelligence" could go, expressed in an article entitled "Can Machines Think?" published in 1950. Would it be possible one day to build a computer that could simulate realistically human emotions, or even to "feel" those emotions electronically? How human could a computer become? It is of course a question that still intrigues us, exemplified by the attribution of human feelings and emotions to Marvin, the Paranoid Android in Douglas Adams's wonderful series *The Hitchhiker's Guide to the Galaxy*, and by the very human-looking Holly in the TV series *Red Dwarf*. Turing actually set a test, which became known logically enough as the Turing Test, to evaluate a computer's ability to "fool" a panel of judges into thinking they were corresponding with a human rather than a computer. In 1990 an American philanthropist, inventor and campaigner,[6] Hugh Loebner, instituted the Loebner Prize for Artificial Intelligence, to be awarded for the first verifiable success in the Turing Test. As at June 2012, the prize has not yet been won, and Loebner himself believes that it will not happen until, in his words, "long after I die". However, testing the ability of computers to imitate human emotions is essentially a sociological test rather than a test of thinking (which was the subject of Turing's original question). There is a sense in which computers can think (albeit as a result of prior human thought) in that they can solve complex problems very fast. Thus, for example, we now have computers that are very good at chess. It was as long ago as 1997 that world chess champion, Garry Kasparov, was beaten by the computer known as *Deep Blue*. The computer used 32 parallel processors to analyse 2,000 million positions per second, enabling it to evaluate possible situations six to eight moves ahead (and sometimes up to twenty moves ahead). It was a very effective chess player but it played the game in a different way from human players. This raises the question of how human-like computers might become; a topic that is discussed more fully in Chapter 9 (section 9.4.2).

8.3 THE AGE OF COMPUTERS: THE DIGITAL AGE

The first personal computers (PCs) were built in the 1970s. They were simple, slow and quite cumbersome to use. Programs (when available) and even whole operating systems had to be loaded, often from tape, before the computer could be used. Nevertheless, they were a great contrast to the rooms full of quietly humming machinery that were familiar to many of those who used computers in the 1960s. Very few pre-written programs were available and many users of these early personal computers became proficient in the use of programming languages. However, improvements were rapid, such that by about 1980, personal computers were several times more powerful than the computer system used in Apollo 11, the spacecraft involved in the first moon landing in 1969.

The age of computers, of which those early PCs were an indication of its start, has seen an invasion of computers into many, many aspects of everyday life in the developed nations. In science, in my own field for example, they are in DNA sequencers, cell culture incubators, constant temperature rooms, purification and separation devices, sophisticated microscopic systems and many other things. In medicine, they are used in implanted devices, in prosthetic limbs and, as we saw in Chapter 7, we are learning to interface computers with the human nervous system. There has also been a powerful link-up between communications and digital technology. Indeed, modern "smart" phones are computers in their own right and have many times more computing power than those early PCs (let alone Apollo 11).

Other aspects of digital communication that we have come to take for granted are email and the Internet. It was in 1971 that the first email was sent. Some commentators have suggested that this invention, by Ray Tomlinson, was the fourth time that a long-distance communications method had contributed to significant changes in society. The first was Morse code

(Morse, 1844), the second, the telephone (Bell, 1876) and the third, wireless radio transmitters and receivers (Marconi, 1895). Interestingly, the names of the first three inventors are all well known but I wonder how many of us have heard of Tomlinson. Perhaps the significance of his invention was not fully realized in 1971 because email took quite a long time to catch on but now we can see that it really has made a huge impact on the way in which we communicate with each other.

Then there is the Internet and the World Wide Web. It is interesting to note that this application of computing was predicted by the science fiction writer Arthur C. Clarke as long ago as 1970.[7] He suggested that via a network based on communications satellites the "accumulated knowledge of the world" would be brought "to our finger-tips" through small desktop computers. He also envisaged that the network would facilitate video-conferencing. This actually happened in 1990 when Tim Berners-Lee, a British computer scientist, launched the World Wide Web (www), which is in effect a powerful information-sharing application that runs on the Internet, the worldwide array of linked computer networks.[8] In 1991, the web was made available to the public, but it was not until 1993 that public use started to take off; once it had taken off, it seems that there was no stopping it.

8.4 HOW THINGS HAVE CHANGED

Like email, the Internet and the World Wide Web have become what seems to be an integral part of modern life; how did we manage without them? Indeed, the "net generation" – those aged 30 and under – find it hard to imagine life without them because, in developed industrialized countries, they have known nothing else (although admittedly, for people at the older end of the net generation, the web was invented during their lifetime, even if, as children, they were unaware of it). But even for those of more mature years, the use of email and the Internet plays a significant role in the way we live. Neither is our use confined to our offices or homes. The Internet is available to us while we are on the move. It is available via hard-wired access or, with increasing frequency, via wireless access (WiFi). What is more, many of us feel cut off if we cannot get Internet access. Going back ten years, it would have seemed improbable that, except perhaps for the most stressed of business executives, people would want Internet access on holiday but that is what has happened. Advertisements tell us that we "can stay in touch while enjoying the sunshine". Laptops, notebook computers and tablets increasingly feature in our hand luggage, while smart phones with Internet access are ever more popular.

The development of computing, information and communications technology (digital technology) has ushered in the most rapid period of change experienced in human society. Although it was the adoption of an agrarian lifestyle some 12,000 years ago that allowed human communities to develop, those communities, until the Industrial Revolution, evolved only slowly. The Industrial Revolution itself certainly initiated a period of change in the way that many worked and lived. However, the changes initiated by the adoption of computer and communications technology are of a different kind simply because they have penetrated so many of our activities, both in leisure and in work. The types of skills needed in manufacturing and commerce differ markedly from those needed prior to computerization. Some work patterns have changed too, and some people have been freed from the need to work in towns or cities. Computer and communications technology has also driven globalization, opening up markets across the world. This is certainly helping to bring some poorer countries out of poverty but I also note that globalization has its negative aspects. These include "land grab" and commercial colonialism (for example by multinational companies) in the poorer countries and loss of jobs in richer countries (as services and manufacture are outsourced to countries where wages are lower). However, this is not the place to discuss the pros and cons of globalization; I simply want to emphasize the role of computing and communications systems in its development.

Changes brought about by the adoption of digital technologies have certainly been rapid. Neither does the pace of change decrease. In almost any application of digital technology, even while the "next generation" is launched, the one after that is under development such that the pace of change in computing and communications is causing accelerated changes in society at large. Life can be difficult for those who do not adapt well to change.

8.5 NETWORKING

Finally, before considering some of the "darker" aspects of computer and communications technology, I need to mention networking. Sites such as Facebook are immensely popular and doubtless help us to feel in some way connected with people, especially those whom we see only infrequently (or perhaps not all). Because of the number of people who use particular social networking sites, those sites can raise revenue by carrying advertisements. Perhaps a little more sinister is the fact that the advertisements can be selected for a particular user, based on their profile, likes and activities. Social networking sites can therefore become "big business", as exemplified by Facebook, which, when floated on the US stock market in 2012, was valued at about three times the GDP of Kenya.[9] There are also what we might call more "professional" networking sites which enable people with particular work interests to remain in contact with each other.

Pages or groups can be rapidly set up for individual causes, a recent example (in June 2012) being a book of condolence in respect of a young professional cricketer who had been killed in an accident. The latter is a small example of a much bigger phenomenon. Campaigning organizations use social networking sites (in addition to email) to alert their supporters of new initiatives and of successes (and perhaps even failures) in campaigning. Petitions are set up online, with the information about them going out by email and by social networking, enabling supporters of a petition to register that support by a simple click of the mouse. The petition can then be sent electronically to its target (which might be, for example, the government), all this being much quicker than gathering signatures on printed pages. Perhaps the most recent spectacular examples of the power of social networking occurred during the "Arab Spring" of 2011, during which despotic regimes were overthrown in several North African countries. In Tunisia and Egypt in particular, Facebook, Twitter and even YouTube were widely used in informing and organizing the anti-government forces – these were, according to several news media, the first revolutions to be conducted over the Internet.

8.6 THE DIGITAL DIVIDE

8.6.1 Introduction

As I have described, digital technology is embedded in almost every aspect of modern life in the industrialized nations. Further, for very many of us, our ability to "go online" means that we as individuals also interact directly with digital technology and can reap the benefits that direct access brings. However, we need to ask how widespread personal access is to digital technologies. What proportion of our population has access to the Internet and does it matter for those who do not? Is there a great divide between industrialized and less-developed countries and if so, is that gap closing?

8.6.2 Digitally divided Britain

Although the majority of people in Britain have access to the Internet, a third of households, representing 10 million people, do not. Public libraries now usually have computers with Internet access, but this is a very long way from the convenience of access at home. Indeed, as at May 2012, just over 8 million people in the UK had *never* used the Internet. Nearly half of these were disabled adults, representing about 35 per cent of the total number of disabled people. Of those without Internet access, 4 million are from the most socially disadvantaged group of people in the country and, overlapping with that group, about 4 million are over 65 and about the same number are unemployed. These miss out on so many advantages that Internet access can bring, including (and this is especially relevant for the poorest people in the country) the price reductions that often go with buying online. Indeed it is estimated that the average household can save between £500 and £600 per year by shopping and paying bills online. There is definitely a digital divide and, in the words of Martha Lane Fox, the government's Digital Inclusion "Champion", "Those being left behind with technology are being left behind across many spheres."[10] The social divisions in British society are abundantly clear.

8.6.3 Industrialized countries and less-developed countries

It was noted earlier that digital technology has played and continues to play a role in globalization, and there is no doubt the technology is embedded at government and institutional levels in even the poorest countries of the world. However, at the level of the individual it is a different story, as we might expect. The poorer the country, the less personal Internet access there is. Access is generally limited to towns and cities so that rural and tribal communities are very unlikely to have

Internet access. They may, however, have access to digital telecommunications and broadcasting technology. I was surprised, as long ago as 1996, to see a satellite "dish" in quite a remote Indian village. Moving forward to 2012, we now note that more people over the world have access to a mobile phone (but probably not a smart phone) than to a toilet. Nevertheless, I doubt whether many of the inhabitants of that Indian village are online even now, despite the enthusiastic uptake of digital technology in India as a country. The data available at the beginning of 2012 showed that overall, 10 per cent of the population of India had Internet access, a figure much lower than, for example, the UK. However, the majority of users were in towns and cities; only 2 per cent of rural Indians had Internet access. The continent of Africa is another interesting example. At the beginning of 2012, about 13.5 per cent of the population of Africa were Internet users. However, this figure hides the rapid change that is taking place because it represents a nearly 3,000 per cent increase on the number of users at the beginning of 2001. Africa is beginning to catch up, and bridging the international digital divide will be one of the factors that help to bring African countries out of poverty. Nevertheless we should note that these figures are overall figures for the whole continent: wealthier countries such as Egypt (26 per cent), Nigeria (29 per cent) and Tunisia (36 per cent) have a far higher proportion of Internet users than the very poor countries in sub-Saharan Africa.

8.7 THE DARKER SIDE OF DIGITAL TECHNOLOGY

8.7.1 Introduction

It is abundantly clear that the digital age has brought benefits to millions of people. Equally, though, many more millions are yet to benefit. However, the "digital divide" is not the only negative aspect of the digital age. Reliance on computers and other forms of digital technology brings its own problems. Some of these are technical, some are related to the many ways in which digital technology may be used for ill rather than good, some affect our social interactions, and, perhaps even more fundamentally, some of the negative aspects may affect profoundly the way we think about other people and even challenge our view of what it is to be human (and thus are clearly related to the overall theme of this book). So, without being in any way "anti-technology", I think that it is important to air some of these problems here. It is far from being an exhaustive treatment, but I hope that the examples given will be both informative and thought-provoking.

8.7.2 Are we over-dependent?

Although many of us accept our dependence on digital technology with very little in the way of questioning, others are more uneasy. If so much of life relies on functioning computers and computer networks, what happens if they go wrong? In the early days of computerization it was quite common to blame the machines for what were really human errors and, in general, such errors could be quickly rectified. However, as the use of digital technology has grown and grown, the consequences of genuine computer malfunction have become ever greater. An example occurred in the UK in 2012 when a fault in a bank's computer system shut down that bank's ATMs and locked customers out of their accounts for several days, such that they were unable pay money out or to receive electronic payments or to put money into their accounts. Even after the computer problem was rectified, some of the knock-on effects for customers were very serious and took some time to sort out. Another serious example occurred in 2004 when one of the computer systems used by the UK's Air Traffic Control Centre went down, effectively grounding, for several hours, outgoing flights from many British airports.

The backlog of flights that resulted took much longer to sort out than the repair of the computer system. A similar but shorter-lived problem occurred in 2008.

In many situations there are back-up systems that will provide at least limited "cover" for malfunctioning components. However, the three examples I have given show that we are very vulnerable to computer malfunction, which equally means that we are vulnerable to attacks on our computer systems by hackers with malicious intent.

8.7.3 Knowing me, knowing you

Some people are very uneasy about the knowledge concerning individuals that is stored in digital systems. As long ago as 1996, I remember watching a debit card reader in Melbourne, Australia, print out my name and home (UK) address from the information embedded in the card. Computer systems store a lot of information about each of us. Some of this is "official", such as the data in our tax returns. At the other end of the scale, our use of a supermarket loyalty card enables the company's marketing division to build up a picture of our shopping habits and even to issue cash-reduction or loyalty-points reward vouchers according to those habits. Further, many of us provide information about ourselves via social networking sites, or via the websites of clubs, societies and other organizations. The extent to which computer systems and Internet-based applications "know" about us as individuals is indeed wide. It is quite instructive (although perhaps a little self-centred) to enter one's name into a search engine such as Google. Although some will find that they are still anonymous, others will be genuinely surprised to find themselves there. So, is unease about all this justified? First, let us note that data about me held on computers no more defines the "real me" than does my genome sequence (Chapter 6) or my job title. This comment is further expanded when we discuss "cyborgs" in the next chapter. Secondly, official data are highly protected and confidential (but nevertheless still vulnerable to human error), while much of the less official information we provide is not publicly available. Thirdly, however, we should note that the information could be used in a more sinister way, even by government agencies in democratic countries. When the UK government tried, in 2009, to introduce identity cards, it was not so much the idea of the cards themselves but the amount of personal information available to government agencies that caused real concern. The distinguished barrister, Bob Marshall-Andrews QC, described the proposal as the greatest threat to civil liberties since before the Magna Carta! In the end, the government did not proceed with the proposal but in less democratic countries, information on individual citizens, including their use of the Internet, is certainly used by government agencies. Thus, one well-known Chinese dissident describes watching a website being first blocked and then erased from her computer screen as she was actually using it. Without wanting to be too alarmist, I suggest that we need to remain vigilant about the way our personal information is used.

Finally, all systems are vulnerable to some extent both to thieves and to hackers, some of whose methods have become very sophisticated. "Identity theft" is a crime encountered with increasing frequency, such that an individual's personal details may be used to make credit card purchases, set up bank accounts (having first raided the *bona fide* account), make applications for passports and so on. As with all human inventions, digital technology is subject to abuse and misuse while nevertheless bringing enormous benefits.

8.7.4 Pornography

In the UK and indeed in the majority of developed industrialized countries, the making of pornographic images and films by adults is not illegal. Distribution of films is regulated by film censors and the display of pornographic images, for example in magazines, is usually limited by local bye-laws. However, the Internet is subject to no such regulation, which means that pornographic images and videos of varying degrees of explicitness are readily available.[11] No longer is it necessary to purchase a "top-shelf" magazine, perhaps in a furtive or even embarrassed manner; all that is needed is a computer linked to the Internet through which, by entry of appropriate search terms, page after page of images plus links to videos is available. Further, much of this material is free to view, although the pay-to-view sites generate, in the USA alone, about $3,000 million per year (as at 2011).[12] Some 12 per cent of websites, containing a combined total of several million pages (over 30 per cent of the total web pages), are devoted to pornography. Further, at least a quarter of these sites use "mouse-trapping", which blocks exit from the site.

In respect of actual "traffic", 25 per cent of search engine requests relate to pornography and 35 per cent of downloads are of pornography; the Internet's most popular search term is "sex". And 8 per cent of emails are pornographic. However, in the UK, the average number of hours spent on news websites is actually slightly greater than the average number of hours spent on pornography websites (and both figures are just a fraction of the average number of hours spent on social networking sites). Not all exposure to pornography is intentional. Many Internet users report completely accidental and unwanted exposure via "pop-ups", hidden keywords, misdirected links and even unsolicited emails.

Accurate data on the number of people visiting pornography sites are more difficult to obtain, with different surveys giving different results. The following numbers, drawn from surveys in the USA and UK in 2011, at least give an indication of the situation. About 75 per cent of men and 33 per cent of women admit to having deliberately viewed Internet pornography. For each gender, about half of those making this admission said that they viewed pornography "regularly" and about 33 per cent of the material viewed regularly is "hard-core". About 90 per cent of teenage boys have viewed Internet pornography and in the USA the *average* age for the first viewing is 11 or 12. In both countries, the largest group, by age and gender, of regular users are men aged between 18 and 24.

So, the Internet has made pornography more readily available. Should this be a matter of concern? There are certainly many social libertarians who believe that we should be free to view whatever we want. If the making of images and films is not illegal, why should we restrict access to them? Further, in some sections of society and in some sections of the media, pornography (at least at the "softer" end of the scale) has become "chic". However, the UK government *is* concerned and at the time of writing is consulting widely on the possibility of a default censorship of Internet pornography, at least of the "hard-core" variety. Needless to say, the Internet service providers are opposed to this, suggesting that it is an infringement of our liberty.

I am among those who share those concerns regarding Internet pornography, and I do so for three main reasons. The first is that pornography reduces people, and especially women, to sex objects. As a Christian I am reminded of some words spoken by Jesus: "But I tell you that anyone who looks at a woman lustfully has already committed adultery with her in his heart."[13] Sexualization of girls at a younger and younger age unfortunately helps to promote this view of women, especially but not exclusively among teenage boys and younger men. I am not convinced by the suggestions that women are empowered by taking their clothes off (with increasing levels of explicit exposure) or by acting in pornographic movies. They may be exploiting a male weakness but, in my view, in doing so they are themselves being exploited. And that is my second point: the use of women (and men) is exploitative, even though as models and actors they undoubtedly earn money. It thus follows on logically that sexual activity is presented as "I want it and I want it now – and I'm going to have it". There was an interesting episode of the American sitcom *Friends* in which two of the male characters, Joey and Chandler, found a TV channel showing a pornographic movie. But, as they commented later, the film led to totally wrong expectations about what is normal behaviour. The bank teller does not take her male customer down to the basement to indulge in animalistic sex; the pizza delivery girl does not, on arriving at the door, throw her clothes off and climb all over the man waiting for the pizza; female colleagues do not dress in extremely low-cut tops and tiny skirts that reveal too much, just waiting for the chance to get a hunky male into the back room. In the porn movie fantasies, sexual activity does not involve any idea of relationship, or even of treating each other as persons. They are just there for instant gratification of desires. And in case my readers think that I make too much of this, I need to add that these attitudes are out there. We are considering in this book whether it is possible to progress "beyond human", whereas the pornography industry clearly treats people as less than fully human and, further, engenders that attitude in others.

My third point about pornography concerns addiction. In the UK it is estimated that 4 per cent of the adult population exhibit addictive or compulsive behaviour in respect of pornography, much of it associated with the Internet.[14] In the USA, estimates vary widely. If addiction is defined as visiting Internet pornography sites for more than ten hours each week, then about 1 per cent of American adults are addicted. However, in surveys based on questionnaires and on interviews of samples of adults, up to 10 per cent of the adult population are deemed to be addicted (but this may include other activities such as "cybersex"). Interestingly, women are over-represented in this group in comparison with the proportion of women who view Internet pornography. This is, in fact, similar to the situation in the UK and in both countries the reason is not clear. Are women more likely to become "hooked"? Are they more honest about themselves? Or are they more aware of the signs of addiction? Interestingly, the US data also indicate that people with a religious faith are at least as likely (and in some surveys more likely) to be addicted as are non-believers. Indeed, Christian leaders seem especially vulnerable.

While there are some who will dismiss this addiction as being of little consequence, Internet pornography addiction[15] is as serious as other addictions. It can have an effect on relationships, on work, on family life, on finances and even on personality. Recovery programmes are available but often need reinforcing with robust Internet filters on all computers to which the recovering addict has access. One former addict, now happily recovered, emphasizes the personal trauma of becoming addicted: "Discovering online sexual material was the worst thing to happen in my life."[16]

Earlier I mentioned networking and file-sharing based on the Internet. These activities are of course available to anyone with Internet access, including criminals. Pornography involving children is illegal, and yet in the USA there are about 120,000 Internet searches for child pornography each day. In June 2012, 190 people who were members of a child pornography network were arrested; most were in the USA but some were in other countries, including the UK. Many thousands of images and hundreds of videos were stored on participants' computers. In the same month, Spanish police arrested 74 people and confiscated computers containing millions of images and videos of child pornography, while a nationwide "crackdown" in the UK resulted in arrests in several different cities. In 2011, one man arrested in the UK for possession and distribution of child pornography had stored 450,000 images on his computer. British authorities estimate that over 20,000 new child pornography images are made available on the Internet every week. One site alone is reported to receive a million hits per month, and the frequency of activities involving child pornography is on the increase. We need to be clear about this. Every indecent or pornographic image of a child represents abuse of that child, leading to a degree of damage and devastation of a young life that is difficult to even try to comprehend. I cannot get out of my head some more words of Jesus: "It would be better for you to be thrown into the sea with a millstone tied around your neck than for you to cause one of these little ones to stumble."[17] The imagery is of course very vivid, but we get the picture: children are very precious. I am sure therefore that my readers, even if they do not share my Christian faith, will share my views of crimes against children. In my view, child pornography, plus the grooming of minors (often via social networking sites and chat rooms) by paedophiles, ranks alongside all other forms of child abuse as being among the most heinous of crimes.

8.7.5 So many friends and yet so lonely

We noted in Chapter 3 (section 3.10) that as countries become more industrialized, more of their citizens live on their own. It is true that many of those who live alone are happy with this arrangement but for many others isolation is a real problem. Further, the feeling of isolation may be exacerbated by patterns of work and even patterns of leisure that result from digital technology. A colleague told me of a journey on the Singapore Metro, on which, in a carriage full of young professionals, everyone had their heads bent over their smartphones "as if in prayer" (not that they would have necessarily been speaking to each other in the absence of smartphones). Further, on arrival at work, each was likely to spend hours in front of a computer screen with little actual human contact. I realized the extent to which the digital age had changed our interactions with each other when a colleague in the next door office started to communicate with me by email, rather than knocking on my (open) door for a chat. That type of trend has clearly continued: in the UK in 2011, people were more likely to communicate by text message than by phone.

Then there are social networking sites. Personally, I enjoy the interactions I can have with friends and particularly with old friends who now live far away from where I am living. Reading each other's "posts" means that we at least have the feeling that we continue to share in each other's lives.[18] I also find the groups with shared professional or leisure interests very helpful, being able to participate in online discussion with several people at the same time, with those people being dispersed, perhaps even across the world. And yet it remains true that none of these interactions involve actual human contact.

In 1989, singer-songwriter Kate Bush produced a very prophetic song, "Deeper Understanding",[19] which portrays the loneliness of a young woman whose main social companion is her computer; she spends her evenings with it as if it were her friend. In a rare BBC radio interview with Roger Scott,[20] she explained:

> *This is about people... well, about the modern situation, where more and more people are having less contact with human beings. We spend all day with machines; all night*

> *with machines.... Press a button, this happens.... And this*
> *is the idea of someone who spends all their time with their*
> *computer and, like a lot of people, they spend an obsessive*
> *amount of time with their computer. People really build up*
> *heavy relationships with their computers.*

If that was true in 1989, it is even more so now. It is indeed
possible for much of our contact with others to take place
via machines. Further, the development of the World Wide
Web/Internet means that many people, and not just those
who live alone, spend many hours online,[21] thus increasing or
causing social isolation. One can have hundreds of "friends"
on Facebook but still feel very lonely. If humans are defined
as social beings, it seems legitimate to suggest that we may
be in danger of becoming something less than fully human.
Further, for some young people, being bullied in the school
playground has been added to (or sometimes replaced) by
cyber-bullying, via social networking sites and emails. For
those young people in particular, the loneliness of the digital
age may be intense and some have been driven to suicide. The
strong trend to individualism in current British society that I
highlighted in Chapter 3 (section 3.10) may have some very
negative effects. It is interesting – and for me encouraging –
to note that there are signs of a reawakening to community
values, not as defined by politicians but by a communitarian
application of true virtue ethics (see Chapter 4). This is
apparent in the writing of, for example, the distinguished
political philosopher Michael Sandel[22] and of the equally
distinguished communitarian theologian Stanley Hauerwas.

8.8 CONCLUDING REMARKS
This chapter has been a series of brief snapshots of the
computer or digital age. In addition to the ubiquity of the
technology, we have also noted that, like all the expressions of

human talent and inventiveness, it can be used for ill as well as good. We have also seen that digital technology is changing the ways in which we interact with each other and may even change our view of ourselves as human persons. This theme comes up again in the next chapter, where, in addition to thinking about further applications of digital technology, we also return to biomedical technology.

NOTES

1. The mention of particular trademarks and brands in this chapter does not imply endorsement; they are simply being used as specific examples.
2. Originally written on a postcard to Robin Gandy. Quoted in Turing's epitaph.
3. From an interview with Roger Scott, broadcast on BBC Radio One, 14 October 1989.
4. I have not forgotten the mechanical devices ("difference engines") built by Charles Babbage in the nineteenth century. However, Turing's machines were electronic and modern computers can be traced back to them.
5. Neither am I forgetting the magnificent work of Bletchley Park's "unsung heroes", the brilliant code-breakers Bill Tutte and Tommy Flowers. I should add further that Flowers' work also contributed to the development of computers.
6. Mainly on behalf of sex workers.
7. In the May 1970 issue of *Popular Science* magazine.
8. These definitions thus differentiate between the Internet and the web. However, the two terms are often used as if they were interchangeable; thus when someone says that they found information on the Internet they really mean that they found it on the World Wide Web. However, in this chapter I have often followed colloquial practice in using the terms interchangeably.
9. Although the share price dropped subsequent to the flotation.
10. At the launch of Go ON UK (http://www.go-on-uk. org), reported on the 21st Century Challenges website (http://www.21stcenturychallenges.org/60-seconds/what-is-the-digital-divide).
11. In many Muslim countries, access to pornography sites is prevented by government-imposed censorship of the Internet.
12. Out of a total of $15 thousand million for the whole pornography "industry".
13. Matthew 5:28, Today's New International Version.

14. It is important here to distinguish between addiction to pornography, which may be fuelled by what is available on the Internet, and addiction to Internet use per se.

15. I also need to mention in passing those "dating" websites that encourage infidelity.

16. Anonymous respondent quoted in Patrick Fagan, "The Effects of Pornography on Individuals, Marriage, Family and Community", Family Research Council, Washington, DC (2009), available online at http://downloads.frc.org/EF/EF09K57.pdf.

17. Luke 17:2, Today's New International Version.

18. But even this can cause problems. One of my colleagues walked out of his 25-year marriage to renew a relationship with a former girlfriend whom he contacted via a social networking site.

19. A longer version of the song was included in her excellent 2011 CD *Director's Cut*.

20. BBC Radio One, 14 October 1989.

21. Some psychologists now recognize Internet addiction as a specific condition that requires treatment.

22. I heartily recommend Sandel's 2009 book *Justice* and his 2012 book *What Money Can't Buy* (both published by Allen Lane, London).

9

TRANSHUMANISM: STRONGER, FASTER, BETTER, OLDER?

There is no stop button in the race for human re-engineering. Science will soon give some of us the tools to make ourselves cleverer and stronger. What will it mean for our humanity?
Madeleine Bunting, in *The Guardian*, 30 January 2006

That there will be change is certain but what that change will be depends in some measure on human choice. In this century we may choose to use our technological ingenuity to unlock our potential in ways that were unimaginable in the past.
Nick Bostrom, in *Better Humans* (ed. Paul Miller & James Wilsdon), 2006

This sort of conceptual cluelessness is rampant in the world of techno-optimism.
Daniel Sarewitz, in *The Los Angeles Times*, 9 August 2005

9.1 INTRODUCTION

In a 2006 article in *The Guardian*, Madeleine Bunting looked beyond the horizon of current biomedical applications to an imaginary scene in 2031. Some of the biomedical technologies have moved on rapidly and have also become more widely used. She pictured a young couple starting a family and who, even before the woman became pregnant, had tough choices about giving their child the best possible start in life. This involved not only the genetic testing of embryos (presumably created by IVF), as described in Chapter 6, but also genetic modification. In the article, it was suggested that one might thus ameliorate the effects of a mutation associated with depression and also add a gene that contributed to intelligence. Drug-based cognitive enhancement, matched to a child's pharmacogenetic profile, is available for all children and also for the elderly (in the latter case in order to reverse any memory loss that comes with age). Further, the young mother will find help to hold down her job in those very demanding early months of motherhood by taking a drug that helps her to go without sleep, if necessary for several days at a stretch.

All this sounds like science fiction, but actually some of it was possible in 2006 when the article was written and more of it is possible now. But while it is possible, is it available? And if it is available, is there equality of access? Bunting envisaged a basic enhancement package, widely available but embodying some parental choice (for example, in the area of genetic modification), alongside of which more sophisticated packages are available for those who can afford them (in her scenario, "The cleverest went to China for the latest technology"). As with so many advantages in life, the best of biological enhancement comes at a price and thus serves to reinforce rather than reduce inequality. This is a topic to which I will return in the next chapter.

In the meantime, the focus is on the applications of biomedical and digital technology, not in therapy but in enhancement. The enhancements that Bunting envisaged are part of a wider array espoused by the *transhumanist* movement. Transhumanists aim to transcend the normal biological limits of human existence, to become in health terms "better than well" and in more general terms more able than most other humans. Should we be concerned, as Madeleine Bunting clearly is? In the light of this question I will look at the relevant scientific developments under four general headings: biomedical, pharmacological, digital and biomechanical.

9.2 TRANSHUMANISM: BIOMEDICAL

9.2.1 Genetics

We noted in Chapter 6 that genetic selection of embryos *in vitro* can just as easily by applied to traits with no medical relevance as it can be applied to heritable diseases. All that is needed is to identify desired traits that are genetically simple enough to be selectable in pre-implantation genetic diagnosis. It was also noted that many desirable traits do not meet this criterion; they are actually too complex to make genetic selection worthwhile. Nevertheless, there are some feasible targets, and some groups within the transhumanist movement support the idea of enhancement via genetic selection and genetic modification. Just a few months after the Olympic Games were held in London, it seems appropriate to discuss this as our example of the possible uses of genetic technologies in enhancement rather than therapy. In relation to sports, we are considering in particular the possibility of "gene doping" to improve performance.

For example, as a long-distance runner, I am interested in the control of the mixture of slow-twitch and fast-twitch fibres in muscles. It turns out that fast-twitch fibres are regulated by a gene called *ACTN3*. People with the non-mutant form of the gene have abundant fast-twitch fibres in their muscles and tend to be good sprinters. People with a mutated form of the gene have fewer fast-twitch fibres and, if they are athletes, are likely to be good at longer distance or even endurance events. However, possession of a particular gene does not on its own make one a Usain Bolt or a Mo Farah. Other features of physiology and anatomy come into play, as do personality and social and environmental factors. Nevertheless, if one wanted to select for a gene that would at least open the possibility to being a sprinter or a 10,000 metre runner, here it is.

Whether any prospective parent would really want to undergo IVF and genetic selection just to increase the possibility of raising a sprinter or a distance runner seems, in 2013, to be unlikely. But what if it were possible to improve the performance of someone who was already an athlete or had already shown the potential to become one? Endurance athletes are already aware of the benefits of doping with erythropoietin (EPO). This peptide hormone regulates the formation of red blood cells such that increased EPO levels lead to an increased red cell count and hence to greater oxygen-carrying capacity. EPO made by recombinant DNA methods is used for treating some types of anaemia. It is also available on the black market, and there is evidence that it is used by some long-distance cyclists and runners to increase their endurance. This is of course contrary to laws regulating the use of drugs in those sports, but EPO doping is hard to detect because it is a product normally found in the body. Nevertheless, by regular testing in and out of competition, it is hoped that unusual "spikes" in EPO content may be detected. This leads us to ask whether increased EPO levels might instead be built in. The phenomenally successful Finnish cross-country skier Eero Mäntyranta has a genetic mutation leading to over-expression of the EPO receptor and hence increased numbers of red blood cells. Indeed, as Professor Chris Cooper of Essex University puts it so succinctly: "His natural red blood cell count was as high as any blood doping or EPO treatment could hope to achieve."[1]

The gene encoding the EPO receptor and the *ACTN3* gene are two of 23 genes that have been implicated in some way in athletic endurance. Based on the frequency of occurrence of the variants among those genes that increase endurance, it is estimated that the ideal endurance athletic genotype would only occur in 1 in 20 million individuals. Further, there is no guarantee that those individuals would be interested in athletics. That being so, attention turns to the possibility of using genetic *modification* to improve athletic performance. Genetic modification of embryos created by IVF is certainly feasible, as shown by the large numbers of GM mammals (mostly mice) used in research. It would have its problems, one of them being that the level of expression of the inserted gene may vary considerably from individual to individual. Nevertheless, we might envisage prospective parents who themselves have some athletic talent using GM techniques, for example, to increase the levels of EPO or EPO receptor.

Use of genetically modified embryos to establish a pregnancy is illegal in the UK. However, what is not illegal is somatic cell gene therapy, the use of GM in particular types of cell in order to correct a genetic defect (as discussed in Chapter 7, section 7.3). It has been suggested that muscle cells may be good targets for gene therapy (thus raising the possibility of genetic enhancement without the need for genetic manipulation of the embryo). The most spectacular example of this is the over-expression in mouse muscle of a gene involved in energy metabolism (the biochemical pathways that convert the energy in our food to a form that can be used by our cells). The mice engineered in this way are known as "marathon mice"; they can run about 25 times further than their non-modified brothers and sisters.

I have so far concentrated on endurance events, reflecting my own preferences within athletics. However, some attention has also been focused on those sports in which muscle bulk is needed. There are mutations that affect muscle mass, exemplified by the Belgian Blue breed of cattle, which produces many more muscle fibres than other breeds. This happens because of a mutation in the myostatin gene, which regulates the amount of muscle that is formed. The mutation also occurs in humans, albeit very rarely (and certainly rare enough to make pre-implantation detection a non-starter). This has led to the suggestion that methods (which may include GM techniques) may be developed to switch off the myostatin genes (thus giving the same end result as the mutation) in people with diseases such as muscular dystrophy. Switching off the myostatin gene would increase the amount of muscle they made. Body builders and others who wish to develop muscle mass are interested in these developments. At present, it is not clear whether a "gene switch-off" therapy that does not involve GM can be developed, but, if it is, there is sure to be interest in it for non-therapeutic applications. One current line of research is to inactivate the myostatin protein itself by using specific antibodies.

Other possible methods of increasing muscle bulk include manipulating the levels of growth hormones and other growth factors. It is already clear from experience with human growth hormone that once such a product becomes available for therapeutic use, a demand (which may be met via the black market) quickly develops for its use in enhancement.

So, to summarize, we can envisage at least four ways of enhancing different types of athletic performance: namely genetic selection of embryos, genetic modification of embryos, genetic "therapy" applied to muscle (which might include switching off or down-regulating genes) and the direct use of pharmaceutical products. All these approaches are technically feasible and, further, can be applied to several other areas in which human enhancement has been considered. It is not just in athletics that these comments apply.

Focusing specifically on the genetic aspects, I have already commented that prospective parents would need to be rather desperate to produce a budding athlete if they were going to put themselves through genetic selection or genetic modification of embryos. However, gene "therapy" of muscles may turn out to be more feasible and in the context of athletics such gene doping would be hard to detect. The procedure would probably need to be repeated, and furthermore we have no idea of the long-term health effects of adding copies of the "marathon mouse" gene to muscle cells or of down-regulating the myostatin gene. We already know that even successful medical applications of gene therapy may, for some, have serious side effects (Chapter 7, section 7.3). So, would it be worth taking on these unknown risks just to improve athletic performance?

What of more general social and ethical attitudes to genetic selection and genetic modification for enhancement rather than therapy? For people who take a "slippery slope" view of ethical thinking, permitting genetic modification of embryos (which has not yet happened) or genetic selection of embryos (Chapter 6, sections 6.1 and 6.2) for therapeutic purposes has already opened the door to their use in human enhancement. But will there in fact be a demand for it? Even with a limited range of choices, and even though selectable genes or genetic modification procedures may only provide slight enhancement, there are some who would opt for such procedures provided they could afford them. This is not cheap technology and its use is likely to be restricted on the basis of wealth. I return to this point below.

In Madeleine Bunting's article from which I quoted earlier, she assumed, at least for genetic selection of embryos, that these procedures would become widely acceptable, although she herself clearly had reservations. Acceptable to some it may be, but does that make it right? The atheist philosopher

John Harris argues that if a particular feature in our child is important to us, then we should be able to choose it. For example, he says:

> *If it is not wrong to hope for a bouncing, brown-eyed, curly-haired and bonny baby, can it be wrong to ensure that one has just such a baby? If it would not be wrong of God or Nature to grant such a wish, can it be wrong to grant it to oneself?* [2]

On the surface this sounds very plausible. But is it? In practice, couples who choose to have children accept and love them as they come. They hoped for a girl, but it was a boy; they hoped for blue eyes but the baby is brown-eyed. The baby is still a gift.

Harris also suggests that if it becomes possible to provide the child with characteristics that give it a distinct advantage in life (as clearly envisaged by Bunting), then that too will be acceptable. He posits that this is no different from buying advantage in private education or in intensive sport or musical training: to Harris, these are simply outworkings of parents' wishes to give their child the best in life, and the genetic version is no different ethically. I have to disagree; a child can later choose to give up sport or ballet and even rebel against his or her school background. Genetic selection and genetic modification are permanent; the child cannot change his or her genetic make-up even if they choose not to realize its full potential (or are prevented by circumstances from realizing their full genetic potential).

This also raises two other enormous issues that society has never properly faced up to. The first relates to equality of opportunity (genetic advantage will be available to the wealthy but not to the poor). Gregory Stock, the influential commentator and policy-maker from the University of California, suggested in his 2002 book *Redesigning Humans:*

Choosing our Children's Genes[3] that the free market should prevail in this area. If parents want to undergo these procedures, society should allow them to do so if they are willing to pay for it. In respect of the uncertainties and risks associated specifically with genetic modification, he suggests that the first few couples to use this procedure would be like "test pilots" and through their experience, problems could be ironed out. When I debated with him in South Carolina in 2006 his view was unchanged. The market should determine what is available, and it is clear that this view is widely held across the USA.

The second point concerns the value we place on individuals with differing abilities and backgrounds. Yes, we have legislation to encourage "diversity" and inclusiveness, but that is a long way from actually valuing diversity. As I have said elsewhere, it is good to install ramps for wheelchairs but we should also love and respect wheelchair users as people. It is good then that the Paralympic Games, which took place just two weeks after the London Olympic Games in 2012, were held in the same wonderful facilities and were also shown on TV.[4] The Olympic Village itself was built around the needs of the Paralympians, the first time this has happened in Olympic history.

For many people, genetic enhancement through manipulation of embryos or gametes strikes at the very heart of an individual's autonomy, identity and dignity. Even though I think that this ascribes much more to genes than is justified (we are far from being just the sum of our genetic make-up), this unease is certainly understandable. It is clearly reflected in attitudes among the British public, who mostly support genetic research, genetic selection and even genetic modification for the detection, prevention and treatment of disease but do not support the idea of genetic enhancement, notwithstanding the views of people like Professor John Harris.

At present, as I noted in Chapter 6, there seems to be no justification for assuming that human genetic research is leading steadily and inexorably towards "designer babies"; there is no indication that this is generally acceptable to scientists, clinicians, or the public, even if there are some individuals in all of those groups who would be comfortable with such developments. In this respect, prevailing views in the UK are very different from the market-oriented views in the USA, although even there widespread use of genetic selection for non-medical reasons is not just round the corner. Nevertheless, as Madeleine Bunting's look to the future indicates, it is important that the ethical debate continues, keeping pace with scientific progress. We need to be ethically prepared, wise before rather than after the event.

9.2.2 Cloning

There has long been a fascination with the idea of human cloning, exemplified by Ira Levin's novel/Franklin Schaffner's film, *The Boys from Brazil* (in which Adolf Hitler was cloned), Fay Weldon's novel, *The Cloning of Joanna May* (in which a man has paid scientists to make several clones of his wife), Kazuo Ishiguro's novel, *Never Let Me Go* (in which people are cloned to be organ donors) and even a sequence in Bill Watterson's wonderful cartoon series, *Calvin and Hobbes*. One of the remarkable things about the Levin/Schaffner and the Weldon plots is their scientific foresight. The authors understood what cloning would involve, despite their work being published before the birth in 1996 (announced in 1997) of the world's most famous sheep, Dolly (*The Boys from Brazil* was produced in 1978 and *The Cloning of Joanna May* in 1989).

The cloning of Dolly was a remarkable scientific achievement, but it precipitated a storm of protest that eventually cooled to a reasoned ethical debate. I participated extensively in that debate, both in print and via radio and

TV, but here I simply want to focus on the aspects that relate to transhumanism. Why would we want to make a genetic copy of another human being? The answer presumably is that having generated a desirable genotype by one of the procedures outlined above, we now want to copy that genotype (which was actually one of the motivations for cloning sheep). Leaving aside my oft-repeated comment that we are much more than our genotype, what are the ethical issues involved? Philosopher John Harris (again) suggests that there are absolutely no ethical objections to human cloning and that it should be permitted on the grounds of reproductive rights or, in his phrase, "procreative autonomy". As might be expected from earlier comments on genetic modification, Gregory Stock's view is again that the market should be the determining factor, but in this case there is not widespread agreement with him across the USA. Indeed, the majority view across the medical and scientific communities is that reproductive cloning of humans should not be attempted, although there are some who dissent from this view.

In Bill Watterson's cartoon sequence on "the duplicator", the little boy Calvin urges his toy tiger, Hobbes, not to let old-fashioned ethical considerations get in the way of scientific advance, as if science were aloof from ethics. But of course there are ethical issues here of which, for me, one of the most important is *commodification*. This is the genotype I want, and cloning ensures that I will get it. The child's genetic make-up fulfils completely the genetic wishes of someone else. Referring back to Chapter 4, this is clearly not in line with Kant's categorical imperative that we should not use another human being as an instrument to fulfil our own wishes, nor is it in line with the "Golden Rule" – do unto others as you would be done by. In terms of Christian virtue, commodification of another human being is not loving our neighbour as ourselves. Alongside this major ethical consideration, there is also the matter of risk. Over a decade's experience of therapeutic cloning (that is, cloning in order to generate embryonic stem cells) shows us that the success rate is very low. If we then add in the problems associated with using a cloned embryo to start a pregnancy and then carrying the embryo/foetus to term we are in totally unknown territory. The immense difficulties experienced in cloning any primate suggest that the process carries many risks.[5] With our current state of knowledge, attempting reproductive cloning with humans seems to me, putting it bluntly, to be using the carrying mother as experimental material. Nevertheless, Christian medic Gareth Jones has on several occasions suggested that human reproductive cloning will inevitably come. He may be right, but I think that it is not just round the corner. And if a human clone were born, we should not regard them as any less human than someone whose origins are more conventional.

9.2.3 Other reproductive technologies

Although these generally lie outside the remit of the transhumanist movement, there are some futuristic reproductive technologies that are being discussed in popular science publications. As I mentioned briefly in Chapter 7, the possibility is presented of producing babies without sex. Egg cells and sperm cells have both been made from stem cells, leading one national newspaper to state: "Scientists re-write rules of human reproduction."[6] More specifically, sperm cells have been produced from both mouse and human embryonic stem cells. The mouse sperm cells performed well in IVF, leading to the establishment of pregnancies and the birth of baby mice. However, if this is ever to help infertile men, the procedure needs to work with either adult stem cells or with induced pluripotent stem cells (see Chapter 7). This has not yet been done. For eggs, researchers have used ovarian stem cells to generate eggs, even if the ovarian stem cells came from post-menopausal women. Experiments are currently in progress to assess whether the eggs can be fertilized in IVF. Some commentators have suggested that by constructing artificial Y chromosomes, sperm could also be made from female stem cells. This would make men redundant in the reproductive process and could be used by lesbian couples who wished to have a baby boy but did not wish to involve a man in the reproductive process.

One further development is that stem cells have been used to generate a womb lining into which seven-day human embryos successfully implanted. Some commentators go as far as saying that this will lead, perhaps within 40 years, to artificial wombs so that babies can be grown outside the body, a procedure known as *ectogenesis*. Although this seems, and indeed is, very futuristic, I first heard of this idea in discussion with a very thoughtful American biomedical scientist in the early years of this century.

My own reactions to these developments are, first, in respect of making eggs and sperm, that we continue to devote extensive resources to helping people who, for one reason or another, are unable to have babies, a topic that I discussed in Chapter 7. Secondly, I have grave ethical misgivings about ectogenesis. It recalls the incubation of foetuses in Aldous Huxley's novel *Brave New World*, in which varying the conditions could lead to differing levels of intelligence and ability. It also makes it very easy to terminate the life of the growing foetus – just switch off the artificial womb. Human foetuses become commodities. So, why is it being considered at all? What is the need for ectogenesis? I quote from the fertility expert and social ethicist Anna Smajdor:[7]

> *Rather than putting the onus on women to have children at times that suit societal rather than women's individual*

> *interests, we could provide technical alternatives to gestation and childbirth so that women are no longer unjustly obliged to be the sole risk takers in reproductive enterprises. In short, what is required is ectogenesis: the development of artificial wombs that can sustain foetuses to term without the need for women's bodies. Only by thus remedying the natural or physical injustices involved in the unequal gender roles of reproduction can we alleviate the social injustices that arise from them.*

So, according to Smajdor, the biological role of women is itself unjust. Women need to be able to get on with their lives rather than take time out for pregnancy just because society requires them to reproduce. It is an argument that is difficult to sustain. First, women and men are biologically different (differences that can be traced back to the origins of sexual reproduction at least 800 million years ago) and have different roles in reproduction. To ascribe the value-laden term "unjust" to these differences is inappropriate. Secondly, many women happily embrace the role of motherhood. Thirdly, how many women are there who have children just to meet societal requirements (expectations of prospective grandparents notwithstanding)? So, it may come down to the inconvenience of pregnancy (even if a woman wants to have children), for example, in relation to career progression. In respect of the last point, society is in general much more sympathetic to career breaks than it was twenty years ago. Further, for some who wish to have children without the inconvenience of pregnancy, there is the option of surrogate motherhood.[8] Overall, Dr Smajdor's views seem to take feminism (and I have already declared myself to be a Christian feminist: Chapter 3, section 3.5) to extremes to which it should not and indeed logically cannot go.

The other justification for research on ectogenesis is that it may help those women who wish to have children but whose wombs, for various reasons, cannot sustain a pregnancy. This raises again the discussions about "a right to a child" (see Chapter 7, section 7.2). Even though I recognize the pain that some couples experience because of their infertility, I suggest that devoting scarce resources to this extremely "high-tech" method of helping a small proportion of childless couples is not justified. And again, if a couple are really desperate, the option of surrogacy is always open.

Finally, I have misgivings about the possible abuses of ectogenesis. While the Brave New World scenario of producing children with different abilities by modifying foetal incubation conditions is at present very far-fetched (we do not yet know the conditions that will be required to bring a foetus to term), it is something that cannot be ignored. However, even without that, ectogenesis goes a long way down the road of commodifying the foetus. It becomes an entity with which, by virtue of the incubation method, we can do what we please. If the couple no longer want the baby-to-be: no problem, just switch off the artificial womb. Whatever we think of abortion (and I know that there will be a range of views among my readers), this seems to remove much of the moral content from discussions about termination of pregnancy.

Nevertheless, like so many aspects of modern biotechnology, all this comes with its own baggage of hyperbole (hype). Thus, in one of the UK's serious newspapers, a banner headline read "Why sex could be history",[9] while elsewhere in the same edition a trailer for the article suggested that the work of a particular scientist means that the "end of sex is near". It is exaggerations like these that have brought science into disrepute, albeit that it is not scientists who are making these claims. I doubt whether either the headline or the trailer is remotely true. Sex is certainly not on the way out and the reasons for that have nothing to do with technology.

9.2.4 Ageing

As was mentioned in Chapter 7, human lifespans are currently increasing across the globe. Old age is often accompanied by degenerative diseases of various types, and much research on ageing is aimed at understanding the factors that precipitate degeneration. However, one branch of the transhumanist movement, led by the Cambridge scientist Dr Aubrey de Grey, believes that we can do better than that. Seven important molecular and cellular changes associated with ageing have been identified and de Grey believes that by reversing these changes, the human lifespan can be extended significantly, certainly to several hundred years and possibly indefinitely. Further, this would not be a very extended old age with declining abilities but a life in which we are, so to speak, forever young. This all sounds like hype and/or science fiction, but de Grey and his colleagues in the SENS Foundation[10] are definitely serious about this. It is difficult to know what to make of this in ethical terms, but I will make two brief points. First, if ever this research does yield significant results, will the benefits (if in fact they are benefits) be available for all, or is this yet another case of the haves and the have-nots? Secondly, assuming for the moment that this was widely available, with the world's population already above 7,000 million, how would we cope if people started living much longer? It might be that, as in the 1976 film *Logan's Run* set in the twenty-third century, people will be killed when they reached a certain age, in order to prevent overpopulation (in the film, the age was 30 rather than several hundred). This may be a solution, but it raises many questions about the wisdom and the ethics of the SENS Foundation's research. Finally, a more personal question for my readers: Would you like to live for several hundred years or more, even supposing that you would be free of all the symptoms of ageing?

9.3 TRANSHUMANISM: PHARMACOLOGICAL

In recent decades it has become abundantly clear that drugs manufactured initially for therapeutic purposes are often readily adopted for enhancement. I have already hinted at this in section 9.2.1. Taking human growth hormone as an example, the use of genetically modified bacteria to produce the hormone led to it being widely available for treatment of growth hormone deficiency. It also quickly found its way onto the black market and was used in attempts to increase height and weight, especially in younger people engaging in sports where these attributes would be advantageous. The same is true of anabolic steroids, again manufactured for therapy, including, for example, their use in female-to-male gender reassignment in cases of gender dysphoria. However, these hormones are widely available, probably even more so than growth hormone, and are used to build up muscle bulk and strength. In all competitive sports, use of growth hormone or steroids is illegal, and over the past three decades there have been several high-profile cases in which elite athletes have been banned from competition and stripped of any titles they have won because they have been caught using these hormones. Nevertheless, they are still used by "body builders" despite concerns about the safety of long-term use.

In the example discussed above, enhancement involves actually modifying physique as part of the enhancement process. However, it is entirely possible to change many aspects of human performance and behaviour without any modification of the body itself. Indeed, for hundreds if not thousands of years humankind has been using different forms of biochemical intervention, including alcohol, caffeine (as tea or coffee), aspirin (in the form of willow bark) and psychotropic drugs (often in the form of extracts from plants or fungi). Even in this short list we can see the possibility of modifying behaviour (alcohol), increasing alertness (caffeine), relieving pain (aspirin) and enhancing awareness or inducing different mental states (psychotropic drugs). In a sense, all these may be regarded as enhancement. However, the possibility of more directed enhancement is now possible, again because of the non-medical use of drugs first developed for medical applications. There are several examples of this, but I will mention just two.

The first is methylphenidate (Ritalin), developed as a prescription drug for children with ADHD (attention deficit hyperactivity disorder) in order to improve cognitive function, including mental alertness and concentration span. Its use is somewhat controversial and it is widely regarded as being over-prescribed, being given to children who do not have ADHD but are just rather boisterous or lively. Further, significant amounts of the prescribed drug find their way into a non-regulated market where it is purchased by anxious parents who wish to improve the academic performance of their teenaged offspring and by college and university students wishing to enhance their own mental abilities.

The second is modafinil. This drug increases wakefulness and is prescribed medically for narcolepsy and for obstructive sleep apnoea. It also has a legitimate non-medical use in that shift-workers, military personnel, pilots and nurses are often prescribed the drug to prevent tiredness and enhance alertness. Indeed, pilots flying sorties in the Gulf Wars of 1990–1991 and 2003 used modafinil to maintain their alertness, as do some pilots on commercial long-haul flights. However, like Ritalin, modafinil has found its way into the non-prescription market and, like Ritalin, is used by students to help them concentrate. Thus, in a survey of 1,000 students at Cambridge University, 1 in 10 admitted using Ritalin or modafinil or Adderall[11] (an amphetamine-based drug used in a similar way to Ritalin) to help them in their studies or during the examination "season". Indeed, some used modafinil for weeks at a time. In addition to these students, up to a third of those questioned said that they had seriously considered using such drugs but had not actually done so.

What are we to make of all this? In my time at university, some of my fellow students took caffeine tablets to help them stay awake when they were doing long hours of revision or when they worked through the night to complete an assignment. A few years later, I had a colleague who used caffeine tablets on long night-time drives to visit family. Is using modafinil and Ritalin any different? In some ways it is not different; modafinil is fulfilling the same function as caffeine and is probably more efficient. However, in other ways it is different. Obtaining prescription drugs (in the USA, regulated drugs) without a prescription is illegal,[12] but users, including those Cambridge students, get round this problem by buying them from unregulated sources via the Internet. Obviously purchase of these drugs costs money and, once more, advantage is accruing to those who can afford it. It is, however, very difficult to know how to regulate this use. As one student put it, are we going to see urine samples being taken during the exam season, rather as they are during athletics meets, in order to see who is "clean" and who is not?

9.4 TRANSHUMANISM: DIGITAL

9.4.1 Human–digital interfaces and cybernetics

Cyborgs – *cyb*ernetic *org*anisms, totally realistic humanoids that are really complex machines (but may be part-human) run by equally complex internal computers – have appeared many times in science fiction writing and films. Among the latter, *Blade Runner*, *AI*, the *Star Wars* series, the *Terminator* series and the *Cyborg* series provide good examples. However, cybernetics is also a fast-moving branch of computer science in which, according to some commentators, we are moving from fiction to fact. That does not mean that a true cyborg is likely to be developed in the next few years but it does mean that we are developing ways of interfacing digital devices with the human body. In Chapter 7, I discussed the progress in using the thought processes of a paralysed person first to move a cursor on a computer screen and more recently to control an artificial hand to move a drinking cup. I also mentioned the very sophisticated new generation of computer-controlled prostheses – known colloquially as bionic limbs – that are able to achieve a high degree of flexible and controlled movement.

These applications of cybernetics fall clearly into the area of restoration – restoring a function to someone who has lost it or who has never had it. A more recent and totally fascinating example of this concerns the British musician and artist Neil Harbisson. He was born with no colour vision at all but, working with a colleague, has developed a head-worn camera that can, in real time, convert colours into sound waves that Harbisson can hear. Specific tones are associated with all the colours and shades that the human eye can detect (and some that the human eye cannot see, i.e. infrared and ultraviolet). Harbisson had to learn the note associated with each colour but once he had done that, recognizing colour was no longer a process of memory but, as he puts it, "became a perception". Harbisson calls the device an "eyeborg" and, because he now regards it totally as a part of who he is, has persuaded the UK Passport Office that his passport photograph should show him wearing it.

Neil Harbisson refers to himself as a cyborg, which, since he is actually a human who is interfaced with a small digital device, seems rather far-fetched. However, this is very much the language of the community of scientists and enthusiasts who support the development of human–digital interfaces. In the UK, one of the most enthusiastic proponents is Professor

Kevin Warwick of the University of Reading.[13] Over the past fifteen years he has had different types of silicon chip transponders implanted into his forearm. The first of these, inserted in 1998, enabled him to open security doors and turn lights on because the detectors on the door locks and light switches recognized the information in the chip. This led him to call himself the world's first cyborg, which to me sounds even more far-fetched than Harbisson's self-description. Nevertheless, as Warwick pointed out, such devices might be a secure means of carrying credit card information and could even be loaded with "cash" (which could only be used in outlets that recognized the inserted chip). This idea has actually come to fruition in the form of the Verichip (about the size of a rice grain), which is used, mainly by the more "important" guests, to be recognized at the door and to pay for drinks at nightclubs in several cities, including Barcelona, Glasgow and Rotterdam. However, it has a much wider use as a security device for workplaces, enabling "wearers" to be recognized as bona fide staff members and to open security doors, in a similar way to Warwick's 1998 device.

Warwick's second implanted device was more sophisticated. It enabled him to control an electric wheelchair and an "intelligent" artificial hand, using an interface between the device and his nervous system (the neural interface). The implant was also able to detect and measure the nerve signals transmitted along the nerve fibres in Warwick's arm, and to create artificial sensation by stimulating nerves via individual electrodes within the array. Finally, the implant could also communicate electronically with a similar implant in the arm of Warwick's wife Irena.

We can recognize in this some of the medical and restorative applications of digital technology that I have discussed earlier. However, the community of cyborg enthusiasts wants to extend use of this technology far beyond the medical realm. It is suggested that by enhancing human capabilities via human–digital interfaces we can take human evolution to a higher level. As a biologist I find a lot to criticize in that statement because I can see no way in which being interfaced with a micro-computer is equivalent to a heritable variation on which natural selection can work within a population. Be that as it may, Warwick and his associates say that this evolution is essential; otherwise machines will take over the planet (but see the next section and Chapter 8). It is a rather Nietzschean scenario, with man becoming superman. Thus they suggest that the technology which enables paralysed people to move computer cursors and artificial limbs could be developed further, leading to brain implants that will facilitate transfer of thoughts between individuals. This leads to a scenario in which networks of enhanced individuals communicate with each other in a special way. There has even been speculation that via a specialized brain interface we may one day be able to download people's memories onto a silicon chip (this does of course presuppose that we can identify and isolate the components of brain activity that make up a person's memories).

Can we make a reasoned ethical response to all this? Anyone with a shred of fellow feeling for other human beings will surely welcome the medical and restorative applications of this technology, even those as far out as Neil Harbisson's eyeborg. Yet I get the impression – an impression that is shared by other commentators – that the real cyborg enthusiasts are not really interested in medical applications but rather are seeing how far they can push the technology. It is almost as if we see geeky boys playing with their cybertoys. However, let me assume that they are indeed serious in their intent; how then should we react, especially to the idea of thought transference? I suggest two specific areas for concern (a third, more general, area – namely that this will be technology only for the rich – is relevant to almost everything in this chapter). The first is that a small group of people with mutual thought transfer capabilities would certainly be in a position to exert power over others. Secondly, without any of us knowing how or even whether this technology will work, it certainly raises the possibility of thought control (of which Pink Floyd sang negatively[14]). Such an invasion of an individual's inner world would be very sinister. Even at the level experienced by Tom Cruise in the film *Minority Report*, where voices in his head, combined with holographic images, urged him to buy this or that, it is clear that thought control is unacceptable under almost any ethical system we care to name. It removes the last vestiges of freedom – the freedom to be me inside my head – with all that this entails. This is not going "beyond human" but is making others less than human. It would be best if such developments were nipped in the bud. It is thus disturbing to learn that the US Department of Defense is funding research on electronic thought-reading and thought-control techniques. My own hope is that the research is not successful.

There are also practical considerations. Anyone who has attempted to analyse their thought processes during a conversation will realize that there is constant activity in conscious and unconscious thought going on all the time, in addition to the verbal statements. If thoughts were indeed transferred, we would get a huge amount of noise, among which the statement or question or comment would be difficult to discern. I am sure that the successes that have been achieved in thought control of cursors and artificial limbs need the almost total focus by the subject on the matter in hand. This does not happen in conversation. Secondly, holding a conversation by thought transfer removes all the non-verbal elements of communication – body language, tone and loudness of voice, speed and cadence of speech. It is in this context that Daniel Sarewitz's highly critical statement was made: "This sort of conceptual cluelessness is rampant in the world of techno-optimism."[15] For example, Sarewitz asks, how can two opponents or even enemies negotiate with each other without the benefit of non-verbal communication? Even in a telephone call, although observation of body language is not possible, all the elements relating to voice and delivery are there. In fact, thought transfer seems to eliminate the warmth of human contact from communication; once again, it is not going beyond human but is something less than human. Thought transfer may turn out to be a very unsatisfactory method of communication, if indeed it ever happens.

9.4.2 Conscious, intelligent computers?

There is a lot of talk about intelligent computers with consciousness. Kevin Warwick seems so convinced that computers will have the potential to rule the world that we need to evolve in order to counter this. In the world of artificial intelligence, Moore's Law is often cited as suggesting an unstoppable march to machine consciousness.[16] The more processing power we can fit on a chip, the closer we approach, it is said, human-like intelligence and consciousness. Nick Bostrom, co-founder of the World Transhumanist Association, suggests that "we can predict with a high degree of confidence that hardware matching that of the human brain will be available in the foreseeable future" and that this will lead to real artificial intelligence. "There is no reason," he writes, "why the computational algorithms that our biological brains use would not work equally well when implemented in silicon hardware."[17]

However, several distinguished computer science experts, including Professor Lionel Tarassenko at Oxford and Professor Peter Robinson at Cambridge, disagree with this. I noted in the previous chapter that although computers can do many things much better and much faster than humans can, no machine has yet passed the Turing Test. Yes, we have computers that recognize speech, but the recognition system is not equivalent to the human auditory system. There are computers that can recognize faces, but again the most up-to-date software does not work in the way that humans recognize faces. Computers can be taught to recognize a range of human emotions based on facial expressions and, to some extent, tone of voice. However, recognizing emotions is not the same as experiencing emotions. Computers lack empathy and emotional intelligence. In respect of artificial intelligence, Tarassenko refutes the idea that Moore's Law leads automatically to consciousness. Machine intelligence may perform much better than human intelligence in many areas, but it does not work in the same way as the human brain. The problem with Bostrom's statement is that it is based on a reductionist view of both humans as organisms and the brain itself, assuming that it works along the lines of the computational algorithms of computer technology. However, this is not so. Artificial intelligence is built on a bottom-up information flow. Biological systems, of which the brain is the most complex, receive and generate information in bottom-up, top-down and even sideways flows. Silicon architecture can never reach this level of complexity. Even though they are everywhere, computers are not about to take over the world.

9.5 TRANSHUMANISM: BIOMECHANICAL

In Chapter 7, I mentioned Claire Lomas who, although paralysed from the chest down, walked (very slowly) the London Marathon course with the aid of a robotic walking suit. Development of robotic suits or "exoskeletons" is proceeding very rapidly. They are becoming lighter and more versatile and enable the wearer to do many things that they would otherwise be unable to do. Further, they are not being developed only for people who are paralysed. Thus, the designers of exoskeletons suggest that, among a range of applications, they may be worn to help with tasks that involve handling heavy equipment. It will be interesting to see how much they catch on.

9.6 THE "SUPER-SOLDIER" PROGRAMME

In 2008, the US Department of Defense announced its $3,000 million "super-soldier" programme in which the aim is to use technology and biology to achieve "transhuman performance goals". Development of robotic suits or "intelligent" exoskeletons is certainly part of the programme, and it is envisaged that the suits will eventually enable soldiers to run at the speed of Usain Bolt for several hours, leap two metres vertically, crawl up walls and carry heavier and more powerful weapons, while at the same time keeping the soldier cool. The programme also includes use of all the biochemical enhancements that I have mentioned already, including drugs to increase muscle bulk, maintain wakefulness, enhance cognition and even block, for up to 30 days, the sense of pain. When the programme was announced, the director proudly stated: "My measure of success is that the International Olympic Committee bans everything we do."[18] It all sounds rather sinister, not least because military personnel will be used as experimental subjects. One wonders how much choice they will have in the matter.

9.7 CONCLUDING COMMENTS

The transhumanist movement certainly makes some big claims for itself, but in my view many of these are exaggerated; they are hyperbole. Looking at Bostrom's statement at the head of this chapter, for example, one gets the impression that societal and technological change have never happened before but that change is certainly coming. In fact, as has been made obvious right through this book, human society changes all the time, as does technology. At present, change is happening very fast and some people may feel that they are running to stand still, but change itself is not a new thing.

I also believe that human enhancement is not a new thing. Prostheses of various types, albeit very unsophisticated, date back to several hundred years before the Christian era. Devices and machines to help in daily activities, in military action and in leisure pursuits also date back a long way. Boomerangs and other curved hunting sticks may have been invented 30,000 years ago. They are found in many places in the world (not just in Australia); King Tutankhamen, for example, who died over 3,000 years ago, had a large collection of boomerangs. Another example is the woomera, a spear-throwing device used by Australian Aborigines, which was invented about 5,000 years ago. Then there is the wheel, which as described in Chapter 1 was invented initially for use in pot-making in about 4500 BC and a few hundred years later adapted for use in transport. I could go on and on here, but will not; the point is made.

Perhaps what we do need to say is that as science has developed, so human enhancement has become more sophisticated. Thus knowledge of genetics makes possible the processes of genetic selection and genetic modification; knowledge of human biology and of pharmacology facilitates specific biochemical enhancements. Developments in computing, neurobiology and biomechanics have led to vastly improved prostheses and to robotic suits or exoskeletons. But are there any trends or developments that lie outside this general picture? Yes, certainly – I think that if there was a sudden step-change in human lifespan or if thought transfer and thought-control techniques were developed, or if ectogenesis was actually developed, then we would be in new territory, territory for which we are currently unprepared. However, it is a moot point as to whether these developments will ever happen.

So, what I have discussed in this chapter is a series of mainly biotechnological developments, many of which have applications in medicine and in healthcare. However, on close investigation it becomes clear that even applications in medicine are not universally available. In systems of social medicine such as the NHS, funding may not and often does not cover the more expensive developments. In the more commercially based systems such as that in the USA, access to the more sophisticated or expensive applications will depend on how much a person pays for their health insurance policy, remembering that 50 million Americans cannot afford health insurance at all. Even if President Obama's healthcare initiatives ("Obamacare") are finally put into practice (they are bitterly opposed by the Republicans) they will not give these poorer Americans access to highly sophisticated techniques.

Once again then we have, through the eyes of technology, a clear view of the divisions in human society; those divisions between the haves and have-nots are visible in the industrial, developed nations of the global north, even before we consider the wider world, including the global south. Transhumanism implies transcending our humanity, but does it do so? It certainly increases the capabilities of humankind (and in doing so represents the latest phase in a long history) but transcend our humanity? I think not. Indeed, the limited availability of many of the developments means that some humans are treated as being worth less than others. As a Christian I am reminded of the words of the prophet Micah: "And what does the Lord require of you? To act justly, to love mercy and to walk humbly with your God."[19] With those words ringing in our ears (at least metaphorically), we move on to the last chapter.

NOTES

1. See http://www.runswimthrowcheat.com.
2. In *Clones, Genes and Immortality*, Oxford: Oxford University Press, 1998, page 194
3. Published by Profile Books, London.
4. At this point, it is appropriate to honour the memory of Dr Ludwig Guttman, whose excellent work on rehabilitation of injured servicemen at Stoke Mandeville (recognized by the award of a knighthood) led to the establishment of the Paralympic Games.
5. For up-to-date information on cloning, see http://www.genome. gov/25020028.
6. *The Independent*, 7 April 2012.
7. A. Smajdor, "The Moral Imperative for Ectogenesis", *Cambridge Quarterly of Healthcare Ethics* 16 (2007), pages 336–45.
8. A recent high-profile example was Rebekah Brooks, former chief executive of News International, whose daughter Scarlett was born (in January 2012) to a surrogate mother.
9. *The Guardian*, 17 August 2012.
10. SENS: Strategies for Engineering Negligible Senescence.
11. Note that modafinil is a generic name while Ritalin and Adderall are specific trade names.
12. In 2004, modafinil was added to the list of banned substances in sport and, since then, the British sprinter Dwain Chambers has been among those caught using it.
13. I am not going to discuss here the work of the Canadian cyborg enthusiast Steve Mann because it seems to me that most of the functions of his wearable computers have been supplanted by the smartphone. More information on Mann can be found in J. Bryant, L.B. la Velle and J. Searle, *Introduction to Bioethics*, Chichester: John Wiley and Sons, 2005, page 82.
14. In the song "Another Brick in the Wall", 1978.
15. In *Los Angeles Times*, 9 August 2005.
16. Moore's Law is actually an observation: during the history of computing hardware, the number of transistors in integrated circuits doubles about every two years.
17. In *Better Humans*, edited by Paul Miller and James Wilsdon, London: Wellcome Trust/Demos, 2006, pages 42 and 44.
18. Quoted in *Live Science*, 26 February 2011: http://www.livescience. com/12991-10-outrageous-military-experiments.html.
19. Micah 6:8, New International Version.

10

BEYOND HUMAN?

Each new power won by man is a power over man as well. Each advance leaves him weaker as well as stronger. In every victory, besides being the general who triumphs, he is also the prisoner who follows the triumphal car.
C.S. Lewis, from *The Abolition of Man*, 1947

I hold these truths to be self-evident, that all men are created equal.
Thomas Jefferson, *US Declaration of Independence*, 4 July 1776

… Who is my neighbour?
Luke 10:29

10.1 INTRODUCTION

The journey that this book has traced has been a long one. I have asked what it means to be human and how our "humanness" has been worked out over the millennia of the existence of our species and, more specifically, during the historical timeline that led from ancient civilizations to where we are today. It is abundantly apparent that humans are capable of good, noble and selfless behaviour and that this can be exhibited at all levels, from the individual right up to whole countries and to international organizations. However, it is sadly equally true that we are capable of evil, base, cruel and egoistical behaviour, which may also be exhibited at all levels of organization. It seems that from earliest times, our history has been marred by wars, conflicts and atrocities, all indicative of, in Robert Burns's well-worn phrase, "man's inhumanity to man".

Against this background I have discussed developments in biomedical technology and biotechnology, with a side-trip into digital technology. I have examined their uses or projected uses in medicine and healthcare (and for digital technology, in wider society) and asked whether any of these may be considered as taking us "beyond human". My general view is that they do not. However, there are other questions to consider. Will these technologies be used for good or ill? If there are benefits, will they be universally available? Are we getting our priorities right?

10.2 THE ANGEL AND THE BEAST

I return to Pascal's wonderful description: we are not angels, although we aspire to be angels; we are not beasts, although too often we behave as beasts (see Chapter 2, section 2.11). Once again we see both sides of our human nature. In this context, it is interesting to note how many writers of serious fiction present a dystopian view of science, or at least of its applications. The list is very long but includes Mary Shelley's *Frankenstein*, Aldous Huxley's *Brave New World*, George Orwell's *1984*, John Wyndham's *The Chrysalids* (with its dramatic imperative "Watch thou for the mutant", inculcated into the society depicted in the book by its religious leader), William S. Burroughs's *Nova Express*, Margaret Attwood's *The Handmaiden's Tale* and *Oryx and Crake*, Kazuo Ishiguro's *Never Let Me Go*, Suzanne Weyn's *The Bar-code Tattoo* and so on. Equally long is the list of films presenting science and technology in a dystopian light (*Jurassic Park*, *Gattaca* and *Never Let Me Go* are but three examples of many). Why is this? Some commentators have suggested that authors and screenplay writers are responding to the hubris, the arrogance of scientists and their confidence in progress. Indeed, in society at large, one way in which modernity (see Chapter 3, section 3.9.1) presents itself in twenty-first-century Britain is in progressivism, almost a worship of technological progress for its own sake. Some of the developments I have discussed in this book may well come into that category, as I indicated, for example, in relation to thought transference and to artificial wombs. Sometimes the old saying "If it ain't broke, don't fix it" should be taken notice of.

On the other hand, the Oxford literary critic Bernard Richards is widely quoted as saying that dystopias are useful because they warn us about what might happen. Nearly all the technologies discussed here are capable of being misused – misused in a way that may indeed treat some people as if they are of less worth than others. It is a sad fact that humankind has a long history of abusing and misusing God's good gifts, including our talents and abilities; so if we can indeed be forewarned about what might happen, then we will have a focus for our ethical and social vigilance.

10.3 FAIR SHARES FOR ALL?

Right at the turn of the century, science communicator Pete Moore produced a very timely and thought-provoking book, *Babel's Shadow*.[1] In it he revisited the old Hebrew story in which human arrogance led to the building of a ziggurat (the Tower of Babel) to reach up to heaven. In doing this, humans incur God's displeasure and he imposes on them a range of different languages; human society becomes fragmented because different groups can no longer understand each other. Of course, the evolution of languages did not happen that way, but the moral of the story is clear. When we become arrogant or self-absorbed, divisions occur and human society tends to fracture. The dystopian tale of the Tower of Babel does indeed tell us what might happen.

Moore went on to discuss the rapidly developing biomedical technologies and cast them as the new Babel because there was a real danger that they would lead to a fracturing of our society. It was highly possible that the benefits of the technology would not be equally available, that some would be able to avail themselves of healthcare benefits while others would not, that some would be able to enhance their opportunities in life while others would not. Thus, as is stated on the back cover of *Babel's Shadow*, "great human technological achievement" could readily "sow division and enmity".

So, twelve years on, has the situation changed? I have cast the iconic double helical DNA molecule as another stairway to heaven, a heaven of personalized genetic medicine, of "genetic health", of gene-based tests, of tissue repair and stem cell technology and of course of millions of pounds or dollars. As in Moore's book, some of these things are happening, while others are still in the future. However, as I have pointed out many times through this text, the benefits of these technologies are not equitably distributed. Even in a single country, the UK, with its system of social medicine, access to some of these technologies is rationed or even denied (for example, in respect of pre-implantation genetic diagnosis) and thus may only be "freely" available to those with private healthcare plans. Then, when it comes to buying advantages, for example through cognition-enhancing drugs, only those who can afford the purchases will be able to benefit. These small examples suggest that we are in danger of becoming a society fragmented in respect of access to some of these technologies. All humans are created equal but, as in George Orwell's classic phrase, "some are more equal than others". Further, there seems to be no political will to address these basic inequalities, so it may well be that the situation gets worse rather than better.

10.4 FIDDLING WHILE HOME BURNS

Let us for a moment look outside the world of high technology and focus on other features of life in the twenty-first century. The population of the world passed the 7,000 million mark sometime around late October/early November 2011. Of that total, about 950 million do not have enough to eat. This is not because the world cannot produce enough food – it can – but because of poverty and of inequalities in distribution. Many people go hungry because they simply cannot afford food. The UN's World Food Programme states that hunger is the world's number one killer. More people die from hunger than the combined total of those who die from malaria, AIDS and tuberculosis. The majority of undernourished people are in less-developed countries (the global south) but significant numbers of them live in developed industrialized countries. If you are reading this in a medium-sized or large city in, for example, the UK or the USA, there will be people, including children, within a few miles/kilometres of where you are, who will tonight go to bed genuinely hungry.

Having in passing mentioned malaria, what are the statistics relating to this disease? Every year, malaria infects somewhere between 400 and 500 million people, of whom about 2 million die. The majority of those who die from malaria are children. Most of these deaths (90 per cent) are in sub-Saharan Africa. If this level of infection and mortality occurred in Europe or the USA, there would be an outcry – something must be done, it would be said. However, in practice, malaria has been one of the poor relations of medical research, with rather less spent on it than elements of medicine in the developed nations (the global north) that have the potential to help relatively few (in comparison) people. It is therefore excellent news that the Bill and Melinda Gates Foundation is now supporting research on malaria, with the express purposes of developing a vaccine and of implementing new control measures.

About 4 million children die each year as a result of complications in childbirth, with a further 2 million dying from respiratory infections and 2 million from diarrhoea. These deaths are spread among the countries of the global south, but again many are in Africa. And perhaps the greatest tragedy of all is that 90 per cent of these 8 million childhood deaths could be prevented at relatively little cost.

Added to all this, and despite the appalling number of childhood deaths in the global south, the world's population did not stop growing when it reached the 7,000 million mark. Even though the rate of increase has slowed a little, we are heading in the direction of 9 billion by 2050, at which point, with current agricultural methods, the population will be in excess of that which we can feed.

Finally, to cap it all, our home, our beautiful blue planet Earth, is burning, or at least warming significantly. The atmospheric concentration of CO_2 is fast approaching 400 ppm, from a baseline of 280 ppm before the Industrial Revolution. This is a key factor in driving climate change. July 2012 was the 329th consecutive month of above-average global temperatures. Globally, it was the third hottest July ever and the hottest month ever for North America. Ironically, July 2012 was colder than average in north-western Europe, including the UK, probably because of excess melt water from the Arctic, leading to disturbances in atmospheric conditions, including the position of the jet stream.

At this point, I need to make some comments about science, lest I am misunderstood in what I have written in the next paragraph. In my own career it has been a privilege to carry out scientific research. There is in research a genuine feeling of going into the unknown. But even when we have a result or can form a new hypothesis, the extent of what we still do not know should keep us humble. It was the philosopher of science Karl Popper who said that knowledge is finite but ignorance is infinite. As a researcher I can rightly say that I still haven't found what I'm looking for. Nevertheless, in those moments of discovery, I do indeed feel that I have had glimpses into the work of God, the creator. Furthermore, much of my research has been on plant genes and on the way they work and has thus contributed to fundamental knowledge about plant growth and crop yield. It is good to think that this might contribute in some small way to improvements in crop performance. I am sure too that colleagues working on human genes and gene expression are delighted when their work helps in the improvement of diagnosis or of healthcare practices of the types I have discussed in this book. Overall, I believe that scientific research is a legitimate activity in our society, resulting from our curiosity about the universe and sometimes leading to worthwhile applications.

It is in this area of application that most of our concerns arise. While I do not believe that any area of knowledge is off limits (although some experimental methods certainly are), the application of that knowledge may raise serious and genuine ethical concerns, as has been noted many times in this book: we *can* do this, but *should* we do this? So, imagine now that we can fast-forward several decades and then look back, just as in the film *The Age of Stupid*. Someone from that future time may well comment along these lines: Let me get this right: the world's population was growing towards a point where it would be impossible to feed everyone; already 14 per cent of the world's population was genuinely hungry; millions of children were dying of preventable diseases; planet Earth was experiencing significant and possibly runaway warming – and they were putting resources into research on thought transfer and thought-control technology, on dramatic extension of human lifespan, on artificial wombs and sexless reproduction! What were they thinking of?

10.5 BETTER HUMANS?

The heading of this section is the title of a book that discusses briefly some of the technologies dealt with in this text.[2] The title immediately raises a question: In what ways might we become better? In the developed industrialized countries of the world, we are certainly becoming very much more enabled by the use of technology, we are better provided for in healthcare and in restorative medicine, we are better able to manipulate our metabolism and other aspects of our physiology and so on – but are we better humans? The book that I have just mentioned carries a headline on its front cover: "From smart pills to designer babies and extended life spans, technology now *promises* to transform our very nature".[3] Transform our very nature – well it might be good if that did happen, but I doubt whether it can be achieved through biomedical technology. Let us take another look at the world.

In the UK, official government figures show that domestic violence accounts for about 20 per cent of all recorded crime, with an incident being reported to the police every minute. About 40 per cent of women have experienced one incident of domestic violence (including emotional and psychological violence), and 1 in 4 women have suffered repeated episodes. We should note that up to 16 per cent of men are also victims of domestic violence. Nevertheless, the majority of domestic violence is suffered by women. In any one year, there are about 13 million separate incidents of physical violence or threats of violence against women from partners or former partners. Over 50 per cent of UK rapes are committed by a woman's current or former partner, and, in an average year, two women a week are killed by a male partner or former partner: this constitutes about one-third of all female murder victims. The data for several other European Union countries are comparable.

Then there is the horror of human trafficking. The United Nations describes it as follows:

> *Slowly and painfully a picture is emerging of a global crime that shames us all. Billions of dollars are being made at the expense of millions of victims of human trafficking. Boys and girls who should be at school are coerced into becoming soldiers, doing hard labour or sold for sex. Women and girls are being trafficked for exploitation: forced into domestic labour, prostitution or marriage. Men, trapped by debt, slave away in mines, plantations, or sweatshops.*[4]

Actual numbers are hard to come by. However, a working estimate is that the *minimum* number of people in forced labour, including sexual exploitation, as a result of trafficking at any given time is 2.5 million. If we then add those who are in slave labour without being trafficked, we arrive at a figure of between 12 and 27 million. There are more slaves now than the number taken from West Africa in four centuries of trading.

Finally, a brief overview of conflict across the world. There are still despotic dictators who oppress their people brutally. At least two of these are heads of countries that were part of the Soviet Union until its collapse in 1990. In Syria, as we have been seeing day by day on our TV screens since 2011, the government is willing to engage in indiscriminate bombing in order to crush any opposition (and again the United Nations has been powerless). There are countries under military rule where individual freedoms are minimal. There are war lords; there are civil wars with one side or the other or both committing dreadful atrocities; there have been genocides and ethnic cleansings of horrendous proportions; there are terrorist attacks almost anywhere in the world; there are shooting incidents and mass murders...

All the examples in this section are indicative, in Plato's analogy, that it is the wrong horse that dominates in the driving of the human soul. Indeed, we may well be led to question Mary Warnock's assertion (see Chapter 4, section 4.2) that "the need for an ethical system is a fundamental need of human nature",[5] based on a personal sense of moral good and a tendency to altruism ("when someone begins to see he must postpone his immediate wishes for the sake of the good"[6]). Sometimes it appears that those who do not seem to possess the sense of moral good, nor show any indication of altruism, are more numerous than those who do exhibit virtue. Indeed, the worse side of human nature comes too readily to the fore, and it is going to take a good deal more than genetic selection and smart pills to change that. And, yes, I know that the readers of this book are not war lords or power-crazed dictators or traffickers of young women for sexual purposes, but we still need to acknowledge that alongside all the noble and selfless deeds of which individual humans are capable we also see acts of arrogance and selfishness. Change is certainly needed, but medical technology cannot bring it about. I am sure that different readers have different ideas about how to achieve change. For me, writing from a specifically Christian viewpoint, it is all about the work in me of God's Holy Spirit, enabling me to practise those virtues that I discussed in Chapter 4 (section 4.2).

10.6 POSTSCRIPT

The question mark in the heading of this chapter and in the title of the book invites discussion. It has led me to look at the *possibility* that technology is taking us beyond human, rather than justifying the statement that it is actually doing so. I hope that it will be very clear by now that I do not think that we are being taken beyond our humanity. Our essential "humanness", our human nature with its strengths and weaknesses (some of which have been graphically described in this chapter), remains the same. So, rather than taking us beyond human, I share the concerns of C.S. Lewis expressed in those prophetic words that are quoted at the head of the chapter. The danger actually is that applications of these technologies may treat some humans as being of less worth than other humans. We need vigilance and wisdom in deciding what is right and wrong in this area. And so I end with some words from which I draw inspiration:

> *But the wisdom from above is first of all pure. It is also peace-loving, gentle at all times, and willing to yield to others. It is full of mercy and good deeds. It shows no favouritism and is always sincere.*[7]

NOTES

1. *Babel's Shadow*, Oxford: Lion Publishing, 2000.
2. *Better Humans*, edited by Paul Miller and James Wilsdon, London: DEMOS/Wellcome Trust, 2006.
3. My emphasis.
4. From *Human Trafficking: An Overview*, United Nations Office on Drugs and Crime, 2008, page v.
5. M. Warnock, *An Intelligent Person's Guide to Ethics*, London: Duckworth, 1998, page 90.
6. *Ibid.*, page 89.
7. James 3:17, New Living Translation.

INDEX

"9/11" 62–63
1960s 48, 54–55, 57–59, 61, 68, 98, 132, 185

abortion/termination of pregnancy 57–58, 75, 89, 91, 98–99, 118, 120–22, 124–25, 127, 219
addiction to pornography *see* pornography
Advance Directive/living will 173
aeroplane, invention of 38
Afghanistan 62–63, 75, 161
Africa 16–17, 63, 74, 101, 105–106, 161–62, 169, 191, 239–40, 243
    sub-Saharan 105, 191, 239
African Americans 56, 105, 121
Ageing 68, 152, 220
Agriculture 19–20, 22, 35, 240
AIDS 169, 239
Al-Qaeda 62–63
Altruism 15, 26, 82, 85, 136, 244
Alzheimer's disease 115, 168, 170, 174, 179
America/USA 26, 31–35, 38, 40–41, 43, 47–49, 53–54, 56, 58–59, 61–64, 66, 70, 82, 85–88, 100–101, 105, 112, 117–19, 121–25, 129, 131–32, 135–36, 139, 142, 150, 153–54, 157–58, 164, 166, 169, 184, 195–98, 213–15, 217, 223, 232, 239–40
amniocentesis 98
anabolic steroids 221
Anglo-Saxons 29–30
Apollo 11 185
Aquinas, Thomas 80–81, 83
Arab Spring 189
Aristotle 27–29, 80, 82–84, 94–95, 130–31
Art 14, 17–19, 27–28, 73
artificial insemination/donor insemination 142–43, 147, 178
artificial intelligence 183–84, 228–29
artificial wombs 217–18, 237, 241

Ashkenazi Jews 108–109, 118, 132
assisted reproductive technologies/ ART 142–43
Assyria/Assyrians 27
atheism 26, 33, 36–37, 39, 68–70, 84–85, 112, 138–39, 211
athletics 129, 151, 162, 182, 209–211, 223
Augustine of Canterbury 29–30
autonomy 33 73, 87–88, 128, 130, 147, 171, 173–74, 213, 215

Babylon/Babylonians 21, 27
Bacon, Francis 32, 34
bases, in DNA 100, 107, 110
BBC 84, 178, 200, 202–203
beneficence 87–88
Bentham, Jeremy 81
Berlin 46–48, 50
    Berlin Wall 48
Berners-Lee, Tim 186
Bible 10, 23, 37, 42, 147, 160, 167
Bin Laden, Osama 62–63
bioethics 90, 112–13, 179, 233
biomechanics 160–61, 231
Bland, Tony 171–73
blastocyst 153–55
blindness 96, 108, 150, 160, 162, 165–66, 181
bone marrow 104, 109, 111, 126, 149–50, 152–53, 157–58
boomerang(s) 231
Bostrom, Nick 205, 228–30
brain stem death 171–72
Brave New World 112, 217, 219, 236
breast cancer 109, 115
Britain 16, 22, 26, 28–32, 34–42, 53, 58, 60, 64, 68, 84, 158, 167, 190, 237
    England 29, 31, 35, 37, 68, 176
    Commonwealth 54
    Empire 54, 182
Brown, Louise 143–45
burial 18, 23

Bush, George W. 63
Bush, Kate 181, 200

CAG triplet, in Huntington's disease
    107
Cambridge University 140, 222
Campaign for Nuclear Disarmament/
    CND 58
cancer 50, 109–110, 115, 150, 159,
    168
Canterbury 30, 53
capitalism 35, 46, 82
car (automobile), invention of 36
Caribbean 106
carriers 98, 104–106, 109–109,
    118–19, 121, 125, 136
Celts/Celtic 29–30, 68, 102
    saints 29
cerebral cortex 172
chimpanzee(s) 13–14, 42
chorionic villus 120
Christianity 10–11, 15, 26, 29–30,
    33–34, 36–37, 41–42, 52, 57, 59,
    61, 63, 65, 70, 81–85, 91, 101,
    112–13, 128, 139–40, 157, 172,
    175–79, 196, 198–99, 215–16,
    218, 231–32, 244
    in Roman empire 29
Christian ethics 81, 83, 113, 140
chromosomes 96–97, 100, 112, 136,
    155, 217
    X chromosome 96–97, 100
    Y chromosome 96, 100, 136, 217
Church of England 31, 37, 136
city/cities 19–23, 25–28, 35, 39–40,
    46, 51, 71, 187, 190–91, 199, 225,
    236, 239, 243
civil liberties 194
civil partnership 183
civil rights see rights, civil
Clapham sect 34
Clarke, Arthur C. 186
climate change 66, 240
cloning 11, 67, 147, 153–56, 159,
    214–16, 233
cognitive enhancement 68, 206
Colchester 22
Collins, Francis 15, 101, 110–12, 119,
    123, 138–40
colour blindness 96

commodification 215, 219
communism 39, 46–48, 50, 56
computers 160, 163, 181–88, 190–95,
    198–202, 223–24, 226, 228–29, 233
    laptops 187
    personal computer/PC 185
computer age 182–83
consciousness 14, 160, 228–29
consequentialism/consequentialist
    81–82, 91
consumers 72–73, 139
Copernicus 32
cornea 150, 152, 165
cotton mill 35
Crick, Francis 67
Cromwell, Oliver 34
Cuba 48
cybernetics 223–24
cyborgs 193, 223–26, 233
cybrid embryos/admixed embryos
    153–54, 156
cystic fibrosis/CF 102–104, 106–108,
    112, 117, 120, 122, 149
Czechoslovakia 48, 95

Dalai Lama 15
Darwin, Charles 15, 36, 42, 131
de Grey, Aubrey 220
death 38, 50, 63, 94, 106, 108, 112,
    121, 141, 167, 169, 171–72, 176,
    182, 239, 240
    definition of 171
    in childhood 108–109, 121, 167,
    169, 239–40
Declaration of Geneva 87
Declaration of Helsinki 87
Declaration of Human Rights 80, 175
Deep Blue, chess-playing computer
    184
dementia 106, 168–70
deontology 78–82, 88–89, 91
designer babies 128, 130, 214, 242
Dignitas 174
direct-to-customer genome analysis 135
divorce 31, 71
DNA 67, 100, 107, 110, 112, 114, 121,
    127, 133–35, 137–38, 154, 185,
    208, 238
Dolly the sheep 154, 214
domestic violence 242

dominant genes/mutations 95–96,
    106, 109–110, 170
double helix 67, 133
Down syndrome 98, 120
Duchenne muscular dystrophy 98

Earth, planet 14, 23, 54, 176, 240–41
ectogenesis 217–19, 231, 233
eggs/egg cells 107, 125, 143, 145–46,
    154–55, 178, 216–17
egoism/rational egoism 37, 41, 73,
    81, 83
Egypt/Egyptians 22, 27, 42, 52, 189,
    191
einkorn wheat 20
email 185–87, 189, 195, 200–201
emancipation of women 38
embryo 10, 13, 67–68, 90–91, 113–14,
    121–30, 133, 138, 141, 144–47,
    149, 153–59, 175, 206–207,
    209–211, 213, 216–17
    moral status 123, 126
emotions 14–15, 115–16, 122, 184,
    229, 242
emotivism 85–87
empathy 15, 26, 88–89, 229
enhancement 68, 151–52, 166, 177,
    206–207, 209–211, 213, 221–22,
    230–31
Enigma code 182
Enlightenment, the 32–34, 36, 65, 70
erythropoietin/EPO 208
ethics 26–27, 33, 37, 66, 70, 73,
    77–91, 94, 112–14, 122–23, 135,
    137, 139–40, 142–43, 145,
    154–56, 159–60, 166, 171,
    173–74, 176, 179, 201, 211–13,
    214–15, 217, 220, 226–27, 233,
    237, 231, 244–45 see also bioethics
ethnic cleansing 40–41, 51, 243
eugenics 118, 131–32
European Economic Community/
    EEC 53
European Union/EU 51, 53–54, 75,
    242
euthanasia 91, 132, 173–77, 179
evolution 5, 13, 16, 18–19, 36–37, 42,
    69–70, 101, 131, 226, 237
existentialism 37, 39, 65, 83
exoskeleton(s) 229–31

eyeborg 224, 226

faith 10, 15, 34, 41–42, 58, 65, 69,
    74, 84–85, 102, 134, 166, 175–76,
    179, 198–99
faith schools 34
family 21, 70–72, 94, 98, 116–17,
    119–20, 130, 132, 136, 142, 144,
    146, 156, 170, 172–73, 176, 179,
    198, 203, 206, 223
    family values 71, 144
Fanconi anaemia 109, 111, 126
feminism 57, 218
Fertile Crescent 19
fertilization 90, 121, 124–25, 143, 149,
    153, 156
fibroblasts 159–60
foetus 89–90, 98, 120, 122–25, 135,
    148, 175, 216–19
founder crops 20
France 33, 36, 39, 55–56, 140
Franklin, Rosalind 67, 214
French Revolution 33
fundamentalism 63, 69–70
futile treatment 172–73, 179

Galileo 32
Galton, Francis 131
gametes 107, 141, 143, 145–47, 149,
    151, 153, 155, 157, 159, 161, 163,
    165, 179, 213
Gdansk shipyard 49
gene doping 151, 207, 211
gene therapy 111, 149–52, 165–66,
    209, 211
Genesis 23, 28, 36
genetics 9, 11, 40, 54, 67, 93–95, 97,
    99–103, 105, 107, 109–113, 115,
    121, 127, 131–32, 135, 138–41,
    178, 207, 231
    ACTN3 gene 207, 209
    APC gene 110
    ApoE gene family 170
    BRCA1 and BRCA2 genes 109, 115
    genetic essentialism 137
    genetic medicine 98, 104, 133–34,
        151, 157, 238
    genetic modification (GM) 67,
        99, 112–13, 149, 152, 206–207,
        209–13, 215, 231

genetic selection 90, 129–32,
    207–208, 210–14, 231, 244
genetic reductionism 137–38
HNPCC gene 109–110, 115
genome(s) 100–101, 110–12, 133–40,
    193, 233
genome-wide associative studies 134
genotype(s) 125, 138, 209, 215
Germany 9, 38, 40–41, 46, 71, 132,
    165, 182
Glasgow 167, 178, 225
global north 64, 141, 152, 232, 239
global south 232, 239–40
globalization 64, 187–88, 190
Glorious Revolution (1688) 31, 34
GM crops 66 *see also* genetics, genetic
    modification
God 15–16, 27, 33, 36–38, 42, 58, 65,
    69, 80, 83–85, 112, 140, 166,
    175–76, 181, 212, 232, 237, 241,
    244
Golden Rule 128, 215
Good Friday Peace Agreement 60
Gorbachev, Mikhail 49–50, 74
Greece/Greeks 23, 27–28, 42, 75, 78,
    82, 87, 91, 112
Greek Cypriot(s) 117
growth hormones 151, 210, 221
Guttman, Ludwig 40, 233

haemoglobin 104–105, 117
haemophilia 94–96, 98
Harbisson, Neil 224–26
Harris, John 129, 147, 212–13, 215
Hauerwas, Stanley 83, 201
Hellenistic Empire 28, 42
Henry VIII 31
heterozygote advantage 105
Hezbollah 53
Higgs Boson 67
Hijack/hijacking 61, 62–63, 193–94
Hillsborough 171–72
Hippocrates 87, 94
Hippocratic Oath 87
Hiroshima 40
Hitler, Adolf 40, 46, 214
Holy Spirit 244
Homo sapiens 13, 16–18
hospice/hospice movement 177
hostages/hostage-taking 53, 61

human embryo *see* embryo
human evolution *see* evolution
Human Fertilisation and Embryology
    Act (1990) 91
Human Fertilisation and Embryology
    Authority/HFEA 122, 147
Human Genome Project/HGP 15,
    100, 111–12, 133–34, 139–40
human identity 93
human rights *see* rights, human
humanism 32–33, 36, 84
humans
    biological features 14
    brains 13–14, 68, 107, 117, 138,
        151, 163–64, 170–72, 178, 183,
        226–29
    intelligence 14, 37, 130, 140, 206,
        228–29
Hungary 48
hunter-gatherers 16–17, 20
huntingtin 107
Huntington's disease 106–107,
    114–16, 118
Hussein, Saddam 61, 63
Huxley, Thomas 37

icons 67, 133, 137, 163, 225–26,
    228–29, 238
ICSI/intra-cytoplasmic sperm injection
    145
identity theft 194
image of God 15, 85
imperatives 79, 128, 215, 233, 236
implantation (of embryo) 6, 90, 114,
    118, 120–21, 123–25, 127, 138,
    141, 145, 165, 207, 210, 238
in vitro fertilization/IVF 90, 121–23,
    125, 127, 130–31, 138, 143–48,
    153, 156, 178, 206–209, 216–17
Indian subcontinent 54, 105–106, 191
individualism 70, 72–74, 201
Indonesia 79
induced pluripotent stem cells/iPS cells
    159, 216
Industrial Revolution 21, 34–35, 43,
    70–71, 187, 240
International Trade Center 62
Internet 185–87, 189–91, 193–99,
    201–203, 223
Iran 53, 62

Iraq 21, 61–63, 75, 161
Ireland 5, 35, 40, 53, 57, 59–60, 75
Iron Curtain 46
Islam 15, 30, 52–53, 62–64, 75, 79,
    157, 175, 202
Israel 51–52, 61–62, 78

Jaipur limb 161, 166
Jesus Christ 29, 59, 83, 160, 196, 199
Jews see Judaism
jihad 62, 69, 75
Judaism 27, 29, 40, 51, 52, 108–109,
    118, 132, 157, 175
Judeo-Christian tradition 26, 85
Julius Caesar 28
justice 34, 88, 174

Kant, Immanuel 23, 33, 79, 81, 84, 215
karyotype 96–98, 112
Kasparov, Garry 184
Kennedy, John F. 48, 57
Kennedy, Robert 57
Khrushchev 48
King Æthelbert 30
King James/Authorized version of the
    Bible 167
King Nebuchadnezzar 27
King, Martin Luther 56–57
Klinefelter syndrome 97
Kuwait 61–62

language 14, 31, 50, 55, 80, 86, 112,
    185, 224, 227–28, 237
Large Hadron Collider 67
law 23, 26, 49, 54, 73, 79–84, 89–91,
    98, 116, 124, 127, 145, 149, 154,
    174–76, 179
Lebanon 52–53
lesbian couples 147–48, 217
leukaemia 150
Lewis, C.S. 9, 15, 235, 245
life expectancy 101, 103–104, 107,
    109, 152, 167–69, 170, 220, 231
living will see Advance Directive
locked-in syndrome 163
Loebner Prize 184
logical positivism 86
Lomas, Claire 164, 229
London 58, 64, 67, 150, 162, 164,
    177, 207, 229

London Marathon 164
Luxemburg 174

MacIntyre, Alasdair 83, 86–87
macular degeneration 168
malaria 105, 239
maleficence/non-maleficence 87–88
mammals 13, 15, 101, 125, 154, 163,
    209
Manchester University 129
marathon 164, 182, 229
marathon mice 209, 211
marriage breakdown 71
Marshall Tito 50
Marx, Karl 35
Marxism 39
mathematics 22, 28
Mecca 30
medical ethics 73, 87–88, 90, 173–74
medical genetics 54, 92, 100–101, 110
memes 69
Mendel, Gregor 95–96
Merthyr Tydfil 35, 42
Mesopotamia 21–23, 25
micro-array 134
micro-engineering 160
Mill, John Stuart 81
mitochondria 146
modafinil 222–23, 233
modernism 65
modernity 65, 237
monotheism 27, 29
Moore, Pete 237–38
Moore's Law 228–29, 233
moral code 15, 84, 89, 123
moral relativism 85
moral sense 15
moral significance/moral value 65,
    87, 89–90
morals/morality 55, 58, 80, 84, 91
MORI polls 155
"morning-after" pill 125
Morse code, invention of 185
Muamba, Fabrice 69–70
music 14, 21–22, 137, 212, 224
Muslims see Islam
myostatin/myostatin gene 210–11

Nash, Adam 126
Nash, Molly 126

NATO 51
natural law 80–83, 91
natural philosophy 83
Nazi 9, 40, 108–109, 118, 132
Neanderthals 17, 23
Near East/Middle East 17, 20, 22, 41
Newton, Isaac 33
NHS 139, 148, 232
Nicklinson, Tony 175, 179
Nietzsche, Friedrich 37, 39, 65, 81, 83, 226
Nobel Prize 49–50, 57, 75
Normans 30–31, 42
Northern Ireland 5, 40, 59–60, 75
nuclear bombs/weapons 40, 47–49, 58

Obama, Barak 56, 101, 232
objectivism 37, 82
Olympic Games 28, 42, 75, 162, 207, 213
Olympic Village 61, 213
Oncogene 150
On the Origin of Species by Means of Natural Selection 36

paedophilia 199
pagans 29, 41–42
Pakistan 63–64
Palestine/Palestinian(s) 28, 51–52, 61
Palestinian Liberation Organization/ PLO 36
palliative care 176–77
Paralympic Games 64, 162, 213, 233
paralysis 160, 162, 164, 166
Parliament 31, 38, 90, 124
    European Parliament 53
Pascal, Blaise 41, 236
permanent vegetative state/PVS 171
Persia/Persians 26–28
personhood 38, 124–25, 129, 137–38, 172
phenotype 127
phenylketonuria 108, 117, 122, 127
Pistorius, Oscar 162, 178
Plato 25, 27–29, 41, 83, 131, 244
Poland 48–50, 57–58
Pope John Paul II 49
population 26–29, 21, 34–36, 42, 47, 49, 52, 56, 59, 69–70, 102–103, 105–106, 108–109, 118, 134,
    136, 142, 153, 157–58, 160, 168, 169, 189, 191, 197–98, 220, 226, 239–41
pornography 194–99, 202–203
    addiction to 197–98, 203
postmodernism 65–66, 78, 85–87, 156
Pratchett, Terry 174
pregnancy 89, 98–99, 118, 120–22, 124–25, 127, 142, 144, 146, 148–49, 153, 178, 206, 209, 216, 218–19
pre-implantation embryo 114, 124, 138 141
pre-implantation genetic diagnosis/ PGD 118, 121, 207, 238
prenatal testing 96, 98, 120, 122, 127
printing, invention of 32
progressivism 237
prosthetic limb(s) 160–62, 166, 178, 181, 185
psychotropic drugs 221

Queen Victoria 95
Qur'an 79

radio, invention of 36, 186
Rand, Ayn 37, 82
Reagan, Ronald 49
recessive genes/mutations 95–96, 102, 105, 108–109, 119, 121, 125, 136
recombinant DNA 208
red blood cells 104–105, 153, 208
regenerative medicine 153–54, 157, 160
religion 18–19, 21–22, 27, 29, 31, 34, 36–37, 39, 50, 65–66, 68–70, 82, 84–85, 123
    church attendance/religious observance, decline in 59, 69–70
Religious Right (in USA) 70
Renaissance 32
Republic of Ireland 40
retina 150, 154, 165, 168
retinitis pigmentosa 165
rights 56–57, 80, 88, 91, 113, 124–25, 130, 147, 156, 175, 215
    civil 56–57
    human 80, 124–25, 147, 175
    right to a child 147–49, 219
    right to life 124

Ritalin 222–23, 233
robotic suits/walking suits 164, 181,
    229–31
Roman Catholicism 31, 33, 58, 60, 81,
    143, 144, 157, 172, 175
Roman empire 29–30
Romans 28–31, 41, 91
Royal College of Nursing 172
Russia 39, 46–48, 82

Sandel, Michael 73, 75, 201, 203
Sartre, Jean-Paul 37, 39, 83
sanctity of life 124
Saudi Arabia 62
saviour siblings 125–26
severe combined immune deficiency
    disease/SCID 149–50
scientific method 32, 34, 65
secularism 84, 156
SENS Foundation 220
shari'a law 79
sickle-cell anaemia 104–108, 117,
    120–21, 134, 150
silicon chip 163, 225–26
single gene disorders 96
single nucleotide polymorphism/SNP
    110, 133
single-person households 71
slavery 34, 105, 112, 243
social networking 188–89, 193, 195,
    199–201, 203
Solidarność/Solidarity 49–50, 74
somatic cell nuclear transfer 154
Soviet bloc 41, 46
Soviet Union 39–40, 46–50, 243
sperm/sperm cells 107, 142–43,
    145–47, 216–17
spirituality 70, 138
Stalin, Josef 46
steam engine, invention of 34
stem cells 10, 67–68, 90, 126, 146,
    153–60, 216–17
Steptoe, Patrick 143
sub-retinal implants 165
suffragette 37
suicide/assisted suicide 64, 91, 115,
    173–74, 176, 183, 201
Super-soldier programme 230
surrogate motherhood 144, 178, 218,
    233

Switzerland 132, 169, 174
Synod of Whitby 30
Syria 20–21, 53, 243

Taliban 63
Tay-Sachs disease 108, 117–18
telephone, invention of 36, 186
Ten Commandments 27–28
test-tube babies 142
thalassaemia 117, 150
thought control 227
thought transfer 226–28, 231, 237,
    241
Tigris 21
tools/tool-making 17, 112, 114, 134,
    139, 205
Tower of Babel 27, 237–38
trafficking, human 243, 245
transdifferentiation 157
transhumanism 205–207, 209, 211,
    213, 215–17, 219–21, 223, 225,
    227–33
transplants 104, 109, 111, 126, 152,
    154, 158, 165
Treaty of Maastricht 53
Treaty of Rome 53
trisomy 21 (chromosome imbalance)
    97
trisomy X (chromosome imbalance)
    97
tuberculosis 239
Turing Test 184, 229
Turing, Alan 22, 101, 181–84, 202,
    229, 238
    homosexuality 183
Turner syndrome 97

United Kingdom/UK 40, 47, 60
United Nations/UN 47, 53, 61, 63,
    74, 80, 243, 245
Uruk 21
USA see America

utilitarianism 81–83, 88, 156
Vikings 30
violence, domestic 20, 242
virtue 15, 27, 82–84, 86–88, 201, 215,
    219, 244
    virtue ethics 27, 73, 82–84, 87–88,
        91, 201

Wałęsa, Lech 49
walking suits *see* robotic suits
warfare/war 26–28, 33, 38–42, 45–53,
    55, 57–58, 61–62, 66, 74–75, 87,
    124, 132, 161, 182, 243–44
  Arab–Israeli war 52
  civil war 52–53, 243
  cold war 41, 47–49, 58
  Gulf Wars 61, 222
  just war 124
  Korean War 46–47
  Thirty Year War 33
  Vietnam/Vietnam War 47, 58
Warnock Committee/Report 90–91,
    124, 145, 156
Warnock, Mary 26, 80, 82, 84, 144,
    244
Warwick, Kevin 163, 225–26, 228
Washington 56, 113
Watson, James 67, 137
Wesley, John 34
West Indies 54
wheel, invention of 22, 231
Whitefield, George 34
Wilkins, Maurice 67
William III of Orange 31
World Transhumanist Association 228
World War I 38
World War II 45–46, 51, 57, 74, 87,
    132, 182
World Wide Web 186, 201–202
Wright, Tom 83
writing, invention of 22

Yugoslavia 50–51, 53